VIETNAM: CURRENT ISSUES AND HISTORICAL BACKGROUND

VIETNAM: CURRENT ISSUES AND HISTORICAL BACKGROUND

V. LARGO (EDITOR)

Nova Science Publishers, Inc.
New York

Senior Editors: Susan Boriotti and Donna Dennis
Coordinating Editor: Tatiana Shohov
Office Manager: Annette Hellinger
Graphics: Wanda Serrano
Editorial Production: Jennifer Vogt, Matthew Kozlowski, Jonathan Rose and Maya Columbus
Circulation: Ave Maria Gonzalez, Vera Popovich, Luis Aviles, Melissa Diaz, Nicolas Miro and Jeannie Pappas
Communications and Acquisitions: Serge P. Shohov

Library of Congress Cataloging-in-Publication Data
Available Upon Request

ISBN 1-59033-368-3.

400 Oser Ave, Suite 1600
Hauppauge, New York 11788-3619
Tele. 631-231-7269 Fax 631-231-8175
e-mail: Novascience@earthlink.net
Web Site: http://www.novapublishers.com

Printed in the United States of America

CONTENTS

PREFACE

Vietnam remains a mystery to the American mind. A former enemy which somehow defeated the American war machine with few weapons or uniformed military, Vietnam remains a significant presence in Southeast Asia. This book presents issues important to understanding Vietnam today as well as a historical background on the country.

Chapter 1

THE POLITICS OF REFORM IN VIETNAM, 1986-2000*

Zachary Abuza
Simmons College

In 1986 Vietnam embarked on a radical course of economic reforms to revive its moribund, war-torn economy. The reforms, known as *doi moi*, saw very positive initial results as the country courted foreign investment and began a development strategy based on export-led growth; the country seemed ready to become the next tiger economy. Yet the initial reforms were running out of steam by the mid-1990s and Vietnam became stuck in a transitional system of market socialism. The leadership, deeply divided into ideologically based factions, exacerbated by the collapse of socialism across Eastern Europe, was unable to come to a consensus on how to proceed with the reform program. Deadlocked, they were unable to effectively respond to a series of crises: a faltering economy, rampant corruption, the Asian economic crisis, and a wave of peasant rebellions. Being a one party state, the Vietnam Communist Party is fraught with factionalism (*bung di*) based both on ideology and patron-client ties. The factional nature of Vietnamese politics, compounded by generational rifts, as well as an overwhelming fear of losing ultimate control has hampered Vietnamese decision-making. Until the next party congress is held when there can be a large-scale leadership transition and generational change, bold policies that will rejuvenate the reform program are unlikely to be implemented. Instead, the Vietnamese leadership will continue to implement piecemeal policies that will allow them to muddle through.

1. THE ERA OF *DOI MOI*: THE 6TH PARTY CONGRESS THROUGH THE 7TH PARTY CONGRESS (DECEMBER 1986 TO JUNE 1991)

At the 6th Party Congress, the newly elected General Secretary of the Vietnam Communist Party (VCP), Nguyen Van Linh, embarked on a radical reform economic program

---

* Excerpted from *Asian Political and Economic Issues, Volume IV* by Frank Columbus (Editor). © 2002 by Nova Science Publishers, Inc. ISBN 1-59033-098-6.

known as *doi moi*. *Doi Moi* was launched in the context of a terrible economic malaise. Decades of war, including the costly 11-year occupation of Cambodia, had left the country on the brink of bankruptcy. Despite over $1.2 billion in annual Soviet military assistance, over one-third of the state budget went to security. The centrally planned economy, which favored heavy industry at the expense of agriculture and light manufacturing was faltering. The rapid socialization of the southern economy had caused terrible dislocations and agricultural out put had declined sharply after the land had been collectivized. Inflation was running in the triple digits. In short, war communism was threatening the regime's legitimacy.

Doi moi sought to remedy these imbalances. Chinese styled agricultural reforms were implemented, giving farmers "land-use rights," and contracts, while small-scale private enterprises were legalized. The role of central planning diminished, and prices, except for a few key commodities, were set by market forces. Many inefficient and loss-making state-owned enterprises (SOEs) were merged in an attempt to make them profitable. And finally, Vietnam sought to join the world economy, by courting foreign investment, and accepting its position in the global division of labor, exporting goods in which it had a comparative advantage in producing.

In addition to *doi moi*, there was a loosening of politics and debate, especially for intellectuals and the press. General Secretary Nguyen Van Linh knew that the party and government bureaucracies were unwilling to implement his economic policies, as much of their power came from their ability to control the distribution of goods, services and resources. Market forces would strip that power away from them. In order to cajole the recalcitrant bureaucracy, Linh employed the press and intellectuals to ferret out corrupt officials and cadres who were abusing their power. As he told a group of journalists on 6 October 1987,

> On the days when our party was fighting for power, it depended on the people for support. Now, the possession of power is likely to lead to alienation from the masses, arrogance and high-handedness, greed and embezzlement, bureaucratism and authoritarianism in economic and ideological leadership. All this must be strongly criticized and condemned. [1]

In order to win the support of the intellectuals and journalists, he had to agree to an overall loosening of ideological constraints; this became known as *coi moi*. Journalists and writers were urged by Linh to not "bend their pens," and to report truthfully. Liberalization also occurred in the literary and visual arts, and for the first time Vietnamese artists and writers were no longer constrained by the tenets of "socialist realism." Writers such as Duong Thu Huong, Nguyen Huy Thiep, Bao Ninh and Le Luu became a voice of a generation in Vietnam and won international acclaim.

The reform program experienced fantastic results. Economic growth soared. In just a few years, Vietnam went from being a net importer of food, to the world's third largest exporter of rice. Foreign investment began to enter the market, industrial output resumed, and inflation was brought down to the low double digits.

Despite its obvious successes, the reform program was in jeopardy due to events in Eastern Europe and the former Soviet Union. The lively political and intellectual debates of the late-1980s, were curtailed as the party became overwhelmed in protecting its monopoly of

[1] Nguyen Van Linh, "Let Writers and Artists Actively Contribute to Renovation," 6 October 1987, in *Vietnam Courier*, No. 1 (1988), 12.

power. Newfound press and literary freedoms were curtailed as censorship and party interference returned. Leading advocates of political reform were silenced and purged, as conservatives, who had all along argued that the pace and scope of *doi moi* was to great, regained the upper hand. What little freedom the press had won since 1986, was stripped, as journalists were ordered to toe the party line, and to not "report solely on negative events." The VCP was determined to not let the forces of counter-revolution get a toe-hold as they did in Eastern Europe. The military was called on to reiterate its loyalty to defending the socialist regime and publicly announced that "revolutionary violence," as had been applied in China in the Tiananmen Square Massacre, was justified. At the 9th Plenum, in March 1990, a leading advocate of political reform, Tran Xuan Bach, was sacked from the Politburo, the country's 13-man ruling body, while a leading ideologue was promoted to the body, giving the conservatives a clear upper-hand.

This majority was important for two reasons: First, the current Politburo selects the incoming members of both the Politburo and Central Committee, as well as the General Secretary of the party. Second, the majority would allow the conservatives to select the member responsible for drafting the *Political Report*, the key document presented at the forthcoming party congress that sets the political and economic tone for the next five years. Yet despite this majority, the Politburo was still sufficiently divided to really hamper effective decision-making.

The 7th Party Congress was clearly a compromise for both the conservatives and reformers. On the one hand, the economic reform program was acknowledged to be a success, and the party vowed to continue on with the economic policies of *doi moi*. On the other hand, *coi moi* and any attempt at political or intellectual liberalization was deemed to dangerous and abandoned. The party emphasized that it would do all that it had to in maintaining its monopoly of power and leading role in society.

There was a significant turnover in the leadership: eight of the thirteen members of the Politburo stepped down, while 46 of the 146 member Central Committee (31.5 percent) were newly elected. The party also went to great lengths to ensure a balance in its leadership. General Secretary Nguyen Van Linh stepped down and was replaced by the northerner and conservative Prime Minister Do Muoi, while the southerner and leading reformer, Vo Van Kiet, took the premiership. The Presidency, was assumed by the former Minister of Defense, Le Duc Anh, a staunch conservative from the central region of the country. The regional balance is important in Vietnamese politics, as southerners tend to be stronger advocates for economic liberalization. At the 7th Congress, five of the thirteen members of the Politburo were southerners. And the average age fell from 71 to 64. For the first time, power was truly shared. Though *primus inter pares*, General Do Muoi had to contend with two other top officials who had significant power bases, patronage networks, and reputations as decisive leaders.

2. The Politics of Near Tigerdom: The 7th through the 8th Congresses (June 1991 to June 1996)

Despite the Congress and the overhaul in the party leadership, the party remained terribly divided and in a constant state of stalemate, crippling much of the country's policy-making in the early-1990s. Vietnam's hasty normalization of diplomatic ties in November 1991 following the 7th Congress seemed to reaffirm Vietnam's socialist identity. At the mid-term Party Congress in January 1994, the conservatives again tried to regain the upper-hand in the run-up to the 8th Party Congress to be held in June 1996, by promoting four more people to the Politburo, three of whom were very clearly opponents of the radical reform program.

Conservative maneuverings, not withstanding, the liberal economic reform program continued with steady results. The average annual growth rate was 8 percent between the 7th and 8th Congresses. Foreign trade expanded rapidly, from a paltry $2.94 billion in 1986, to $12.7 billion in 1995. Between 1991 and 1995, exports increased from $2.04 billion to $5.20 billion. The percentage of manufactured exports also rose, in that same period, from 10 percent to 17 percent.[2] Foreign investment poured into the country. Between 1987 and 1996, $23.4 billion was pledged for 1,615 projects, by some 56 countries. In 1996 alone, Vietnam received $2.3 billion in actual investment, up 30 percent from 1995. Staples output increased from 18.38 million tons in 1986 to 27.5 in 1995.[3] Inflation was curbed from its triple digit figures in the mid-1980s, including a high of 774 percent in 1986, to 12.7 percent in 1995. The number of SOEs was cut from 12,296 in 1989 to 5,962 in mid-1995.[4] Yet, the percentage of industrial output to GDP has increased from 36.5 percent in 1991 to 41.9 percent in 1995. From 1991-1995, industrial production increased 88.4 percent, an annual average of 13.5 percent.[5] Vietnam was set for "tigerdom."

Vietnam's foreign policy reflected this outward economic trend. Once the Paris Peace Accords were signed in November 1991, formally ending the Cambodian conflict, Hanoi charged out of diplomatic isolation. It quickly normalized ties with the ASEAN states, Japan and Korea. A fiercely unilateral state, Vietnam resumed ties with multilateral lending institutions, such as the World Bank, IMF and Asian Development Bank. In 1995 Vietnam joined its former adversary, ASEAN, becoming the 7th member of the regional grouping. For the first time Vietnam displayed a willingness to resolve differences in multi-lateral settings. That same year, Hanoi normalized ties with both the United States and the European Union. Vietnam seemed committed to an economic development policy based on global integration and interdependence.

But there were already many underlying problems in the economy that Hanoi was unwilling to confront: 90 percent of joint ventures took place between foreign firms and SOEs. Though not illegal, the government curbed private domestic firms from entering into joint ventures, hoping that if SOEs had foreign partners, they would get a cash injection, be able to export goods, and turn a profit, all without privatization. Although the single fastest growing sector of the economy, SOEs only added 90,000 jobs in that five-year period, despite tax advantages, better access to land and capital. Moreover, the commitment to creating a multi-sector economy was weak. By 1996 only ten SOEs were equitized. Their continued receipt of preferential taxes, access to cheap capital, land, power, and other benefits prevented private sector competition from developing; the firms that are responsible for employing the

---

[2] UNDP, *Catching Up*, 30; World Bank, *Viet Nam: An Agenda for Financial Sector Development* (Hanoi: World Bank, 1995), 4.

[3] Le Van Toan, "An Overview of Vietnam's Economy After 10 Years of Renovation," *Tap Chi Cong San* (*Communist Review*) (February 1996): 25-30, in Foreign Broadcast Information Service, *Daily Reports-East Asia* (hereafter *FBIS-EAS*), 4 June 1996, 77.

[4] Vietnam News Agency (hereafter VNA), 23 June 1996, in *FBIS-EAS*, 25 June 1996, 102.

[5] Toan, "An Overview," 77.

surplus labor. Rather than privatization, Vietnam attempted to merge and reorganize SOEs in an attempt to make them profitable. This had the net effect of "further reinforcing and expanding existing monopoly powers and inefficiencies."[6] Although Vietnam agreed to meet AFTA rules and tariff levels by 2006 when it joined ASEAN, Vietnam continues to offer very high rates of protection to its SOEs. In addition to tariffs, Hanoi continues to employ quotas, monopoly trading companies, and import licenses in order to protect its ailing state sector.

Although the average annual growth of 8-9 percent was spectacular, it was clearly not sustainable unless Vietnam pushed through some major reforms. These included the equitization of and the cessation of government subsidies to the 6,000 inefficient state-owned enterprises, banking sector reform, improving the investment climate by eliminating red tape and corruption, furthering rural reforms, ending discriminatory policies towards the private sector, and liberalizing the foreign trade system. Fearing instability, conservatives in the VCP have prevented the government from implementing these necessary reforms that would lead to a period of economic hardships, increase unemployment and socio-economic inequalities, and thus potentially a challenge to the VCP's rule. Concern for stability is paramount and the idea of implementing reforms that will cause a further loss of jobs is unappetizing in a country that already has some of the highest unemployment in the region. Vietnam acknowledged that it has 3.7 million unemployed workers, over 7 percent of the workforce, and that the number will climb to 8.5 million by 2000.[7]

Vietnam's slowing economy was compounded by the Asian economic crisis. GDP growth, fell from its record high in 1995 of 9.5 percent to 2 percent and has now recovered to just over 4 percent in 1999. Export growth rates also fell dramatically, from 30 percent in 1996, to 20 percent in 1997 but only 5 percent in 1999. Foreign investment fell by 60 percent, and was under $1 billion in 1998. Meanwhile, inflation entered double digits, 9-10 percent while the currency lost 20 percent of its value, yet still remained over-valued. Declining farm prices, have led to drastic declines in rural revenue, while the urban sector is simply not creating enough jobs. The Asian economic crisis also had a devastating effect on the Vietnamese economy, as much of its foreign investment comes from and 70 percent of its trade is with other Asian states. Moreover, Vietnam's competitiveness dissolved in the face of devalued currencies throughout the region, which fell between 30 to 80 percent of their value. In sum, the *zeitgeist* that Hanoi enjoyed between 1994-1996 is gone, which is very alarming as Hanoi has acknowledged that it needs some $45 billion in investment, much of which will come from abroad. Yet, foreign investment in 1997 was $4.5 billion, nearly half the amount of 1996's figure of $8.6 billion. For the first time, former backers such as the World Bank became critical of the speed and scope of the reform program and downgraded Vietnam's growth potential. The Bank's Vietnam Country Director, Andrew Steer warned that although

> Since launching its ambitious reform program in 1986, Vietnam has achieved unprecedented levels of growth. . . However, recent trends showing a slowdown in foreign direct investment, stagnating domestic savings, increasing problems in the banking sector, deteriorating state enterprise performance, and a regional financial crisis that has hurt competitiveness, clearly indicates the need for Vietnam to embark on a greatly deepened economic reform program and speed up progress on its long and difficult transition to a successful market economy.[8]

---

[6] UNDP, *Catching Up*, 25.

[7] Reuters, "Vietnam Plans to Prevent Unemployment Crisis," 29 November 1997.

[8] World Bank, "Vietnam: Deepening Reform For Growth," News Release No. 98/1534EAP, 17 November 1997.

The economic downturn was not the only crisis confronting the leadership, and because of the political stalemate the regime was unable to effectively deal with any of them. The first crisis was the peasant protests in Thai Binh Province, the cradle of the revolution. Peasants began protesting throughout the north protesting arbitrary fees and taxes from land usage to "teacher fees" for their children's schooling, to corvee; an amount that one Vietnamese researcher calculated to total 40 percent of peasants' income.[9] In all, the total amount of taxes and levies collected between January 1994 and July 1997 were more than dong 176 billion (about $16 million) more than had been authorized by the central government. At the same time, loans to local farmers and businesses in the province fell by 40 percent compared to 1996 and unemployment was skyrocketing, already at 200,000. In addition, there were concerns regarding corruption, abuse of power, land seizures, forced contract renegotiations and "commandism." As local party secretaries tended to also be the chairmen of the local people's committee's they were in a position of absolute power. Because of this power, the village leaders were able to redistribute communal lands, which averaged between 10 and 25 percent of a village's land area. Legally, this process is supposed to be conducted through auction, but in reality it is often conducted out of the public's eye, so that the village chief can distribute the land to his family and friends. Although the proceeds from the lease of these "second land use rights" are supposed to be used for social welfare programs, they are often embezzled.[10]

Something had to be done as the protests truly threatened the regime: its legitimacy has always come from the support of the peasantry. As Pham Van Khai warned: "If rural areas remain stable and farmers are happy with their livelihood, our country will be able to ensure stability however serious the difficulties. Therefore, rural stability is the key to national security." The party acted quickly, dispatching 1,200 police and several Politburo members to investigate. In the end, some 1,800 officials were "disciplined," but only 84 party members were expelled and only 30 were sentenced to prison; 62 peasant protestors were arrested for jeopardizing public safety. The Politburo later issued decree 89/CP that authorized military and police units to set up temporary pre-trial detention centers, in which suspects could be held for up to two years without trial.[11]

The second crisis was the rampant corruption and smuggling, much of it conducted by government officials and party cadres. Major drug smuggling operations were discovered to be run by senior members of the Ministry of Interior. Meanwhile, in two major show-case trials, a total of 77 defendants from two state owned enterprises, EPCO-Minh Phung and Tamexco, were investigated for fraud, embezzlement and $280 million in losses; a staggering figure in a country where the average annual income is less than $400. Corruption allegations even reached the highest levels as Politburo member Pham The Duyet was accused, though

[9] See Dang Phong, "Aspects of Agricultural Economy and Rural Life in 1993,"in Benedict J. Tria Kerkvliet, and Doug J. Porter, eds., *Vietnam's Rural Transformation* (Boulder: Westview Press, 1995), 182-183. A 1996 Oxfam study found in one province 8 types of tax imposed by the central government, including land use rights, fishing, salt-making and slaughter, as well as 6 other local "contributions," including corvee. See Oxfam UK and Ireland, *Report on the Financing and Delivery of Basic Services at the Commune Level in Ky Anh, Ha Tin* (March 1996). Peasants, on a nationwide average, must contribute 10 days of labor annually to the state.

[10] Phong, "Aspects of Agriculture," 181.

[11] *Cong An Thanh Pho Ho Chi Minh*, No. 689, 10 November 1998.

later exonerated in an internal party investigation.[12] On top of these show-case corruption trials, there continued to be the systematic abuse of power and petty corruption by low-level bureaucrats, such as that which caused the Thai Binh protests, that really called the regime's legitimacy into question.

On top of this, the regime has to contend with a very youthful population; 60 percent of whom were born after 1975 and have no memory of the war. The party is clearly losing touch with the people in whose name it rules.

In short, despite some remarkable achievements, there were real limits to sustained economic growth without some major new policies. But the political stalemate, crippled any chance that a new impetus for reform could be implemented. Between the 7th and the 8th Congress, the leadership experienced some of its worst infighting. This was fundamentally a debate over how to strengthen and develop the nation. Reformers argued that the way the country could overcome its perpetual poverty and for once no longer be ranked amongst the world's poorest nations was to become fully integrated into the global economy. This meant accepting everything that Lenin railed against: Vietnam would have to accept the liberal neo-classical notions that ruled global economics. Vietnam would have to accept its place in the global division of labor, produce what it had a comparative advantage in. Vietnam would have to rely on agriculture and low-tech, manually intensive products. Vietnam would have to follow the model of the Asian Tigers and adopt an export led growth strategy, which would entail imports. Vietnam would have to borrow from abroad, and court foreign investment. All this meant that the Vietnamese economy would no longer be insulated. And the government would have to stop propping up the public sector and especially SOEs with soft budget constraints. The private sector would have to be freed up so that it could employ the surplus labor force.

Conservatives argued that the way that Vietnam could strengthen itself and become a tiger, was through socialism. State owned enterprises had to be strengthened. To do so, conservatives argued that Vietnam should emulate the South Koreans. They looked at these huge conglomerates, the *Chaebul*, which had diversified (we now know to disastrous degrees), and catapulted South Korea into becoming a industrial powerhouse. Could not Vietnam do the same with its SOEs? Could not the more efficient SOEs take over the less efficient ones so that the Vietnamese economy be run by a few giant all-encompassing *Chaebul*?

The party, which has always prided itself on its unity and consensus style approach to decision-making, was so divided on how to proceed, that there was no attempt even to hide the huge rifts in the party. In late 1995, Prime Minister Vo Van Kiet's "Letter to the Poliburo," which was leaked to the press, argued that "in order to mobilize the genius of all within the party and promote transparency within the party, there must be uncompromising democracy." Kiet went on to lambaste conservatives. He called for shrinking the state-owned sector and increasing private industry, forsaking ties with the remaining socialist states, getting the party out of government affairs, putting national affairs ahead of government affairs. In response, the conservatives dispatched Politburo member Nguyen Ha Phan to lead meetings around the country to attack Kiet's "deviation from socialism." By the 9th Plenum

[12] Faith Keenan, "Dishing the Dung," *Far Eastern Economic Review* (hereafter *FEER*), 13 August 1998, 28. After a three month-long investigation, the State Inspector, Ta Huu Thanh, announced that he had found no wrong doing by Duyet. See Dean Yates, "Hanoi Probed High-Level Graft Cases," Reuters, 4 November 1998. Members of the Inspectorate subsequently intimidated the accusers.

(November 1995), the conservatives seemed to have the upper-hand. Draft resolutions stated that the main lesson of *doi moi* was "to maintain the stalwarthy the leadership role of the Party and to consider the development of the Party as the primary responsibility."

But attacks were no longer merely rhetorical. When the army's Chief of Staff, General Dao Dinh Luyen, gave a long speech in support of Vo Van Kiet and continued economic reforms he was sacked from the Politburo and lost his army post in January 1996. Then the conservative Nguyen Ha Phan was expelled from the Politburo, stripped of his party membership and placed under house arrest for treason in April 1996. Phan, who led the charges against Tran Xuan Bach in 1991 and Vo Van Kiet, was very close to the leading candidate to become the next party general secretary. If Dao Duy Tung was elected, Phan was a leading candidate to become the prime minister. But then Tung, reportedly fell into a coma following the Party's 10th Plenum (April 1996) where he was criticized for "abusing power" and "anti-democratic behavior," as he managed to get unprecedented control of both the personnel appointments and the drafting of the *Political Report* for the 8th Congress. At the Plenum, only 10 percent of the 164 members voted to reelect him to the Politburo, yet until the plenum, he was the leading candidate to replace Do Muoi. Reformers were euphoric as Tung had completely disregarded their position in the *Political Report* and in their personnel selections, both of which were rejected. The party was back at square one, and nearly had to delay the 8th Congress because of a lack of consensus. A compromise to maintain the status quo was reached on 26 June, two days before the start of the 8th Congress: the top three leaders would remain in their posts; a blow for the regularized transition of power since 1986.

3. The 8TH Congress (June 1996)

While this political maneuvering maintained the status quo among the top three leaders, it did not resolve all personnel issues to be discussed at the congress. A 170 member Central Committee was elected, of which 92 (54 percent) were incumbents. Yet the central-level party apparatus saw a loss of power. Only seven, a humbling 8.9 percent of the 72 new members, were center-level cadres, while 67 percent of the Central Committee was made up of provincial and government officials. Center-level party officials and top ideologues fared even worse on the Politburo. Do Quang Thang, Director of the Central Committee's Control Commission and Secretariat member, Le Phuc Tho, Director of the Central Committee's Organization Department, Dao Duy Tung, a top ideologue and Secretariat member, and Vu Oanh, the former Director of the Central Committee's Economics Department were all forced out of the Politburo. In total, three-fourths of the remaining 16 members were either forced out or asked to resign, yet, for the sake of stability, the Central Committee requested that the 8th Politburo keep at least 8 members from the preceding body. In the end, 10 of the 19 now members were incumbents, including, Do Muoi, Le Duc Anh, Vo Van Kiet, Nong Duc Manh, Nguyen Manh Cam, Nguyen Duc Binh, Doan Khue, Phan Van Khai, and Pham The Duyet.

Politburo of the 8th Central Committee

Name, Age, and Region	Concurrent Posts
1. Do Muoi (79) N	General Secretary
2. Le Duc Anh (75) C	President & Chairman National Defense Council
3. Vo Van Kiet (73) S	Prime Minister
4. Nong Duc Manh (55) N	Chairman, National Assembly
5. Le Kha Phieu (64) N	Lt. General, Director, General Political Department
6. Doan Khue (72) C	Lt. General, Minister of Defense (Died on 1/16/99)
7. Phan Van Khai (62) S	Vice-Prime Minister
8. Nguyen Manh Cam (66) C	Minister of Foreign Affairs
9. Nguyen Duc Binh (68) N	Director, National Ho Chi Minh Academy of Politics
10. Nguyen Van An* (58) N	Deputy-Director, CC Organization Department
11. Pham Van Tra* (60) S	Lt. General, Vice-Minister of Defense, VPA Chief-of-Staff
12. Tran Duc Luong* (59) C	Vice-Prime Minister
13. Nguyen Thi Xuan My*(56) N	Deputy-Director, CC Control Commission
14. Truong Tan Sang* (47) S	Secretary, Ho Chi Minh City Party Committee
15. Le Xuan Tung* (60) N	Secretary, Hanoi Party Committee
16. Le Minh Huong* (59) N	Lt. General, Vice-Minister of Interior
17. Nguyen Dinh Tu* (63) N	(died on 6/28/96) Director, CC Science, Technology and Education Commission
18. Pham The Duyet (59) N	Director, CC Mass Mobilization Commission
19. Nguyen Tan Dung* (47) S	Vice-Minister of Interior

* Denotes new member

Although the Vietnam People's Army (VPA) and other security personnel only held 20, or 11.7 percent, of Central Committee seats, the military received the highest number of Politburo seats it has had since the reform program began at the 6th Congress in 1986. Of the 18 members (Nguyen Dinh Tu died during the congress), six were either in the VPA or Ministry of Interior. Aside from the growing role of the "security bloc," the makeup of the 8th Politburo, as expected, was a careful ideological and geographic balance: there was a fairly equal distribution of reformers, conservatives, and moderates while there were ten northerners, 5 southerners, and 3 members from the center.

The average age of the new Politburo was a sprightly 62.2. Two members were in their 40s; 5 in their 50s; 7 in their 60s; and only 4 in their 70s. The average age of Central Committee members fell from around 65 to 55.

The *Political Report* differed greatly from Dao Duy Tung's draft that emphasized that "Leadership without control is tantamount to no leadership."[13] In the redraft, state-owned enterprises and cooperatives were called on to make up only 60 percent of GDP by 2020. New paragraphs were inserted which stated that "profit" was an important criterion in evaluating state owned enterprise performance. There were far fewer references to "hostile forces" and "peaceful evolution," clear victories for the reformers and pragmatic moderates.

13 The *Political Report* was carried in *Quan Doi Nhan Dan*, 30 June 1996, 3,6, in *FBIS-EAS*, 11 July 1996, 71-100.

In sum, the Eighth Congress failed to conclusively address the nagging issues on which the country's economic development hinge. In striving to balance both factions, the party sowed the seeds of future deadlock. And without a change in leadership, there would be no change in policies. What came out of the Congress was a commitment to continued party control and an unwillingness to push through radical economic reform, i.e., stability and caution. As Do Muoi told reporters during the Congress, "I think we will have to accelerate our development. Slow development means hunger, don't you think? But as the same time I want to see efficiency and stability. If reform is too fast we will make mistakes. If you run too fast and there is something in the road you may fall down." Even moderates such as Foreign Minister Cam toed the party line, arguing that "our task is to maintain social and political stability and order. Past experience has shown that we can only have economic development with social and political stability."

4. THE LEADERSHIP TRANSITION: THE 8TH CONGRESS TO THE 4TH PLENUM (JUNE 1996 TO DECEMBER 1997)

Following the conservative's attempted ouster of the Vo Van Kiet at the 8th Party Congress the reformers went on the attack. The opportunity for the reformers first availed itself in November 1996 when President Le Duc Anh suffered a serious stroke. With a leading conservative incapacitated, Kiet actively pushed the reformist agenda. In his 12 March 1997 address to the National Assembly, Kiet advocated for a greater role for the private sector, while calling for more enterprise autonomy and accountability. He spoke of the importance of amassing of wealth and the establishment of a simple and open tax system. But the reformers were not powerful enough to change the party's top leadership in their favor.

The first movement towards a leadership transition came at the June 1997 Plenum. Do Muoi, Le Duc Anh and Vo Van Kiet all removed their names from candidacy for National Assembly seats. Constitutionally, the president and the prime minister, though not the party general secretary, must be National Assembly members, so it confirmed their resignations at the 9th National Assembly in September 1997 were forthcoming. Muoi, who technically could have remained in office until the 9th Party Congress in 2001, seemed determined to stay in office in order to ensure a smooth transition of power.

The Central Committee overwhelmingly approved Vo Van Kiet's protege Phan Van Khai to become the next Prime Minister. Although Khai had originally been slated to become the Prime Minister back at the Eighth Congress, Kiet apparently would not step down without concurrent moves by Le Duc Anh or Do Muoi. But his election was a clear victory for the reformers. Khai, an ardent supporter of reforming the state-owned sector, stated that he would further the reform program. But there was less consensus regarding the presidency; hotly contested by the moderate Foreign Minister, Nguyen Manh Cam, and conservative Minister of Defense, Lieutenant General Doan Khue. Keeping the regional balance in mind, both are from central Vietnam. Cam was able to take credit for a string of diplomatic successes since 1995, but as a career diplomat, he is neither charismatic, nor does he have any military experience which is important as the president is constitutionally responsible for defense issues. Due to these drawbacks, at the June Plenum, only half of the 170 members voted for Cam; not enough for a political system based on "consensus."[14]

As the president is constitutionally the commander-in-chief of the Vietnam People's Army and concurrently the Chairman of the National Defense Council, the highest national security decision-making organ in the country, the post is the natural position within the ruling triumvirate, one might assume, that the military would want to assert itself. President Anh's protege, Minister of Defense Doan Khue trailed closely behind Cam, despite Anh's campaigning. What prevented Khue from becoming President was not so much the effectiveness of the lobbying by the reformers for Cam, but an odd alliance and a slip of the tongue. First, during a trip to France, Doan Khue told President Chirac that after his "promotion" he would welcome the French president in Hanoi. As one commentator noted "Such bragging is frowned upon in a system that stresses modesty and consensus."[15] The second reason was perhaps the strange alliance between the reformers and the VPA's top political commissar, Le Kha Phieu. If a military man became the president, it would diminish Phieu's chances for becoming General Secretary, as the Central Committee would never agree to two of the top three position being held by military personnel. To that end, Phieu and the reformers were united in their opposition of Khue. In the end, it was neither man, but a relative unknown who became president, Tran Duc Luong (60). Luong, a Russian-educated geologist, a Vice-Premier since 1992 and a member of the Politburo since 1996, had remained a little-known technocrat. Though allied with Do Muoi, he was clearly a compromise candidate, as neither the reformers' or the conservatives' first choices had enough of a majority.

The transition left several nagging questions: was there really a transition of power as Vo Van Kiet and Le Duc Anh not only kept their positions in the Politburo, but also on the Politburo's Standing Committee, thus outranking their successors? Could the new president make decisions regarding national security if Le Duc Anh was still around? If the Politburo Standing Committee was indeed the "highest leading nucleus" in Vietnam, what were the implications of the president and prime minister not serving on it? The face saving solution was that Kiet and Anh joined the Central Committee's Advisory Board, originally created to accommodate Pham Van Dong and Nguyen Van Linh in their retirements. Clearly they continue to be powers behind the throne; in Putnam's terms, even without positional power, they continue to have reputational and decisional power. Although Kiet indicated that he would like to retire altogether he would not step down unilaterally and it was clear that Anh wanted to stay on despite his stroke. Kiet warned that he would continue to use his influence if he had to, especially if the less-powerful Khai was under attack from conservatives: "I don't think my work is finished," he told the daily *Thanh Nien*. "If I can do something to contribute to the new cabinet then I will try."

It was publicly agreed upon that for the sake of stability and a smooth transition of power the Standing Committee would remain unchanged, thus Muoi, Anh and Kiet would maintain their power. But in reality no one would step down until it was decided who would become the next party general secretary.

Between September and December 1997 the factions campaigned intensely for their respective candidates for the post of party general secretary. The conservatives fought very

[14] Faith Keenan, "Wait and See," *FEER*, 3 July 1997, 26.

[15] Faith Keenan, "New Crop," *FEER*, 2 October 1997, 16.

hard for they felt that they were being edged out of the ruling troika. For example, although Tran Duc Luong was thought to be allied to Do Muoi, he called for greater reform in his acceptance speech: "The way to overcome all trials and limits and to make the best of our opportunities to build our country and take it forward should be through continuing the policy of renovation systematically, comprehensively, and in a far-reaching way."[16] Luong's pragmatism, coupled with the radically reformist Prime Minister Phan Van Khai, alarmed the conservatives.

If one looks down the Politburo roster, it is clear that there were really few realistic and acceptable choices for General Secretary, for both the reformers and conservatives. The reformers, for their part, initially backed Nguyen Tan Dung, the former Deputy Minister of the Interior. Dung was elected to both the Politburo and its Standing Committee at the Eighth Congress and was considered to be a rising star within the party. But at 47, he was the youngest member of the Politburo, and was felt to have not enough experience to be general secretary, though he is clearly being groomed.

The conservative's problem was that there were very few like-minded people on the 18-member Politburo from whom to chose and whom could win a majority of votes. Doan Khue was unacceptable to most and weakened after his failed bid for the Presidency; Nong Duc Manh, it was already agreed, would remain Chairman of the National Assembly; Nguyen Duc Binh, the Director of the party school was too old and too ideological; a woman was not acceptable, so Nguyen Thi Xuan My was out of the running; Le Minh Huong and Le Xuan Tung were too inexperienced; and Pham The Duyet, though experienced, was not seen as capable enough.

The only credible and acceptable candidate to the conservatives was Nguyen Van An, the Director of the Central Committee's Organization Department. At 59, An was the right age. Heading the Organization Department also put him in control of the party's patronage networks. Russian educated, he had some foreign experience. Although many in the military were concerned that the election of An would leave them out of the ruling troika, Le Duc Anh and Doan Khue did not want Le Kha Phieu to get the position perhaps not for ideological reasons, but for personal ones. The animosity and rivalry towards Phieu dates back to the occupation of Cambodia, when Doan Khue was Le Duc Anh's assistant, while Phieu was the chief commisar, ostensibly second in command. As a result, they campaigned hard for An, even convincing Do Muoi to postpone his retirement until the 5th Plenum in December 1997 so that they would have more time to build-up support. An could have appealed to the reformers, as well, as he was reported to be "reform minded" by the Western press. The question, then, is why was he not elected?

Despite intense lobbying, it appears that An's stature was still too small and he could not win enough supporters, especially within the military. Although Le Duc Anh supported An, it was evident that his power over the VPA was waning and he could not get the military to unite behind his candidate. Indeed, the VPA closed ranks behind Phieu. Although considered a "party man" rather than a soldier, perhaps the VPA thought him to be more conservative and willing to look out for the military's interests than An. More importantly, An's election would leave the military without a voice in the top leadership. A commissar, in the VPA's eyes, was better than no one.

---

[16] Reuters, "Vietnam's New President Backs Reforms, Strong Party," 25 September 1997.

Le Kha Phieu, himself, did not have the necessary backing in the Politburo to get elected even when the military began to support him. He continued to need the support of the reformers, as he did when he blocked Doan Khue's nomination for president. The reformers were willing to back Phieu in return for a greater commitment for economic reform. Phieu toned down his rhetoric and had to publicly call for greater "equitization"-- though not privatization-- of state owned enterprises as well as a greater role for small and medium sized private firms. He stated that despite "differences," socialism and capitalism could "be resolved in a world of peaceful co-existence;" a far cry from his 1996 comments that capitalism was "obsolete" and "would soon be replaced."[17] He tried to assuage foreign investors by arguing that the development of a "socialist market economy" would strengthen the Vietnamese economy and that "Only by doing so will cooperation with foreign partners be effective and successful, and only then will the growth in foreign investment be maintained without sacrificing national independence and socialist orientation. . . The door will never be shut."[18] Likewise he said that he was committed to diversifying the economy, although the "leading role has to be played by the state sector." In another move to appease the reformers, the "stability-minded" Phieu met with a leading dissident, Hoang Minh Chinh, in Hanoi.

With the reformers apprehensively behind him, Phieu began to have the numbers he needed. But what really helped him was the anger that many Central Committee members felt towards Do Muoi's apparent refusal to step down. Phieu, who had already taken over of much of the party's day-to-day affairs from Muoi, could now count enough support to force Do Muoi into retirement. Thus General Le Kha Phieu became the VCP's sixth general secretary in December 1997 the first time a military man has ever held that post.

The difficulty in finding a suitable heir to Do Muoi reflects more than personal rivalries, ideological differences and factional politics. The problem is really systemic as Carlyle Thayer succinctly summed up: "Vietnam lacks men of talent" which has enormous consequences as the top leadership positions "require more than party experience."[19] As cited above, Vo Van Kiet acknowledged that the party is not producing the competent leadership that is needed to develop the country. The 18 months that it took to find a suitable and acceptable person to fill the post of general secretary drove this point home.

---

17 Greg Torode, "Party Leader Faces Tough Baptism," *South China Morning Post*, 3 January 1998.

18 See Le Kha Phieu's speech to foreign investors at the Tan Thuan EPZ, "Party Commitment," *Vietnam Economic Times* (February 1998), 9.

19 Cited in Keenan, "Wait and See," 26.

Politburo of the 4th Plenum of the 8th Central Committee

Name, Age, and Region	Concurrent Posts
1. Le Kha Phieu	General Secretary
2. Tran Duc Luong	President, Chairman National Defense Council
3. Phan Van Khai	Prime Minister
4. Nong Duc Manh	Chairman, National Assembly
5. Pham Van Tra	Lt. General, Minister of Defense
6. Doan Khue	Director, Internal Political Defense Commission
7. Nguyen Manh Cam	Minister of Foreign Affairs
8. Nguyen Duc Binh	Director, National Ho Chi Minh Academy of Politics
9. Nguyen Van An	Deputy Director, CC Organization Department
10. Nguyen Thi Xuan My	Director, Central Control Commission
11. Truong Tan Sang	Secretary, Ho Chi Minh City Party Committee
12. Le Xuan Tung	Secretary, Hanoi Party Committee
13. Le Minh Huong	Minister of Interior
14. Pham The Duyet	Director, CC Mass Works Commission
15. Nguyen Tan Dung	First Vice-Prime Minister
16. Pham Than Ngan *	Lt. General, Deputy Minister of Defense, Director General Political Department
17. Phan Dien *	Director, CC General Office
18. Nguyen Minh Triet *	Deputy Secretary, Ho Chi Minh City Party Committee
19. Nguyen Phu Trong *	Editor, *Tap Chi Cong San*, Deputy party chief of Hanoi

* Denotes new member

5. Rejuvenating the Economy

The new leadership made some initial attempts to rejuvenate the economy, but the effects of the Asian flu were too great and the leadership too divided to make the hard policy choices needed to reform the economy. On the one hand, the new General Secretary, Le Kha Phieu, was indebted to the reformers, and made some overtures to their economic policies: "We understand that the way ahead is full of thorns so we have no choice other than continuing the acceleration of the *doi moi* course in a comprehensive and concerted way in he orientation to socialism of we want to bring our country further forward."[20] Likewise he stated that he would carry-through economic policies in order to double 1996's GDP by the year 2000. Warning that "We should not indulge in self-satisfaction and sleep on our laurels," he said, "the only chance for the country to move forward is comprehensive, uniform renovation along the socialist line."[21] A few weeks later, he gave a speech at the country's most successful export processing zone in Ho Chi Minh City where he tried to reassure investors

[20] Kyodo, "Vietnam Party Leader Says Renewal Only Choice," 5 January 1998.

[21] "Party Chief Le Kha Phieu on Significance on Fourth Plenum Meeting," VNA, 5 January 1997, in *FBIS-EAS*, 14 January 1998.

that there would be no conservative-led retrenchment and that Vietnam would continue to court foreign direct investment: "We must persist and push ahead with the renovation cause. That is a consistent policy."[22]

Prime Minister Phan Van Khai also went out of his way to ensure foreign investors, by hosting a public meeting and issuing a series of new foreign investment reforms. "Your loss is our risk and our loss," he told the foreign investors, reiterating that, "Enterprises with foreign investment are integral parts of the Vietnamese economy."[23] Khai attacked bureaucratic red tape and corruption, and announced a hotline for foreign investors to call when confronted with corruption. But these were not enough.

Vietnam's reluctance to reform clearly played a part in the 60 percent reduction in foreign investment in 1998, and by October 1999 60-70 percent of foreign firms reported losses from their Vietnamese operations.[24] Vietnam's future economic growth is dependent on continued and deepened reform, but these reforms, such as privatization of state-owned assets, will challenge the authority of the state as well as its ideological underpinnings. The Asian economic crisis also had a devastating effect on the Vietnamese economy, as the leadership responded in piecemeal fashion; liberals promising reform while conservatives argue that Vietnam can weather the storm without changing. Indeed, the Central Committee's 5th Plenum, in July 1998, emphasized the mobilization of $7 billion in domestic capital to supplant the fall in foreign investment. Conservatives within Vietnam's leadership blamed the Asian economic crisis on capitalism, and believed that Vietnam's lack of integration was a blessing in disguise. Reformers, on the defensive, blamed the crisis on "crony capitalism," imperfect markets and too much government intervention. For two and a half years, there has been no major decision by the Politburo, which has been completely deadlocked since the 8th party congress in 1996. There is tremendous resistance to implementing these necessary reforms from within the conservative-dominated politburo.

By all measurable accounts the Vietnamese economy is in poor shape. It is growing too slowly to create jobs for the million new entrants to the workforce each year. Exports are falling, though imports have leveled off, Vietnam is not importing capital equipment, FDI has fallen off, the dong is overvalued, the banks are indebted, 46 percent of SOEs are in the red and being subsidized at huge public expense, foreign debt is still high, unemployment is already a problem, government expenditures are already in the red and inflation is on the rise. It is time for some drastic action. Foreign investors have been fleeing, and those that have stayed have raised the alarm. Even the World Bank and IMF have held up some $500 million in loads until Hanoi adopted a "more comprehensive approach to reform." The Prime Minister, Phan Van Khai has raised the alarm, but the Politburo has been unable to come to a decision.

It is in this context that Hanoi's unwillingness to conclude a trade agreement with the United States must be seen.

---

22 AFP, "Party Chief Says Vietnam Welcomes Foreign Investment," 23 January 1998.

23 Nguyen Ngoc Chinh and An Dao, "Your Loss is Our Loss," *Vietnam Investment Review*, 9-15 February 1998, 1; and Nguyen Ngoc Chinh, "Pledging Sweeping Reforms For Investors," *Vietnam Investment Review*, 9-15 February 1998, 4-5.

24 Reuters, "Majority of Foreign Firms Report Losses in Vietnam," 13 October 1999.

6. Rejection of the Trade Deal

In October 1999, the Politburo of the Vietnamese Communist Party (VCP) rejected a trade deal with the United States; an agreement in principle that had been reached in July 1999. In the context of diminished exports and foreign investment since the onset of the Asian Economic Crisis in 1997, the Politburo's rejection of a deal that would have paved the way for the doubling of exports to the United States is surprising. Indeed, ever since the United States lifted its economic embargo on 4 February 1994 and the two sides normalized diplomatic relations in 1995, the Vietnamese requested a trade agreement that would give them MFN status instead of having to go through the annual Congressional approval process. The Vietnamese looked for a deal that would give them the same degree of market access that America's Asian allies enjoyed during the Cold War. The Americans, however, refused as trade deficits have become a charged political issue and American firms have demanded equal access. Trade talks, which began in 1995, went through nine rounds. The Vietnamese demanded special treatment, which they felt America was morally obliged to give them, both because of the war and because of their developing country status. American negotiators refused, and indeed got their Vietnamese counterparts to agree to a very inclusive trade deal that included investment, intellectual property and services. Only with the intervention of several liberals on the Politburo who felt that the trade deal, even with concessions to the Americans, was necessary to revive the moribund Vietnamese economy, was the agreement in principle reached. But the full Politburo rejected it. To understand the deal you must understand that the Politburo debate has little to do with tariffs and trade with its former foe the United States. It must be seen as part of a much larger debate regarding the future of the Vietnamese reform program.

And it was because the agreement would start to undermine the socialist economic foundations and end subsidies to state-owned enterprises that the Politburo was so unhappy with the agreement and deadlocked from the start. Though inefficient, the 6,000 state-owned enterprises are the cornerstone of the socialist economy, despite the fact that between one-third to one-half operate in the red. The leadership cannot fathom any policy that would limit subsidies or subject them to increased foreign competition because unemployment rates in Vietnam are already near 10 percent, and even by April 1998, over 8 percent of the 1.8 million SOE employees had been laid off. In addition, at current population growth rates, Vietnam must create between 600,00-700,000 jobs per year.[25] Whereas reformers want to scrap the inefficient SOE system and free up the private sector, conservatives believe that the collapse of the SOE system will lead to mass unemployment and political unrest. The SOE system is at the heart of the regime's legitimacy and must be defended at all costs. As one Vietnamese diplomat was quoted as saying, "If the agreement improves trade, that's one thing, but it also pushes reform. That's what makes us hesitate. We must determine the steps of reform."[26]

The VPA, which has vast industrial and commercial holdings to augment its diminished budget, was also against the trade deal. Increased competition would threaten its market share

[25] Ari Kokko, "Vietnam: Ready for Doi Moi II?" *ASEAN Economic Bulletin*, Vol. 15, No. 3 (December 1998): 319-327, esp. 325.

[26] Keenan, "Opening Doors."

and competitiveness, that is so critical to the military's overall budget.[27] By 1998, total revenue of the military's 164 enterprises surpassed $600 million,[28] and one estimate is that 100,000 of the military's 572,000 troops are engaged in full-time economic activity.[29] Since 1989, VPA firms have entered into approximately 30 joint ventures capitalized at $302 million, involved in industrial areas such as ship repair and construction, car assembly, building materials, hotels and entertainment centers, and food stuffs. The military operates an airline and its trying to establish a rival telecommunications service to challenge the Ministry of Post and Telecommunications' monopoly.

The second reason that the trade deal was rejected has to do with the current deadlock in the Politburo. There are several aspects to this. First, the top three leaders, General Secretary Le Kha Phieu, Prime Minister Phan Van Khai and President Tran Duc Luong, really don't have the authority (and more importantly the patronage networks running through the party, government, and military) that their predecessors did. The Vietnamese political system is based on patron-client ties: the relationship between two or more individuals of unequal rank or stature. In return for support and protection, the client owes his patron unquestioned loyalty and support. Because Do Muoi, Le Duc Anh and Vo Van Kiet came to power during the war years, they all wore party, military and government hats. The party-military-government elite at that time really was an elite. There were ideological and strategic differences and personal rivalries to be sure, but it was a small group, who went through a formative period together. And they all had very broad experience. The current leadership, the fourth generation, came of political age during a period of stagnation when their predecessors refused to give up power- most importantly their patronage networks- the nomenklatura. They were brought up through the ranks because they were "clients" who never had enough authority or opportunity to really be "patrons" in their own right. What gave Le Duc Anh authority and power as president, was not his positional power, in Putnam's terms, but his decisional power. As a senior general and former Minister of Defense, he had vast patronage networks throughout the military. Though constitutionally as powerful as his predecessor, Tran Duc Luong has little power over the military that he technically commands because he does not control any of the patronage networks throughout the military. He has never promoted anyone or done anything to ensure unwavering loyalty to him. Similarly, because Le Kha Phieu was a compromise candidate, and came in without patronage or clear support. He is a weak leader who needs to appeal for the support of both reformers and conservatives. He tends to sit on the fence, weighing in at the last moment, and trying to build consensus between these disparate factions. Because of this he is perceived as a weak leader. He endears himself to neither faction.

---

[27] With the withdrawal from Cambodia and the loss of all Soviet subsidies beginning in 1989, the VPA was significantly downsized in both size and budget. Once over 1 million men and commanding over one-third of the national budget, in addition to an average annual $1 billion in Soviet aid, the military's size and budget was slashed by 50 percent. The military's budget fell annually hitting a low of $800 million (5.7 percent of GDP) in 1994, before rising to $1 billion in 1999 (3.7 percent of GDP), a far cry from the $2.3 billion (18 percent of GDP) in 1989. Per capita military expenditure was only $12 per soldier, the lowest in a region experiencing unprecedented growth in military budgets and acquisitions. As 70 percent of the Vietnamese military budget goes to salaries, only 30 percent is left for maintenance and upkeep of existing weapons systems as well as new acquisitions. As many of Vietnam's weapon systems are at the end of their service life, the military feels that it needs a major refurbishment of its arsenal.

[28] Hanh Dung, "Military Enterprise," *Viet Nam Economic Times* (December 1999). The Military's 300 enterprises were reduced to 164 through closures and mergers in late-1997 through early-1998.

[29] Huw Watkin, "Proud Military Slips into Decline as Aid Dries Up," *South China Morning Post*, 7 July 1999.

Moreover, this generation of leaders was brought up in "line," i.e., Phieu was just a military political commisar, nothing else, his entire career. Tran Duc Luong was a geologist, and though a well connected one, simply a line ministry geologist. Phan Van Khai, again, rose through the economic ministries and commissions. In short, their experience is deep but not wide. Their predecessors' experience was wide not deep. They rotated through different positions across different branches of government-party-military during the war years. Do Muoi, for example, served as a labor leader, in various economic ministries, as prime minister, and in various party positions. Vo Van Kiet served as a top communist official in the south, a long-time member of the Central Committee, head of the State Planning Commission, and various other posts before becoming Prime Minister. These long and varied careers introduced them to a lot of people. And power in Vietnam is nothing but personal. The current leadership had no such broad experience, and it shows.

In short, the current top leadership does not have the leverage or personal pull over their colleagues. And they cannot pressure or influence their colleagues from below- because they do not know those underlings. At the 4th Plenum, in December 1997, the top three leaders, Le Duc Anh, Do Muoi and Vo Van Kiet, resigned from the Politburo; yet they were appointed "advisors" to the Central Committee. To this day, they use that position to make their presence known. Former General Secretary Do Moui casts a long shadow over Le Kha Phieu, weighing in when he feels like it, and he has always been against the trade deal with the Americans. Likewise, Phan Van Khai, continues to rely on the support of his patron Vo Van Kiet.

One also has to look at the composition of the Politburo to explain its current deadlock. The Politburo is carefully chosen with one factor in mind: balance. Balance between regions (especially north and south), age, ideological proclivities, sector, job or career path, and incumbency. The Politburo includes a diverse range of opinions and views, factored by regional, generational and bureaucratic politics. By this very fact, new policies are hard to implement as the stability and the status quo are the paramount concern.

The current Politburo has some real reformers, but also some real hardliners, and clearly the tilt is in the conservatives' favor. Though there are a few reformers, they're young and don't have too much political capital. They seem unable or unwilling to act in the face of older, more entrenched conservatives. This younger group of reform minded leaders include Prime Minister Phan Van Khai (3), Vice Prime Minister Nguyen Tan Dung (14), Truong Tan Sang (10) and Nguyen Minh Triet (17), the new Ho Chi Minh City Party Secretary. This group is very well educated, they have considerable experience- especially in economic issues. And they also have some cross-sector experience. For example, Nguyen Tan Dung is a 20-year veteran of the army and a former Vice Minister of the Interior, who has served as Central Bank Governor and Vice Prime Minister, responsible for the economy. Phan Van Khai held a large number of posts in the various economic ministries including the umbrella, State Planning Commission. Truong Tan Sang served as the Party Secretary in Ho Chi Minh City before being brought to Hanoi to run the Central Committee's Economic Commission in early 2000.

The reformers are young, and clearly going places, but they do not have the power base or political capital to take on the conservatives at present. Phan Van Khai, who has real liberal credentials, has been a terrible disappointment. Not just because he cannot get his policies through the conservative dominated Politburo, but because he must play up his conservative credentials to mollify them. He is very vulnerable to appearing too liberal, too reformist, because conservatives see a direct correlation between reform and corruption, and a cloud of corruption hovers over Khai because of his son's misdeeds. To be sure, after conservatives launched a major anti-graft campaign at the 6th Plenum (January-February 1998) the first major purge was of Khai's own Vice Minister Ngo Xuan Loc.[30] The reformers are very vulnerable.

The conservatives are powerful and there are more of them. But they are also much older, nearing the age of retirement, and many have questionable staying power past the next party congress in 2001, because of mismanagement in their sector, or because their patrons have passed on. The fact that so many of them- perhaps seven- are lame ducks is very important in understanding the current impasse. For example, General Scretary Le Kha Phieu (70) may be held responsible for the country's current economic malaise. He has been far more pragmatic than anyone expected him to be, but as he has sat on the fence on many issues, conveying the image of a weak leader. He has endeared himself to neither faction. President, Tran Duc Luong (65) lacks charisma and leadership, and is moreover, very close to the aging Do Muoi. That relationship could hurt Luong when Muoi passes on. Nguyen Manh Cam's (72) star is fading, now that he has retired as Minister of Foreign Affairs. Cam most likely will not be reelected to the next Politburo, unless the Central Committee feels it needs a party elder for "stability." It is likely that Cam will be appointed Vice President to replace the outgoing Madame Nguyen Thanh Binh. Nguyen Duc Binh (74) is as hard core an ideologue as they come, and as head of the party school he controls one of the most powerful patronage networks. He's getting old and a lot of people want him off the Politburo because he is too ideological. Nguyen Thi Xuan My (61), the party disciplinarian, is obviously not doing a great job. She has been disciplining more than she is deterring. Her continued presence will have more to do with how successful the current anti-corruption drive goes in regaining some of the party's lost legitimacy, than with the token presence of the Politburo's first and only woman. She is in her late-50s and could be on the next Politburo, but only if some of the graft is dealt with. Le Xuan Dung (65) has taken some heat for the economic slowdown in the capital- including the mass exodus of foreign investment. He is also rumored to be in poor health. Pham The Duyet (65) is the only true proletarian on the Politburo, a former union leader. Despite being acquitted of corruption charges, in 1998, he's been under a cloud. Duyet has been the Politburo member in charge of dealing with the peasant protests in Thai Binh. Supposedly, few officials have been arrested or punished. If peasant protests resume or spread to other provinces, Duyet could be held accountable. Moreover, like Tran Duc Luong, he is one of Do Muoi's protégés; this relationship could hurt him when Do Muoi passes on.

In short, of the 18 Politburo members, there are quite a few definite and potential vacancies, many of whom are conservative. Because the Politburo tends not to newly elect more than 50 percent of its members, seven or eight new members is foreseeable. This will really be an opportunity for the balance of power to tilt towards the reformers. Until the new congress, there will be few substantive decisions coming from the Politburo. Without a change in personnel, there cannot be a fundamental shift in policy. At present, there are simply enough conservatives who can block the deal- and more importantly- the continuation of the reform program and a commitment to greater economic globalization.

In the meantime, the reformers have attempted some damage control as they do not want to lose the initiative to the conservatives. If they cannot move the reform process forward,

[30] Adrian Edwards, "Closed Minds," *FEER*, 9 December 1999, 26.

they know that they have to prevent conservatives from reversing the gains that have been made since 1986 until the 2001 Party Congress. First, Hanoi has continued the tariff waiver of US imports. In an attempt to force the American hand to conclude the trade deal, in 1998 Hanoi passed a law that would increase all tariffs by 50 percent on imports from countries that did not accord MFN trade status to Vietnam. Then, as a gesture of good will, Hanoi waived the tariff hike for American imports in 1999. The tariff, which would have been dropped with the signing of the trade agreement, legally will take affect in 2000. When the Politburo did not sign the agreement, Vietnamese Ministry of Finance officials were quick to go on the record and announce that although no decision had been made, "The principle now is to maintain good trade relations between Vietnam and the US."[31] Second, senior Vietnamese leaders, such as First Vice Prime Minister Nguyen Tan Dung, have assured their American counterparts that the Politburo would eventually sign the agreement. Dung, who has overall responsibility for economic issues on the Politburo, is a leading reformist and a contender to become the next party General Secretary. He met with Assistant Secretary of State Stanley Roth at the APEC summit where President Clinton was hoping to sign the agreement with Prime Minister Phan Van Khai.

There will be a lot of infighting and jockeying between conservatives and reformers to see who will be responsible for the drafting of the Political Report of the 9th Congress and controlling the nomination lists for the Central Committee and Politburo membership. There is always a lot of politicking behind these issues. To be sure, the Politburo still has not been able to reach any consensus regarding who will fill Doan Khue's seat, now vacant for almost two years. Not much will happen until the next party congress in late 2001. It is possible that they move the congress up if urgent issues are at hand, but more likely, it will be delayed like the last one because they will not have been able to agree on the political report, policies, personnel changes on the Central Committee and Politburo beforehand. This was the case, for example, with the 7th Plenum in August 1999, which was delayed five times because they could not reach a consensus.

Likewise, at the 8th Plenum, in November 1999, which was scheduled to discuss the rejected trade deal and the future course of the reform program, economic integration and the trade deal were never even discussed because they are simply too divisive at present. The VCP is terrified at the idea of being divided. If one analyzes the VCP's reaction to the events in Eastern Europe in 1989, it was the collapse of communism in Hungary that most concerned Hanoi. In Hungary it was not exogenous forces that pressured the party to step down, such as the Catholic Church or independent labor unions, or intellectuals, but "reform circles" within the Hungarian Communist Party. These circles eventually became independent parties. As Hanoi does not have to worry about large student movements, a large and independent Church presence, and independent unions, it does worry about intra-party dissent and division. The leadership, at present, is unwilling to take on major ideological policy issues that could jeopardize the unity of the party.

---

[31] Reuters "Hanoi Yet to Discuss U.S. Tariff Waiver for 2000," 25 October 1999, and Reuters, "Vietnam Undecided on U.S. Tariff Waiver for 2000," 12 October 1999.

7. Conclusion

The economic reforms of *doi moi* revived Vietnam's moribund economy and poised the country to become the next tiger economy in Southeast Asia. No longer diplomatically isolated, the Vietnamese embarked on an externally-oriented development plan, seeking to develop through export led growth and by courting foreign investment; to do so, Hanoi revamped its confrontational foreign policy, normalizing ties with Japan, the United States, the ASEAN states and China. The collapse of socialism across Eastern Europe and the Tiananmen Massacre in 1989, however, alarmed many in the VCP's leadership that the reform program was going too quickly. While economic reforms were allowed to continue and the country enjoyed high growth rates in the early to mid-1990s, all debates over political liberalization were silenced as the party sought to ensure its leading role in society. Yet the initial reforms were running out of steam by the mid-1990s and Vietnam became stuck in a transitional system of market socialism. The leadership, deeply divided into ideologically based factions, was unable to come to a consensus on how to proceed with the reform program. In short, there was no consensus on what economic course the country should pursue. Deadlocked, they were unable to effectively respond to a series of crises: a faltering economy, rampant corruption, the Asian economic crisis, and a wave of peasant rebellions. The factional nature of Vietnamese politics, compounded by generational rifts in the leadership, as well as an overwhelming fear of losing ultimate control has really hampered Vietnamese decision-making. The Politburo's rejection of the trade agreement with the United States magnifies the weaknesses in the system; that the party leadership is so deadlocked over an issue that will bring such tangible results and will help to rejuvenate the economy that has been in a down turn since 1995.

Until the next party congress is held when there can be a large-scale leadership transition and generational change, sometime in 2001-2002, bold policies that will rejuvenate the reform program are unlikely to be implemented. Instead, the Vietnamese leadership will continue to implement piecemeal policies that will allow them to muddle through. Vietnam currently has very weak leaders at a time when the country desperately needs bold measures.

Ironically, the next generation of leaders will probably have more power and authority than the current leadership, for two reasons. First, they were promoted and hand picked not by the current leaders, but by the past group. They have had a lot of support and patronage. Second, and more importantly, as they are all relatively young, they will have been in top positions for a long time, and rotated through many different postings and bureaucracies; they have both depth and breadth of experience. This gives them a long time to promote and train proteges- a cadre of loyal supporters across many different bureaucracies. Only with stronger leaders, will Vietnam have the political will to make the hard policy choices to reform the economy and get it back on track to becoming the next "tiger" economy.

Chapter 2

VIETNAM'S TRANSITION TO A MARKET ECONOMY

Raymond J. Ahearn

SUMMARY

As Vietnam's *doi moi* economic reform program enters its 10th year, a political struggle within the ruling Communist Party continues to take place over the pace and scope of the reforms. Reformers in the party are pushing for a further increase in the role of the private sector in economic activity, while conservatives want the state to continue to play the dominant role in Vietnam's development. The eighth National Party Congress, scheduled for June 1996, could clarify which group has the upper hand. The outcome of this leadership struggle could have important implications for Vietnam's full integration into the world trading system as well as for U.S.-Vietnamese economic relations.

BACKGROUND

Vietnam's reform program, known as *doi moi* or economic renovation, began in 1986 in response to deteriorating internal and external conditions. At home, the economy was in desperate straits, afflicted by hyperinflation and widespread food shortages. Abroad, the Soviet Union, its most loyal ally, was cutting back on its large foreign aid programs.

In these circumstances, Vietnam's leaders adopted pragmatic, albeit partial, reforms to regain economic growth. The main stated objective was to replace a centrally planned economy, dominated by state-run enterprises, with a "regulated market economy." The internal contradiction of a controlled free market is indicative of divided views within the Vietnamese Communist Party leadership over how much reliance should be placed on the private sector.

At the heart of the reforms adopted in the late 1980s were measures that eliminated price controls on most key goods, established land use rights for farmers, clarified the legal status of private businesses, and tightened government spending. As part of the latter attempt, efforts were made to limit subsidies to state-owned enterprises (SOEs) by providing them greater autonomy in production, investment, and pricing decisions. The authorities also moved to open the economy to foreign trade and investment and to attract foreign assistance.

DOI MOI RESULTS TO DATE

Vietnam's economy has prospered since the reforms commenced in 1986. After years of negative growth, economic activity increased on average by 3.9% form 1986-1990 and by 7.6% from 1991-1993. The economy grew by 8.8% in 1994, and by 9.8% in 1995. Another year of 9-10% growth is forecast for 1996 rates of growth that have led to much media speculation that Vietnam is primed to become the next Asian tiger.[1]

Vietnam, however, remains a very poor country with a per capita income level around $230 at nominal exchange rates.[2] An estimated 36 million people (about half the population) live below the poverty line, and the country is basically at the level of development where Thailand was 30 years age. Nevertheless, the living standards of most Vietnamese have improved dramatically in the last 10 years and most Vietnamese reportedly feel that the government is moving the country forward.[3]

In terms of specific sectors, the agricultural reforms, which were aimed at transforming the state-run collective farms into private, family-based production units, have been most successful to date. Over the past decade, Vietnam has overcome its dependency on food imports to regain its historical position as a net food exporter. Rice production has led the way. Vietnam is currently the world's third largest rice exporter, after Thailand and the United States. In addition, more family-based farms, which now account for over 90% of to5tal production, are growing exportable cash crops such as coffee, corn, rubber, sugarcane, and cashew nuts. The extension of long-term leases for farmers to till the land is widely credited with creating incentives for farmers to make the requisite capital investments in the land.

In addition to family-based farm units, small and medium size enterprises (SMEs) have proliferated as government policy towards private enterprise has become more tolerant. An estimated 25,000 SMEs now dominate service industries such as real estate, restaurants, transportation, and tourism, and account for a growing proportion of light manufacturing, mostly in consumer goods. Some statistics suggest that SMEs, which are capitalized at an average of only $17,000, account for 40% of industrial output, and employ two-thirds of the labor force.[4] While official government data can be unreliable, these firms appear to be the most dynamic sector of Vietnam's economy despite important handicaps.

Gaining access to capital is the most critical handicap SMEs face. To obtain capital from banks, these firms (particularly those that have no connection to the overseas Vietnamese or Chinese communities) must put up hard assets for collateral that are worth twice the value of the loan. Even then, they can borrow only short-term – less than one year – and at relatively

---

[1] World Bank data.

[2] Because much of the economy does not involve cash transitions, real incomes are considerably higher.

[3] Bulman, Robin. "Vietnam Remains Poor Despite A Wealth of Progress Made," *Journal of Commerce*, March 21, 1995, p. 3.

[4] Comer, Bruce. "SMEs – Vietnam's Engine for Growth", *The Vietnam Business Journal*, Vol. 2, Nov-Dec. 1994, pp. 20-23.

high rates. While the country has attracted several billions of dollars in foreign aid and investment, very little has reached Vietnam's small companies in terms of joint ventures.[5]

Despite progress in closing down some 6,000, mostly small and town-based SOEs since *Doi Moi* commenced, Vietnam still operates an estimated 6,500 SOEs. The largest SOEs dominate strategic sectors of the economy such as banking, construction, energy, telecommunications, steel, and chemicals.[6] Altogether, the SOEs reportedly still account for 75% of Vietnam's assets, obtain about 65% of the bank credit, and employ a third of the labor force, but they account for only 49% of the country's GDP and do little for new job creation.[7]

To improve the efficiency of the SOEs, the government is trying to put together several dozen conglomerates, known as general corporations, in industries such as steel, coal, power, and textiles. Patterned after the South Korean model of huge conglomerates of *chaebol*, the government hopes that combining several SOEs in the same field will allow them to compete more effectively internationally while at the same time retaining control over their activities.[8]

So far the government has resisted outright efforts at privatization, but it has established a pilot "equitization program" in which it has sought to issue shares for 21 small state firms. The hope is to raise money, while retaining majority control. So far the program has had little success, but the government is set to list 200 companies for equitization this year.

Regarding external economic relations, Vietnam's reforms have opened up the country further to foreign trade and investment. Combined with inflows of capital, expanding trade ties with countries in the region have helped Vietnam weather its drastic reduction in commercial ties with the former communist countries of the Soviet bloc. As trade with the former Soviet Bloc countries dropped from 80% of Vietnam's total trade in the 1980s to under 10% today, trade with other Asian countries – led by Japan and Singapore – has more than taken its place.

Since a liberal foreign investment law was passed in 1987, Vietnam has attracted close to $19 billion in foreign commitments covering nearly 1,500 projects. Asian countries – Taiwan, Hong Kong, Japan, Singapore, South Korea, and Malaysia – account for nearly 70% of the investment commitments or approvals. While approximately 80% of the projects have been started, most in the form of joint ventures with wholly or party-owned state enterprises, only 30% of the capital has been disbursed. Bureaucratic delays in getting licenses, a murky legal status on land-use rights, pervasive corruption throughout the bureaucracy, a poor infrastructure, and lack of managerial skills are among the explanations frequently cited for the gap between project approvals and actual disbursement of capital.

DEBATE OVER ECONOMIC POLICY

Although the Vietnamese Communist Party has relinquished some of its control over the economy as part of the doi moi reform process, it still exercises near absolute political power. Decisions are made collectively and behind closed doors. Opposition to the Communist Party

---

[5] Ibid., p. 21.

[6] Schwarz, Adam. "The Way We Were: Breaking Up Is Hard To Do for Vietnamese State Firms, *Far Eastern Economic Review*, March 2, 1995, p. 58.

[7] Schwarz, Adam. "Economic Monitor: Vietnam", *Far Eastern Economic Review*, April 25, 1996, p. 52; and Chamber of Commerce and Industry of Vietnam.

[8] Schwarz, Adam, "Steps in the Dark", *Far Eastern Economic Review*, October 26, 1995, p. 52.

rule, in the streets or in the press, is not tolerated. Political and religious dissidents are jailed or otherwise repressed. While a new party constitution promulgated in 1992 makes it possible that the party could become more representative of different interest groups in the future, key decisions are made by a handful of party officials.[9]

Vietnam today, however, is not the highly regimented, centralized, and doctrinaire Communist state that it was a few decades ago. People may not have political freedom, but the *Doi Moi* process has weakened the position of the party, particularly in economic and social affairs. In these areas, the Vietnamese people appear to have considerable personal freedom. Provincial and local officials also have considerable power, and often act contrary to decrees issued from Hanoi. Top party leaders are most often described as pragmatists who are focused on two overriding objectives: bringing economic prosperity to Vietnam and maintaining the party's monopoly on political power. The pace and scope of the economic reforms, however, is a matter of serious divide among Vietnam's ruling elite.

Two camps are now locked in debate running up the eighth Vietnamese Party Congress, scheduled for this June. One group of so-called "reformers" advocates more active policy reforms that support development of a stronger private sector, the contraction of the largely inefficient state sector, and the country's economic integration into the world economy. A second group of "conservatives" worry that an increase in the pace of economic reforms could have negative consequences for Vietnamese society, including the potential to undermine the party's monopoly on power through an increase in societal demands for political reforms.

The reformers, led by Vo Van Kiet, the prime minister and party's third ranking official, judge that the economy is not a critical crossroads. They believe that if the economy is to keep growing at current rates over the next five years, around $40 billion of investment capital will have to be raised from both domestic and foreign sources. To raise half of the capital domestically, a major transfer of resources out of the state sector into the private sector would be necessary. Mobilizing foreign capital will require that investors and aid donors be convinced that the reform process is moving forward with a restructuring of the legal, financial, and administrative foundation of a market economy.

Conservatives, led by President Le Duc Anh, tend to be more wary of opening the country to foreign influences as well as any rapid rush towards economic reform. Their immediate concerns are focused on the side-effects of economic reform, particularly on the widening income gap between the mostly peasant population of the countryside – who tend to be strong supporters of the Communist Party – and the population of the cities, and on an erosion of "moral values." Their longer-run concerns are fixated on deflecting threats to their monolithic authority and control.

To deal with the income gap, many conservatives advocate higher taxes, more restrictive land-use laws, more centralized control of businesses, and a reduction of the autonomy with which local People's Councils can authorize joint ventures. All these steps arguably go against the main direction of the *doi moi* reform process and would have a dampening effect on foreign direct investment.[10]

---

[9] Goodman, Allan E. "Vietnam in 1995: It Was a Very Good Year," *The Washington Quarterly*, Spring 1996, pp. 137-150.

[10] Goodman, Allan E. p. 145.

Conservatives are also opposed to any fundamental restructuring of the SOEs. As the economy has experienced rapid growth without any radical restructuring of the state enterprises, conservatives believe that Vietnam's economic development can be state-led. In addition, the possible displacement of hundreds of thousands of war veterans (a key party support group) employed by SOEs is a more important consideration to this group than the growth-impeding aspects of SOEs.

In the run-up to the Communist Party congress, a draft report issued by the party has been widely interpreted as bolstering the position of the conservatives. While the report does not call for the reversal of economic reforms already put into place, it argues that the state sector should play the leading role in the country's industrialization process, with a goal of increasing the state sector's contribution to GDP from around the 40% level today to 60% by 2020. The report also urges that resources should also be concentrated on developing the state sector in key areas such as the financial system, insurance, trade and other service industries.[11]

A campaign against "social evils," launched in February 1996, has also been widely reported in the press as an indication of growing conservative influence. This campaign, which has included attempts to limit prostitution, corruption, and the use of only foreign names in advertising, has unsettled many foreign investors and may be contributing to a drop in foreign investment approvals.[12]

It is, however, uncertain whether the conservatives are gaining the upper hand. In the prelude to previous party congresses, similar signs of conservative rumblings have surfaced, only to be followed by a return to the status quo after the party congress. In addition, some sings point to a possible growing ascendancy of the reformer camp. These include the dismissal in April 1996, of conservative Politburo member Nguyen Haa Phan, and a commitment by the party to bring "younger" members into the Centralized Committee.

POLICY IMPLICATIONS

In assessing the leadership conflict, most analysts believe that the political consensus in favor of *Doi Moi* is unlikely to be reversed. As the legitimacy of the Communist Party depends on rising living standards induced by rapid economic growth, few analysts believe that ideology will prevail over this imperative.

A number of external forces also make it likely that the rhetoric of Vietnam's leadership will continue to be socialist while its practice continues to be increasingly capitalist. For example, Vietnam's membership in the Association of South East Asian Nations (ASEAN) and its application to become a member of the World Trade Organization (WTO) are strong forces for keeping the country moving in the direction of a more market-oriented economy. For Vietnam, membership in both groupings will help it gain wider access to markets and increase its acceptability to international investors. In addition, preconditions for loans established by the World Bank, and the Asian Development Bank provide strong pressures for continuing the reform process.

---

[11] Chua, Reginald. "Vietnam Sets Lofty Goals for Economy While Maintaining State's Primary Role," *New York Times*, April 20, 1996, p. A8.

[12] Grant, Jeremy. "Investment in Vietnam Drops," *Financial Times*, May 6, 1996, p. 7.

Continuing divisions among the top leadership, however, are likely to ensure that the pace of Vietnam's transition towards a market economy will not be smooth. A likely scenario, barring a crisis, is for a continuation of the two-steps forward and one-step back routine where the state sector will continue to play a large role and where small entrepreneurs will continue to operate somewhat handicapped.

Despite the considerable progress made over the past decade, Vietnam's transition towards a market-oriented economy has a long way to go. In this context, Vietnam's leadership struggle could affect the movement towards normalization of commercial relations with the United States.[13]

Currently, a number of statutory provisions preclude Vietnam from being eligible for preferences such as most-favored-nation (MFN) treatment, Export-Import Bank trade financing, and Overseas Private Investment Corporation (OPIC) insurance guarantees for private investment. To become eligible for the restoration of these economic benefits, Vietnam would have to make a number of fundamental reforms in the areas affecting SOEs; emigration; labor policies; government control over trade and investment flows and Vietnam's legal system. In addition, human rights and press freedom could be important considerations as well.

The Clinton Administration recently provided the Vietnamese authorities with a framework paper detailing a list of steps Vietnam would have to take in order to enter into a trade agreement with the United States – a necessary action before Vietnam could be granted MFN treatment. Many of the steps involve a reduction of the Vietnamese government's still heavy control over trade and investment flows as well as improvements in its legal system.

How fast Vietnam may undertake these reforms, many of which are required as well for admission to the WTO, could be affected by the policy and ideological struggle being waged among Vietnam's top leadership. The outcome of the party congress, thus, will be monitored closely by the U.S. government and private sector.

[13] For a full discussion, see *Vietnam-U.S. Relations*: *The Debate Over Normalization*, CRS Issue Brief 93081, Updated May 1, 1996 (By Robert G. Sutter).

Chapter 3

THE VIETNAM-U.S. BILATERAL TRADE AGREEMENT

Mark E. Manyin

BACKGROUND

On July 13, 2000, after nearly five years of bargaining, the U.S. and Vietnam announced they had signed a bilateral trade agreement (BTA).[1] On June 8, 2001, President Bush submitted the agreement, which requires congressional approval, to Congress. Following President Bush's transmission, joint resolutions (H.J.Res. 51 and S.J.Res. 16) were introduced in both chambers, and referred to the House Ways and Means Committee and the Senate Finance Committee. On September 6, 2001, the House approved the agreement by voice vote. The Senate passed the agreements, by a vote of 88-12, on October 13, 2001 (Roll Call 291). On October 16, 2001, President Bush signed the agreement into law (P.L. 107-52). Vietnam's National Assembly ratified the BTA on November 28, 2001, by a vote of 278-85, and Vietnamese President Tran Duc Luong singed the agreement into law on December 7. It entered into force on December 10, 2001 when the two countries formally exchanged letters of implementation.

The BTA is a major step toward fully normalizing U.S.-Vietnam commercial relations, as it restores reciprocal most-favored-nation (MFN, also known as normal trade relations [NTR]) treatment between the two countries, and commits Vietnam to undertake a wide range of market-oriented economic reforms.[2] Extending MFN treatment to Vietnam is significantly reducing U.S. tariffs on most imports from Vietnam.

---

[1] The text of the agreement – along with a separate Annex on Services and two separate letters on investment – may be found on the home page of the United States Trade Representative [http://www.ustr.gov] and on the home page of the United States – Vietnam Trade Council [http://www.usvtc.org]. The While House has prepared a "fact sheet" on the BTA. It may be found at: [http://www.usinfo.state.gov/regional/ea/vietnam/whtrd713.htm].

[2] In 1998, legislation was enacted to replace the term "most-favored-nation" treatment in existing and future legislation with the term "normal trade relations" (NTR). The former term is used in this report for reasons of historical continuity and because of its continued use in international trade relations, including in U.S. bilateral trade agreements. See CRS Issue Brief IB93107, *Most-Favored-Nation (Normal-Trade-Relations) Policy of the United States* by Vladimir N. Pregelj.

CONGRESS' ROLE IN THE NORMALIZATION OF U.S.-VIETNAM TRADE RELATIONS[3]

Following the victory of communist North Vietnam over U.S.-back South Vietnam in 1975, the United States ended virtually all-economic interchange with unified Vietnam. The commercial restrictions included not only those that previously had been imposed only on North Vietnam (see the following section), but also a halt to bilateral humanitarian aid, opposition to financial aid from international financial institutions (such as the World Bank), a ban on U.S. travel to Vietnam, and an embargo on bilateral trade.

Washington and Hanoi gradually began to normalize relations in the early 1990s, following improvements on the issues of Vietnam's activities in Cambodia and American prisoners of war (POWs) and missing-in-action (MIA) personnel in Vietnam.[4] In 1994, President Clinton ordered the lifting of the trade embargo against Vietnam. The following year, the two countries established ambassadorial-level diplomatic relations. In 1998, President Clinton granted Vietnam its first waiver from the requirements of the so-called **Jackson-Vanik amendment** (contained in the Trade Act of 1974, Title IV, section 402), which prohibit the President from normalizing commercial relations with selected socialist and formerly socialist countries if they do not meet certain requirements regarding freedom of emigration. Presidential waivers were also granted to Vietnam in 1999, 2000, and 2001. Congress may reject the annual waiver by passing a joint disapproval resolution. Each time waivers have been granted to Vietnam, the House has defeated disapproval resolution. (See **Figure 1**.) As explained below, until the U.S.-Vietnam BTA goes into effect the waiver does not change Vietnam's current, non-MFN, trade status with the United States. Instead, it allows the U.S. Overseas Private Investment Corporation (OPIC) and the U.S. Export-Import Bank to support U.S. businesses exporting to and/or operating in Vietnam

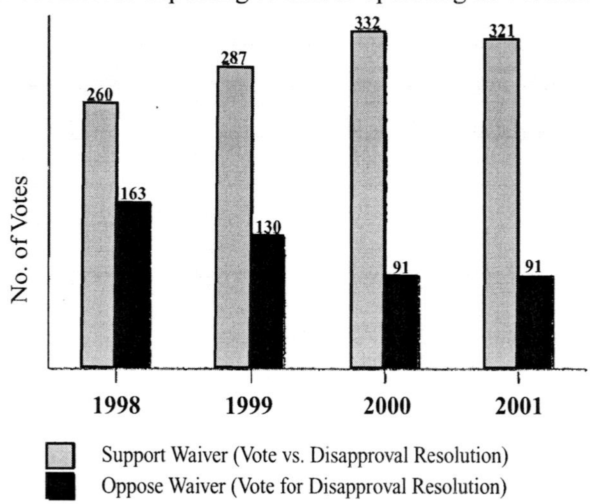

Figure 1. House Votes on Vietnam's Jackson-Vanik Waiver, 1998-2000

---

[3] Vladimir Pregelj, CRS Specialist in International Trade and Finance, provided extensive assistance with this section.

[4] For a more detailed account of the history of U.S.-Vietnam normalization, see CRS Issue Brief IB98033, *The Vietnam-U.S. Normalization Process*, by Mark Manyin.

Restoration of Temporary MFN Status to Vietnam

The U.S. denied MFN treatment to communist-controlled areas of Vietnam in August 1951. At that time, under Section 5 of the Trade Agreements Extension Act of 1951, MFN tariff rates were suspended for all countries of the Sino-Soviet bloc.[5] When communist North Vietnamese forces unified the country in 1975, MFN status was suspended for the entire country.

In 1974, the U.S. issued strict conditions for restoring MFN status to those non-market economies (NMEs) subject to Section 5 suspension (in practice, the new conditions applied to virtually all countries in the former Sino-Soviet bloc). Under Title IV of the Trade Act of 1974, MFN treatment may be restored to NME countries after two requirements have been met:

a. The President issues a determination that the country is not in violation of the freedom-of-emigration requirements of the Jackson-Vanik amendment.[6] To date, Vietnam has not been found to be in full compliance with Jackson-Vanik requirements. Alternatively, subject to certain conditions, the President may waive these requirements, as Presidents Clinton and Bush have done since 1998. Jackson-Vanik waivers must be renewed annually, and Congress may reject them by passing a joint disapproval resolution.
b. The completion of a bilateral trade agreement that contains certain required provisions, including a reciprocal MFN clause. Such an agreement requires approval by the Congress (and by the Vietnamese National Assembly). Once the BTA is approved, the President can extend *temporary* MFN tariff treatment to Vietnam. The MFN treatment would be temporary because it is contingent upon Vietnam meeting the requirements described in the previous paragraphs – *i.e.,* either obtaining a Presidential determination or a Presidential waiver, both of which are valid only for one year and are subject to congressional review.[7] This is the same process through which Congress has reviewed China's temporary MFN status.

---

[5] Section 5 of the Trade Agreement Extension Act of 1951 (65 Stat. 73), which Congress passed in response to the outbreak of the Korean War, required the President to suspend the application of MFN tariff rates to the Soviet Union and all countries or areas under the control of international communism. Yugoslavia, a non-Soviet bloc country, was the one exception. For more on the history of the U.S.'s MFN policy, see CRS Issue Brief IB93107, *Normal-Trade-Relations (Most-Favored-Nation) Policy of the United States*, by Vladimir Pregelj. Currently, the U.S. denies MFN treatment to only six countries – Afghanistan, Cuba, Laos, North Korea, and Yugoslavia (Serbia and Montenegro).

[6] After the issuance of a determination of full compliance with the Jackson-Vanik amendment's freedom-of-emigration requirements, the President must issue semiannual reports to Congress arguing that the relevant country is not in violation of the freedom-of-emigration requirements. The President's end-of-year report is subject to congressional disapproval by joint resolution.

[7] Note that Vietnam's MFN treatment would be temporary regardless of whether it received a Jackson-Vanik waiver or a Presidential report that Vietnam is in full-compliance with the Jackson-Vanik amendment. In the case of the latter, the President's annual year-end report would be subject to congressional review, and therefore could be rejected by a joint disapproval resolution.

Congressional Procedures for Considering a U.S.-Vietnam BTA.[8]

To go into effect, Title IV bilateral trade agreements must be approved by a joint resolution of Congress. Once the President transmits the agreement to Congress, a resolution must be introduced in both Houses. The resolutions are subject to special expedited procedures, under which amendments are not permitted in either chamber.

Additionally, there are deadlines of 45 session-days for committee consideration (by the House Ways and Means and the Senate Finance Committees), and 15 session-days for floor debate in both chambers. Because the approval resolutions are revenue measures, the Senate must vote on a House-passed resolution, and Congress would have a *maximum* of 90 session-days to act on the resolution: 45 days for consideration by the House Ways and Means Committee; followed by 15 days for floor debate in the House; followed by 15 days for consideration of the House-passed resolution in the Senate Finance Committee; followed by 15 days for floor debate in the Senate.

As with most trade agreements with non-market economies, the U.S.-Vietnam BTA will remain in effect for a 3-year period and will be extended automatically unless renounced by either party. Additionally, each extension will require a presidential determination that Vietnam is satisfactorily extending reciprocal MFN treatment to U.S. exports.

After the BTA: Extending Permanent MFN Treatment to Vietnam

Following the BTA, the next step toward normalizing U.S.-Vietnam commercial ties is restoring permanent MFN status (also know as permanent NTR or PNTR status) to Vietnam, a process that will require Congress to "graduate" Vietnam from the group of non-market economies that are denied unconditional MFN treatment. This would be done by terminating the application of the relevant Title IV provisions to Vietnam, as has been done for several countries, including Bulgaria, the Czech Republic, Slovakia, Hungary, and Romania. In May 2000, the House voted to give permanent MFN status to China once it joins the World Trade Organization.

Vietnam and the World Trade Organization (WTO). Vietnam applied to joint the WTO in 1995. Many observers believe that Vietnam is a number of years away from meeting the requirements for WTO membership. In March 2001, Vietnam's Trade Minister expressed his government's goal of acceding to the WTO by 2004. As a practical matter, countries seeking to enter the WTO must obtain the consent of all WTO member countries. Typically, these bilateral negotiations focus on tariff concessions and other market access issues that will govern bilateral trade relations after the applicant becomes a member. Thus, at some point in the future, Vietnam and the U.S. are likely to engage in another set of negotiations about the changes Vietnam must make to its trade regime before the U.S. will support Vietnam's application for WTO membership. Upon completion of this agreement, it is likely that the U.S. president will ask Congress to extend permanent MFN treatment to Vietnam, much as

[8] For more on this topic, see CRS Report RS20717, *Vietnam Trade Agreement: Approval and Implementing Procedure*, by Vladimir Pregelj.

President Clinton did after completing WTO accession negotiations with China in November 1999.[9]

Table 1. Vietnam's Path to Commercial Normalization with the United States

Step	Action
Step 1. Removing the U.S. trade embargo	In February 1994, President Clinton ordered the embargo on Vietnam lifted.
Step 2. Granting an annual waiver of Jackson-Vanik restrictions on OPIC and Ex-Im Bank operations in the country.[10]	President Clinton issued waivers for Vietnam in 1998, 1999, and 2000, as did President Bush in 2001. Each time, disapproval resolutions were defeated in the House.
Step 3. Signing a bilateral trade agreement, subject to Congressional approval, that includes an extension of conditional MFN treatment.	An agreement was signed in July 2000. It was approved by Congress and signed into law by the President in 2001. Vietnam has yet to ratify the agreement.
Step 4. Restoring permanent MFN status by passing a law "graduating" Vietnam from its status as a non-MFN country.	Presumably, this step will be taken if and when Vietnam joins the World Trade Organization (WTO).

U.S. and Vietnamese Interests in a Bilateral Trade Agreement

U.S. Interests in a Bilateral BTA

U.S.-Vietnamese trade and investment flows are extremely low. Although Vietnam is the world's 13th most populous country, with nearly 80 million people, for the past several years annual U.S. exports have hovered in the $200-$300 million range (see Table 2), a figure roughly equivalent to three days' worth of exports to Japan, and roughly one-fifth the amount the U.S. exported to South Vietnam in 1970.[11] Major U.S. exports to Vietnam include aircraft, fertilizer, telecommunications equipment, and general machinery. Cumulative foreign direct investment (FDI) by U.S. companies in Vietnam is also low, valued at about $1 billion, making the United States the ninth-largest source of investment in Vietnam.

[9] If Vietnam acceded to the WTO before the U.S. extended to it permanent MFN status, its WTO membership could place the U.S. in violation of the WTO requirement that unconditional MFN treatment be applied to all WTO members. The U.S. could avoid this by invoking the WTO's non-application article (Article XIII) prior to Vietnam's accession to the WTO. Thus, if Vietnam were to join the WTO, Hanoi's accession would not in and of itself alter the status of U.S.-Vietnam trade relations, which would continue to be governed by Title IV of the Trade Act of 1974, as well as the U.S.-Vietnam BTA. However, the U.S. would not be guaranteed all the benefits of Vietnam's accession to the WTO, including the use of the WTO's dispute resolution mechanism to deal with U.S.-Vietnam trade disputes.

[10] Alternatively, as described earlier, this step could be taken through a Presidential determination that Vietnam is in full compliance with the Jackson-Vanik amendment's freedom-of-emigration requirements. Along with China and Belarus, Vietnam has not been certified to be in full compliance with the Jackson-Vanik requirements.

[11] In 1970, the United States exported $342 million to South Vietnam. Adjusted for inflation, this amount equals approximately $1.5 billion today.

Table 2. U.S.-Vietnam Trade, 1994-2000 (millions of dollars)

	U.S. Imports from Vietnam	**U.S. Exports to Vietnam**	**Trade Balance**
1994	50.45	172.22	121.77
1995	198.97	252.86	53.89
1996	319.04	616.05	297.01
1997	388.19	277.79	-110.40
1998	553.41	274.22	-279.19
1999	601.90	277.30	-324.60
2000	827.40	330.50	-496.90
Major Imports from Vietnam	Shrimp, footwear, coffee, petrol products, cashews		
Major Exports to Vietnam	Industrial & office machinery, footwear parts, telecommunications equipment, fertilizer, cotton		

Source: U.S. Department of Commerce. Data are for merchandise trade on a customs basis.

To boost U.S. exports and investments, U.S. negotiations demanded that Vietnam provide more comprehensive and detailed concessions in the areas of services, investment, and market access than had been obtained in previous bilateral trade pacts with other Jackson-Vanik countries. As discussed in the following section, it appears the U.S. successfully obtained most of these negotiating objectives.

Following the signing of the agreement, Clinton Administration officials and business representatives were careful not to argue that the BTA will significantly boost U.S. exports and investments to Vietnam in the short term. Rather, they stressed that U.S. exporters and investors will benefit most in the medium to long-term, as Vietnam continues market-oriented reforms, becomes more developed and integrated into the global economy, and as Vietnam phases in more and more of the BTA's requirements. Moreover, exports to and investments in Vietnam are expected to increase as Hanoi and other members of the Association of Southeast Asian Nations (ASEAN) – a 10-country, 500-million person market – follow through on commitments to reduce trade barriers by 2006. Ultimately, U.S. trade and investment opportunities in the future will depend on: a) Hanoi's implementation of the BTA; b) Vietnam's progress on moving toward a more market-oriented economy; and c) Vietnam's rate of economic growth.

In the short- to medium-term, the BTA will require Vietnam to improve the climate for foreign investors. U.S. businesses in Vietnam will receive legal protections that are unavailable today. More sectors will be open to U.S. multinationals. Additionally, the BTA will help make the Vietnamese business environment more predictable and transparent. Currently, a frequent complaint from foreign executives in Vietnam is the lengthy delay in obtaining investment licenses from the government. To make matters more difficult, foreign investors often are not aware of all the regulatory requirements for obtaining licenses, leading to complaints of arbitrary treatment by local and central government authorities.

Many of the agreement's proponents also contended that the bilateral trade pact will nudge Vietnam toward a more democratic society by committing the government to enact market-oriented reforms, weakening the government's tight political controls, solidifying the rule of law, integrating Vietnamese enterprises more fully into the global economy, and economically empowering individuals. BTA proponents also pointed out that the agreement will help to bring Vietnam closer to compliance with WTO rules, facilitating Hanoi's eventual WTO accession. Once Vietnam joins the WTO, its trade policies will be subject to even greater international scrutiny and disciplines. Strategically, BTA backers argued that the U.S.-Vietnam BTA, together with BTAs recently completed with Cambodia and Laos, will promote regional stability by smoothing the integration of Indochina into the regional and global community.[12]

Arguments against the BTA

The agreement's critics argued that Vietnam's government is likely to fall short on implementing the agreement and/or is likely to erect new, hidden barriers to imports and foreign investment, while low-cost Vietnamese exports – particularly textiles – to the U.S. will increase. Some U.S. trade unions criticized the pact's lack of provisions on minimum labor standards and environmental protection. Vowing to fight the agreement in Congress, AFL-CIO President John Sweeney in July 2000 argued that "it [the BTA] is missing what we've been championing – core labor standards, human rights and environmental protection." Textile manufacturers and other groups said they would lobby Congress and the Administration for changes to safeguard their industries from low-priced Vietnamese imports.[13] Many observers, including labor groups, also opposed the pact on human rights grounds, arguing that human rights considerations should take priority over trade ties and/or that Hanoi's ruling elite would capture most of the gains from increased globalization. Indeed, on the same day the House approved the BTA, is also passed the Vietnam Human Rights Act, (H.R. 2833, by a vote of 410-1), which would ban increases (over FY2001 levels) in non-humanitarian aid to the Vietnamese government if the President does not certify that Vietnam is making "substantial progress" in human rights. The act allows the President to waive the cap on aid increases. In its most recent annual review of Vietnam's human rights situation, the U.S. State Department reported that Hanoi continues, "to repress basic political and some religious freedoms and to commit numerous abuses," notably "not tolerating most types of public dissent."[14]

Vietnam's Interests in a BTA

After recording impressive growth for much of the 1990s following Hanoi's launch of the *doi moi* (economic renovation) reforms, Vietnam's economy has slowed since the 1997-1999 Asian financial crisis, which originated in nearby Thailand. Annual economic growth declined from a peak of 9.5% in 1995 to 4.8% in 1999 and 6% in 2000. foreign direct

---

[12] Testimony of Ambassador Charlene Barshevsky before the Senate Foreign Relations Subcommittees on International Economic Policy and Asia-Pacific Affairs, August 4, 1999. Note that Congress has approved the U.S.-Cambodia BTA, which is now in force, but has yet to approve the agreement with Laos.

[13] "U.S. Labor Vows Fight Against Vietnam Trade Pact," *ABCnews. com*, accessed July 17, 2000; see also "Clouds Part Over Vietnam's Bumpy Road to Reform," *Reuters*, July 18, 2000.

[14] U.S. Department of State *2000 Report on Human Rights Practices in Vietnam*, released February 26, 2000, available at [http://www.state.gov/drl/rls/hrrpt/2000/].

investment – a major stimulus for the country's growth – dwindled from over $8 billion in 1996 to $600 million in 1999, the lowest level since 1992.[15]

It is likely that the deterioration in Vietnam's economic fortunes played a major role in jump-starting the BTA talks with the U.S. in the spring of 1999, as a significant portion of Vietnam's leadership come to see increased U.S. investment and MFN access to the U.S. market as major ways for Vietnam to reverse its declining growth rates. As of December 2000, the United States was only the ninth largest source of foreign investment in Vietnam and absorbed less than 5% of Vietnam's exports. The bilateral trade agreement presumably will increase these levels considerably by conferring to Vietnamese exporters the same tariff rates that are applied to other MFN-recipient countries. The World Bank has estimated that Vietnam's exports to the U.S. will rise to $1.3 billion – more than 60% over 2000 levels – in the first year of MFN status, as U.S. tariff rates on Vietnamese exports would fall from their non-MFN average of 40% to less than 3%.[16]

Obtaining MFN status is likely to dramatically transform the product mix of Vietnam's exports to the U.S. Since the trade embargo was lifted in 1994, most of Vietnam's exports to the U.S. have been in items that either receive duty-free treatment (zero tariffs) or that have identical tariffs for MFN and non-MFN countries. In the short term, the BTA is likely to increase Vietnam's exports of labor-intensive manufacturing with large differences between the MFN and non-MFN tariff rates. Judging by Vietnam's leading exports to the European Union and Japan (see **Figure 2**), exports of the following items are likely to increase substantially: garments, leather products, footwear, household plastic products and processed foods.[17]

Vietnam's Clothing Exports

In particular, Vietnam's clothing exports are expected to increase dramatically. Vietnam currently exports few apparel products to the U.S. – less than $40 million in 1999 – because of the higher, non-MFN, tariff rates it faces. In contrast, Vietnamese garment exports to Japan and the 15 countries of the European Union in 1999 totaled more than $500 million and $640 million, respectively (see **Figure 2**). Based on the experience of Cambodia, which was granted MFN status by the United States in 1996, the World Bank estimates Vietnamese apparel exports will increase nearly tenfold – to $384 million – in the first year after receiving MFN status.[18]

The BTA agreement contains no provisions on Vietnamese textile exports to the U.S., but the safeguard provision would allow the U.S. to impose quotas on textile imports in the event

---

[15] For more on Vietnam's economic situation, see CRS Report 98-551, *Vietnam: Economic Reforms and Commercial Relations with the United States*, by Raymond J. Ahearn, and CRS Issue Brief IB98033, *Vietnam-U.S. Relations*, by Mark Manyin.

[16] Fukase, Emiko, and Will Martin, *The Effects of the United States Granting Most-Favored-Nation (MFN) Status to Vietnam*, (Washington, DC: World Bank Development and Research Group, 1999). In a 1998 report, the World Bank estimated that half of the projected increase in exports to the U.S. will consist of clothing items. The rest is likely to consist of manufactures and processed agricultural goods. See World Bank, *Rising to the Challenge*, 1998, available at [http://www.worldbank.org.vn/rep1/rep001.htm].

[17] EUROSTAT Internal and External Trade of the EU Database; *2000 Japan Statistical Yearbook; AsiaPulse*, [http://sg.dailynews.yahoo.com/headlines/asia/], accessed on August 18, 2000.

[18] Fukase and Martin, *The Effects of the United States Granting Most-Favored-Nation (MFN) Status to Vietnam*, p. 12.

of a surge of imports. In private, U.S. and Vietnamese officials have said they expect to begin negotiating a bilateral textile agreement, which presumably would set quotas for Vietnamese textile exports, soon after a Congressional vote on the BTA. Some Members of Congress have called for the Bush Administration to publicly commit to negotiating a textile agreement, and have pressed for a commitment that such an agreement would include provisions that would link the size of Vietnam's quotas to progress in its labor rights.[19]

Passing a trade agreement would also bring Vietnam one step closer to receiving U.S. trade benefits under the generalized system of preferences (GSP), which allows many imports from less-developed countries to enter the U.S. market duty-free.[20] Furthermore, Vietnamese officials see the bilateral trade agreement as an important stepping-stone to joining the WTO, providing them with non-discriminatory access to all WTO members. Not only do they regard the BTA as necessary to obtaining U.S. support for Vietnam's application for WTO membership, but they also see the processes of negotiating and implementing the agreement as useful for raising Vietnam's legal, regulatory, and economic systems to the WTO's standards.

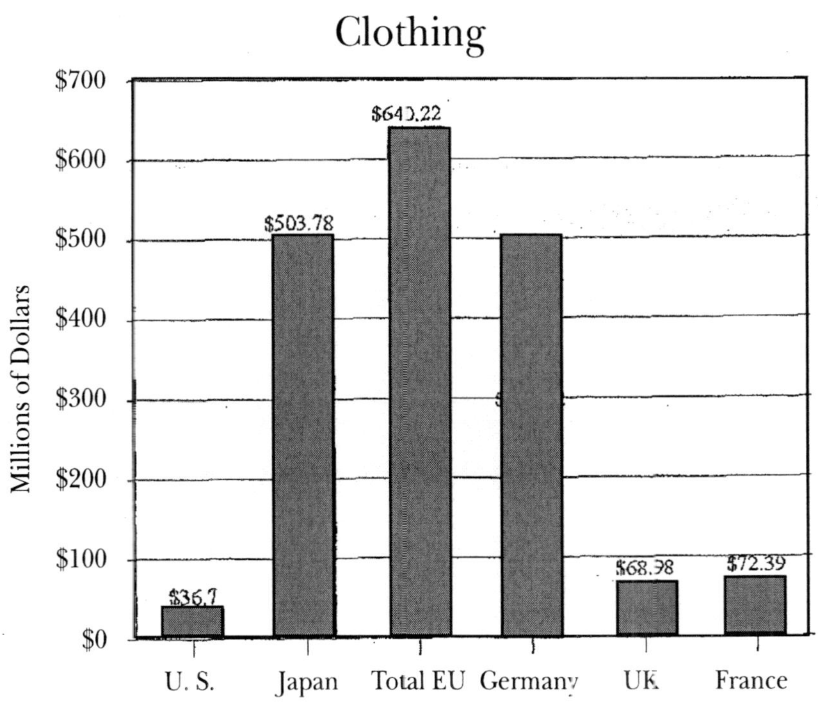

Figure 2. Imports from Vietnam, Selected Countries & Products, 1999

[19] *Inside U.S. Trade*, May 25, 2001.

[20] Under Section 502 of the Trade Act of 1974, to be eligible for GSP treatment, Communist countries, in addition to meeting other conditions required of recipient developing countries, must receive MFN treatment, and belong to the WTO and the IMF. Paragraph I:3:8 of the Vietnam-U.S. BTA states that "the United States shall consider Vietnam's eligibility for the Generalized System of Preferences."

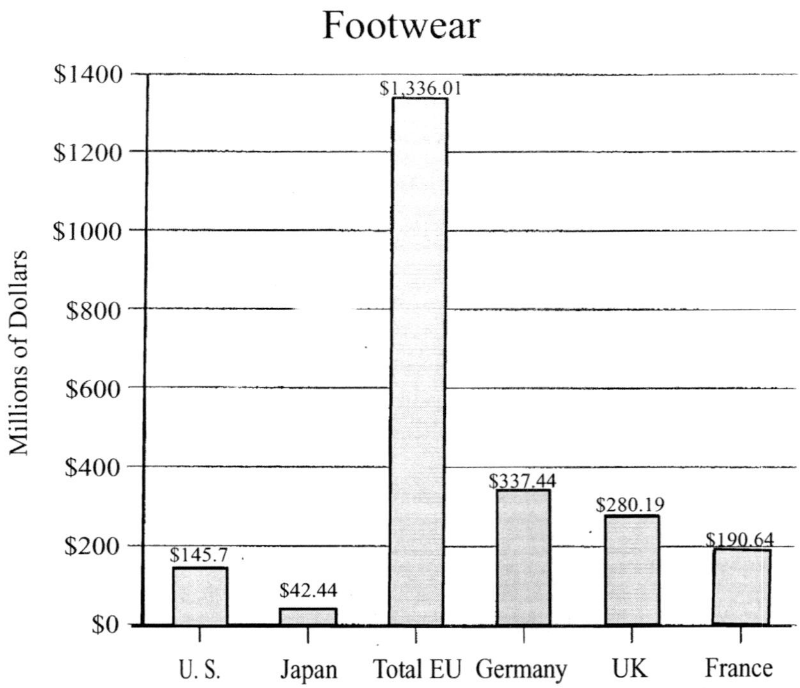

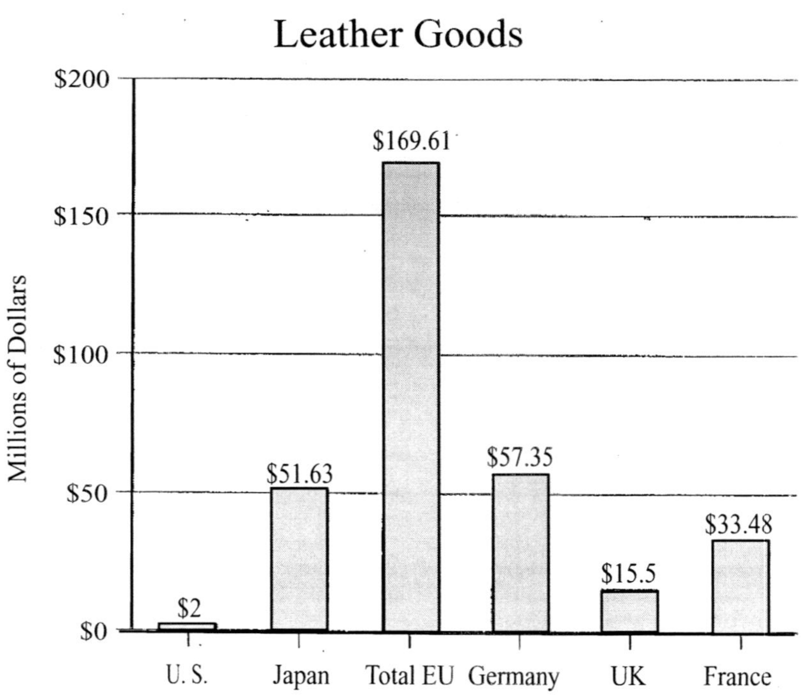

Figure 2. Imports from Vietnam, Selected Countries & Products, 1999 (continued)

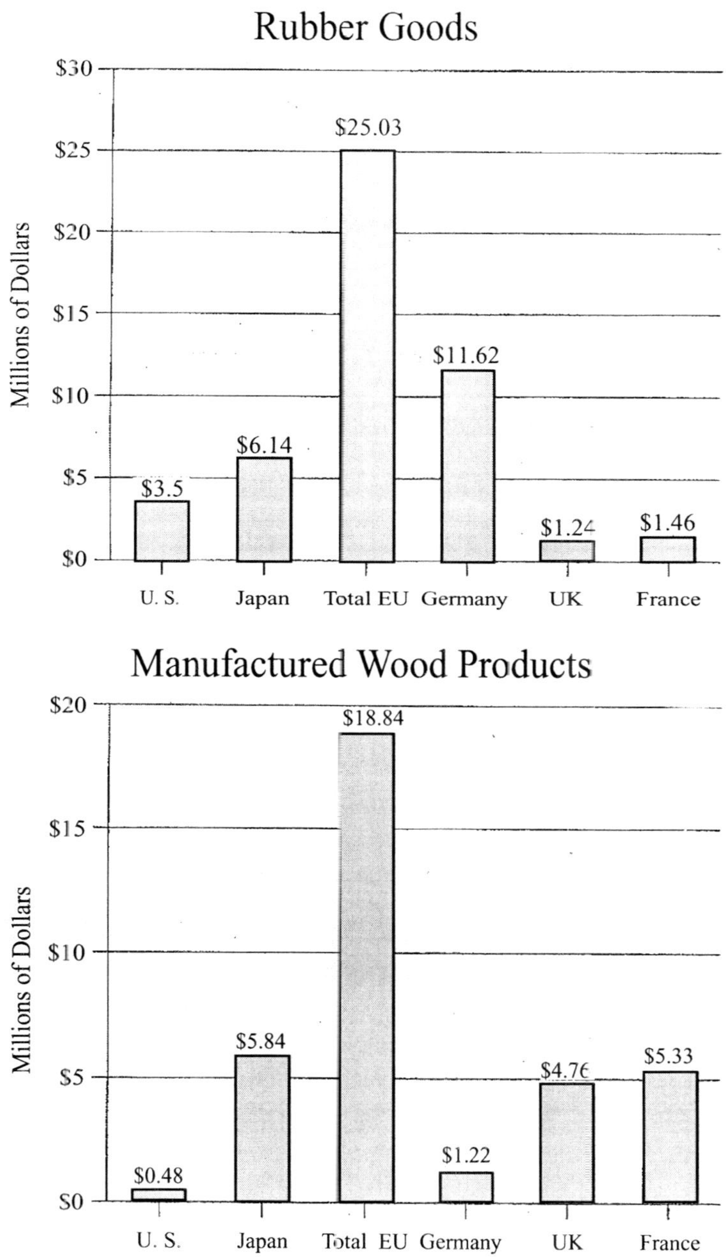

(Source: U.S. International Trade Commission, EUROSTAT, and Japan Tariff Association)

Figure 2. Imports from Vietnam, Selected Countries & Products, 1999 (continued)

Overview of the Vietnam-U.S. Bilateral Trade Agreement

The trade agreement consists of four parts: market access, trade in services, intellectual property rights, and investment.

1) Market Access

Vietnam has agreed to take the following steps to open its markets:

- guarantee most-favored-nation (MFN) treatment to U.S. goods;
- treat imports the same as domestically produced products (also known as "national treatment");
- eliminate quotas on all imports over a period of 3 to 7 years;
- make its government procurement process more transparent;
- allow for the first time all Vietnamese enterprises to trade all products;
- allow for the first time U.S. companies and U.S.-invested companies to import and export most products (to be phased in 3-6 years) (Presently, foreign companies have to rely on licensed Vietnamese importers, most of which are state-owned enterprises.);
- ensure that state enterprises comply with WTO rules;
- adhere to WTO rules in applying customs, import licensing, technical standards, and sanitary and phytosanitary measures.

Tariff Concessions

The U.S.-Vietnam BTA is unique in that, in contrast to previously negotiated bilateral trade agreements between the U.S. and Jackson-Vanik countries, it includes specific commitments by Vietnam to reduce tariffs on approximately 250 products, about four-fifths of which are agricultural goods. Typically, the cuts range from 33% to 50% and are to be phased in over a three-year period. Vietnam's tariffs are not considered to be extremely high for a developing country (the U.S. Foreign Commercial Service estimates that Vietnam's average tariff line is 15%-20%).

Also in the area of market access, the agreement includes a **safeguard** provision that will allow either side to raise tariffs temporarily if it encounters a surge of imports.

2) Intellectual Property Rights

Vietnam has pledged to phase in the World Trade Organization Agreement on Trade-Related Intellectual Property Rights (TRIPs) over 18 months. The bilateral TRIPs agreement goes above and beyond the WTO's TRIPs agreement by including Vietnamese commitments to protect satellite signals within 30 months.

3) Trade in Services

In the areas of services, Vietnam has committed to uphold WTO rules such as MFN, national treatment, and disciplines on domestic regulation. Additionally, Vietnam has agreed to allow U.S. companies and individuals to invest in markets in a wide range of service sectors, including accounting, advertising, banking, computer, distribution, education, insurance, legal and telecommunications. Most sector-specific commitments are phased in over three to five years. Vietnam's commitments in three of the largest U.S. service sectors – banking, insurance, and telecommunications – are highlighted below.

Banking Services

Vietnam agreed to the following liberalization measures: for the first nine years after the agreement goes into effect, U.S. banks may form joint ventures with Vietnamese partners, with U.S. equity between 30% and 49%. After nine years, 100% subsidiaries are permitted.

Insurance

Under the BTA, for "mandatory" insurance sectors (such as automobile and construction-related insurance), after three years Vietnam will allow U.S. companies to form joint ventures, with no limit on the U.S. equity share. After six years, 100% subsidiaries are permitted. For life insurance and other "non-mandatory" insurance sectors, after three years joint ventures are permitted, with a limit of 50% U.S. equity. After five years, 100% subsidiaries are allowed.

Telecommunications

Under the BTA, for higher-end telecommunications services (such as Internet, e-mail, and voice mail services), Vietnam will permit joint ventures after two years, with a 50% cap on U.S. equity participation. Internet services have a three-year phase in period. For basic telecommunications services (such as facsimile, cellular mobile, and satellite services), joint ventures are permitted after four years, with U.S. companies limited to a 49% stake. For local, long distance, and international voice telephone services, joint ventures are permitted after six years, with a 49% cap on U.S. ownership. Vietnam agreed that it will consider increasing the U.S. equity limits when the agreement is reviewed in three years.

4) Investment

Regarding **investment**, the U.S.-Vietnam trade agreement includes guarantees of MFN treatment, national treatment, transparency, and protection against expropriation. Additionally, Vietnam pledged to implement the following changes in its investment regime:

- Investment screening: Currently, foreign businesses must obtain government approval to invest in Vietnam. Under the BTA, investment screening will be phased out for most sectors within tow, six, or nine years, depending on the sector involved.

- Profit repatriation: Presently, Vietnamese enterprises have greater freedom than foreign multinationals to convert their Vietnam-earned profits into hard currency. The State Bank of Vietnam must approve the conversion of currency on behalf of foreign businesses, and the Bank does not give permission to convert currency to foreign-invested companies.[21] Under the BTA, foreign multinationals will receive the same rights for profit repatriation as Vietnamese firms; however, Vietnam's currency is still not fully convertible.

- Capital contribution floors: Currently, the U.S. stake in a joint venture must be at least 30%. This requirement will be eliminated in three years.

- Personnel requirements for joint ventures: Presently, Vietnam requires that certain board members of joint ventures be Vietnamese and requires that certain types of decisions be made by consensus (thereby granting veto power to the Vietnamese board members). Under the BTA, within three years Vietnam will allow U.S. multinationals to select top executives without regard to nationality.

- Trade-related investment measures (TRIMs): Vietnam has agreed to eliminate within five years all TRIMs that are inconsistent with the WTO, such as local content requirements.

5) Transparency

Vietnam has agreed to adopt a fully transparent commercial regime by allowing comment on draft laws and regulations by ensuring that advance public notice is given for all such laws and regulations; by publishing these documents; and by allowing U.S. citizens and corporations the right to appeal rulings.

Vietnam's Implementation of the BTA

It is an open question whether the Vietnamese government has the will or the wherewithal to implement the pervasive reforms required by the U.S.-Vietnam bilateral trade agreement. Implementing the agreement will require cooperation at the local government level, where central control often is weak and corruption is rampant. An unprecedented level of cooperation among governmental ministries will also be required. Powerful vested interests – particularly the state-owned enterprises and the Vietnamese People's Army – undoubtedly will put pressure on local and central government officials to erect new barriers to foreign competition.

[21] United States Foreign Commercial Service, "Country Commercial Guide: Vietnam," July 15, 1999.

In a sign that the government is determined to push ahead with market liberalization despite the obstacles, Vietnam's trade ministry has already begun preparing draft laws and regulations on reshaping the country's trade regime. In January 2001, the Ministry of Trade issued a directive allowing foreign-invested enterprises to directly export most items.[22] The Trade Ministry also has finalized regulations to cancel most import-export licensing requirements for virtually all Vietnamese and foreign firms.[23] Additionally, all ministries have been ordered to identify all laws and regulations that must be changed in order to implement the trade agreement.[24]

Comparison with the 1999 "Agreement in Principle"

In July 1999 the U.S. and Vietnam announced an "agreement in principle" on a BTA, but for nearly a year Vietnam delayed finalizing the deal because of intense divisions among the Vietnamese Communist Party (VCP) leadership (see the following section for an analysis of the reasons for Vietnam's hesitation). The Clinton Administration did not release the full terms of the July 1999 agreement in principle. According to one negotiator, the only significant differences between the final BTA and the 1999 agreement lie in the area of trade in services (Chapter III and Annex G), specifically in the area of telecommunications.[25]

Telecommunications

In general, the 1999 agreement in principle would have allowed U.S. companies the right to obtain a majority (51%) stake in certain Vietnamese telecommunications sectors after a certain number of years (often referred to as the "phase-in" period). Following the November 1999 U.S.-China agreement on China's WTO accession – which granted U.S. companies the right to a 49% maximum stake in Chinese telecommunications enterprises – the Vietnamese negotiators demanded that they receive similar equity caps. The U.S. agreed to this concession, but in exchange received significantly shorter phase-in periods. Vietnam also agreed to consider increasing the U.S. equity limits when the agreement is reviewed in three years.

Two telecommunications sectors, wireless and basic voice services, illustrate the differences between the1999 and 2000 documents. In wireless telecommunications, under the 1999 agreement Vietnam would have allowed U.S. companies the right to set up joint ventures after three years, with a 51% maximum stake for U.S. companies. Under the 2000 BTA, Vietnam is to grant U.S. companies the right to set up wireless joint ventures after two years (three years for Internet services), with a 50% cap on U.S. equity participation.

In the areas of basic voice telecommunication services (local, long distance and international phone service), press reports indicate that the 1999 agreement would have phased-in a right to invest after 11 years, with a 51% maximum stake for U.S. companies.

---

[22] "Trade Amendments Set to Assist Foreign Companies," *Vietnam Investment Review*, January 8, 2001.

[23] "With an Eye on WTO, Vietnam to Relax Trade," *Australian Financial Review*, February 14, 2001. the Ministry reportedly is awaiting final governmental approval of these regulatory changes.

[24] Memo from the Office of the Vietnamese Prime Minister, "Re: Preparatory Tasks After the U.S. and Vietnam Agreement," November 21, 2000.

[25] July 2000 interview with U.S. government official.

Under the 2000 BTA, Vietnam is to allow U.S. companies to set up joint ventures after six years, with a 49% cap on U.S. ownership.

Insurance

According to press reports, under the 1999 agreement Vietnam would have permitted U.S. companies to invest in its insurance sector in two to six years. The phase-in period varied by insurance sector. Details are unavailable on foreign equity caps.[26] Under the July 2000 BTA, Vietnam is to grant U.S. companies the right to set up 50-50 joint ventures in its insurance sector after three years, and wholly owned (100% stake) ventures after five years.

Market Access

The final BTA includes commitments by Vietnam to reduce tariffs on approximately 250 products, about four-fifths of which are agricultural goods. 1999 press reports implied that the agreement in principle contained 330 tariff items scheduled for tariff reduction. A U.S. official involved in negotiating the agreement, however, has argued that this number is incorrect, stating that the tariff changes in Annex B of the final BTA are essentially the same as those agreed upon in 1999.

Comparison with Past BTAs

In negotiating bilateral trade deals with Jackson-Vanik countries, U.S. negotiators generally have tried to break new ground with each successive agreement. As one indication of that policy, the 1979 agreement China was less than 10 pages, while the far more comprehensive U.S.-Vietnam BTA is more than ten times that length. The Vietnam-U.S. BTA goes beyond past agreements in its more detailed commitments in the areas of services and investment. Furthermore, Vietnam's tariff concessions represent a new development. Previous Jackson-Vanik BTAs contained few or no market access commitments because in those negotiations the U.S. proposed to carry out tariff discussions at a future date, not as part of the final BTA itself.[27]

Vietnam's Ambivalence toward Economic Integration

Though the U.S. and Vietnam reached an agreement in principle on the BTA in July 1999, for nearly a year Vietnam delayed signing the deal. What were the reasons for Vietnam's hesitancy?

---

[26] "USTR Lays Out Key Issues to be Resolved in U.S.-Vietnam Trade Deal," *Inside U.S. Trade*, July 30, 1999.

[27] November 1999 interview by the author with trade policy expert Craig VanGrasstek, President, VanGrasstek Communications.

Internal Factors

Consensus-Based Decision-Making

Vietnam's official reason for the delay was that it needed time to vet the agreement among decision-makers in Vietnam. Vietnam's consensus-style of decision-making and the weakness of the country's current leadership probably extended this betting process: The BTA is the most extensive agreement Vietnam has ever negotiated, and the assent of virtually all officials involved in implementing the deal was required before Hanoi would take such a radical step. Furthermore, the weakness of the country's current top leaders – VCP General Secretary Le Kha Phieu, Prime Minister Phan Van Khai, and President Tran Duc Luong – made it difficult for them to forge a consensus on such a controversial issue.[28]

Questions from Vietnamese Conservatives

Ever since the Vietnamese Communist Party's (VCP) 8th Party Congress in 1995, disagreements between reformers and conservatives in Vietnam's 19-member Politburo – the country's supreme ruling body – have paralyzed economic decision-making. As the bilateral trade agreement with the U.S. requires Vietnam to jump-start its reforms and deepen its integration into the global economy, it is not surprising that the Politburo also has been divided over whether to finalize the deal.

The conservatives fear that economic reform will undermine the "socialist foundations" of the country's economic and political systems, and thereby erode the VCP's legitimacy and monopoly on power. They also fear that Vietnam's sovereignty will be eroded by increasing Vietnam's economic dependence on the West and by increasing Vietnam's vulnerability to regional economic downturns such as the 1997-99 Asian financial crisis. Among their specific concerns, conservatives worry that shifting to a more market-oriented economy will force the Politburo to curtail subsidies to the country's state-owned enterprises, the backbone of the socialist economic system. Many conservatives are understandably worried that further rationalization will raise unemployment rates, which already exceed 10%, according to some estimates. Social and political pressure on the Party has already been heightened in recent years by peasant uprisings and widespread accusations of government corruption. High-level U.S. pressure on Vietnam for its human rights record, applied during Secretary of State Madeleine Albright's September 1999 trip to Vietnam, is said to have further rankled conservative forces opposed to the trade agreement.

In January 2000, a group of reform-minded leaders were transferred to key economic and political posts. These moves, combined with the BTA signing, the unveiling of a new Enterprise Law, the passage of new amendments to the Foreign Investment Law, and the opening of Vietnam's first stock market on July 20, 2000, may be signs that Hanoi's policy logjam is breaking up in the reformers' favor.

---

[28] Zachary Abuza, "Leadership Transition in Vietnam since the Eighth Party Congress The Unfinished Congress," *Asian Survey*, (December 1998).

Opposition from Vested Interests

Parochial interests also may have played a role in Vietnam's deliberations. According to many sources, Vietnam's military leaders have been among the staunchest opponents of the BTA. Many argue that the military – known as the People's Army of Vietnam – is worried that the trade deal will threaten its vast commercial interests. According to one estimate, the business enterprises of the People's Army of Vietnam generated over $600 million in revenue in 1998, a figure equivalent to nearly 60% of the entire military budget.[29] Evidence of the military's influence can be seen in Vietnam's bargaining position on telecommunications liberalization during the BTA negotiations. Hanoi demanded an eleven-year phase-in period for FDI liberalization in cable communications, a sector in which the People's Army has invested heavily since 1995. In contrast, Vietnam's negotiators were willing to accept a four-year phase-in for cellular communications, an area in which the Ministry of Defense has few investments.[30]

External Factors – Balancing China and the U.S.

Yet another hypothesis is that Hanoi was concerned that a trade deal with the United States would antagonize China. Beijing and Hanoi recently have strengthened their ties, and conservative elements in Hanoi may be wary of upsetting Beijing by appearing too closely aligned with the U.S. In particular, the Vietnamese leadership may have wished to avoid jeopardizing negotiations with China over a land-border treaty, negotiations that were not concluded until December 1999. There are also reports that Chinese leaders warned the Vietnamese not to conclude the BTA before Beijing had finalized its own WTO accession negotiations with the U.S., talks that were concluded in November 1999. However, some analysts and Administration officials reject this reasoning as a stalling tactic by the Vietnamese, who are said to often use the Chinese as an excuse for delaying foreign policy moves about which they are uncertain. As one observer has pointed out, Chinese opposition did not prevent Vietnam from joining the Association of Southeast Asian Nations (ASEAN) in 1995.[31]

Most observers agree that, apart from the issue of unsubstantiated Chinese pressure, the China factor played a positive role in spurring the Vietnamese to move forward, due to Hanoi's fears of increased economic competition with Beijing following China's likely accession to the WTO in 2000 or 2001.

---

[29] Huw Watkin, "Proud Military Slips into Decline as Aid Dries Up," *South China Morning Post*, July 7, 1999, and Huw Watkin, "Military Puts Boot in as Treaty with US Seen Growing Threat to Business Empire," *South China Morning Post*, September 14, 1999.

[30] Zachary Abuza, "The Politics of Globalization: Explaining Vietnam's Rejection of the U.S. Trade Deal," (Boston, MA: Simmons College, 2000), p. 20.

[31] Abuza, "The Politics of Globalization," p. 21-22.

Chapter 4

VIETNAM TRADE AGREEMENT: APPROVAL AND IMPLEMENTING PROCEDURE

Vladimir N. Pregelj

SUMMARY

The procedure leading to the entry into force of the U.S. trade agreement with Vietnam, including a reciprocal extension of nondiscriminatory treatment, calls for its approval by the enactment of a joint resolution of Congress, considered under a specific fast-track procedure with deadlines for its various stages, with mandatory language and no amendments. After favorable reports on the legislation in both houses, H.J.Res. 51, approving the nondiscriminatory treatment, was enacted on October 16, 2001; the agreement also was ratified by Vietnam on December 4, 2001, and entered into force by exchange of notices of acceptance between the two parties on December 10, 2001. The functional sequence of the legislative and executive steps involved in the implementation of the agreement is described in this report.

BACKGROUND[1]

After protracted negotiations and a one-year delay after its adoption in principle, the United States and Vietnam signed, on July 13, 2000, a comprehensive bilateral trade agreement. The key statutory purpose of the agreement is the restoration of nondiscriminatory tariff treatment[2] ("normal-trade-relations" (NTF), formerly, "most-favored-nation" treatment) to U.S. imports from Vietnam, suspended since 1951. Hence the agreement contains a

[1] For detailed background information on the U.S.-Vietnam trade agreement, see CRS Report RL30416, *The Vietnam-U.S. Bilateral Trade Agreement*, by Mark E. Manyin.

[2] Although the internationally adopted term "most-favored-nation treatment" has been replaced, in all current and future U.S. statutes, under Section 5003 of P.L. 105-206, by the term "normal trade relations" or a similar expression, its functional equivalent – nondiscriminatory treatment – has been retained in the relevant legislation, while the term "most-favored-nation treatment" remains in universal international use.

provision reciprocally extending the NTR treatment and certain other provisions required by law for trade agreements with non-market economy (NME) countries. In addition, it contains comprehensive specific commitments by Vietnam in matters of market access (e.g., reduced tariff rates on imports from the United States), intellectual property rights, trade in services, and investment, such as the United States already has in force as a matter of general trade policy. To enter into force, the agreement must be approved by the enactment of a joint resolution of Congress.

Restoration of NTR treatment to Vietnam as an NME country is also contingent on Vietnam's compliance with the freedom-of-emigration requirement of the Jackson-Vanik amendment (Section 402) of the Trade Act of 1974.[3] In the case of Vietnam, such statutory conditions; such waiver may be disapproved by the enactment of a joint resolution of Congress. The President has issued such waivers for Vietnam since mid-1998, but in to instance has a disapproval resolution, if introduced, been passed by Congress, allowing the waiver to continue in force.

IMPLEMENTING PROCEDURE

The statutory requirements and legislative procedure leading to the enactment and entry into force of a trade agreement with a non-market economy (NME) country, including Vietnam, are set out in detail in Section 151, 404, 405, and 407 of the Trade Act of 1974 (P.L. 93-618), as amended. Section 151 has been enacted as an exercise of the rulemaking power of either house and superseded its other rules to the extent that they are inconsistent with it. Its provisions can be changed by either house with respect to its own procedure at any time, in the same manner and to the same extent as any other rule of that house (Section 151(a); 19 U.S.C. 2191(a)).

All alphanumerical statutory references cited in this report are to sections of the Trade Act of 1974. While care has been taken to reflect accurately the meaning of the statutes, consulting the actual language of any statue is recommended in case of any ambiguity.

Functionally, the consideration and enactment of the approval resolution and the implementation of the agreement follow a specific expedited ("fast-track") procedure explained below. Additional information, based on past practice of implementing trade agreements with NME countries in general, but applicable also to Vietnam, is provided in footnotes

(1) Enactment Necessary

The agreement can take effect only if approved by enactment of a joint resolution (Section 405(c); 19 U.S.C. 2435(c)).

[3] For detail on the Jackson-Vanik amendment, see CRS Report 98-545 E, *Jackson-Vanik Amendment: A Survey*, by Vladimir N. Pregelj.

(2) Transmittal of the Agreement of the President to Congress

The text of the bilateral trade agreement with Vietnam must be transmitted by the President to both houses of Congress, together with a proclamation[4] extending nondiscriminatory treatment to Vietnam and stating his reasons for it (Section 407(a); 19 U.S.C. 2437). While there is no statutory deadline for the transmittal of the proclamation and the agreement to Congress after its signing, the law requires that the transmittal take place "promptly" after the proclamation is issued.[5]

(3) Mandatory Introduction of Approval Resolution

On the day the trade agreement is transmitted to the Congress (or, if the respective house is not in session on that day, the first subsequent day on which it is in session), a joint resolution of approval (Sec. 151(b)(3); 19 U.S.C. 2191 (b)(3)) must be introduced (by request) in each house by its majority leader for himself and the minority leader, or by their designees (Sec. 151(c)(2); 19 U.S.C. 2192 (c)(2)).[6]

(4) Language of Approval Resolution

The language of the resolution is prescribed by law (Sec. 151(b)(3); 19 U.S.C. 2191(b)(3)) to read, in this particular instance, after the resolving clause:

"That the Congress approves the extension of nondiscriminatory treatment with respect to the products of Vietnam transmitted by the President to the Congress on June 8, 2001."[7]

(5) Committee Referral

The resolution is referred in the House to the Committee on Ways and means and in the Senate to the Committee on Finance (Sec. 151(c)(2); 19 U.S.C. 2191(c)(2)).

(6) Amendments Prohibited

No amendment to the resolution, and no motion, or unanimous-consent request, to suspend the no-amendment rule, is in order in either house (Sec. 151(d); 19 U.S.C. 2191(d)).

---

[4] Although the proclamation is issued at the time of transmittal of the agreement to Congress, its entry into force is specifically delayed to the date of the exchange of notices of acceptance of the agreement by its two parties.

[5] Trade agreement with Vietnam and other required documents were transmitted by the President to Congress on June 8, 2001. They have been published as House Document 107-85.

[6] S.J.Res. 16 and H.J.Res. 51 to approve the trade agreement with Vietnam were introduced respectively, on June 11 and 12, 2001.

[7] Although the language of the approval resolution mentions only nondiscriminatory treatment, other relevant statutes make it clear that the enactment of such resolution is required for the approval of any agreement containing the extension of nondiscriminatory treatment.

(7) Committee Consideration in the House[8]

If the Ways and Means Committee has not reported the resolution within 45 days[9] after its introduction, the Committee is automatically discharged from further consideration of the resolution, and the resolution is placed on the appropriate calendar (Sec. 151(e)(1); 19 U.S.C. 2191(e)(1)).

(8) Floor Consideration in the House

a. A motion to proceed to the consideration of the approval resolution is highly privileged and non-debatable; an amendment to the motion, or a motion to reconsider the vote whereby the motion is agreed or disagreed to, is not in order (Sec. 151(f)(1); 19 U.S.C. 2191(f)(1)).
b. Debate on the resolution is limited to 20 hours[10], divided equally between the supporters and opponents of the resolution; a motion further to limit debate is not debatable; a motion to recommit the resolution, or to reconsider the vote whereby the resolution is agreed or disagreed to, is not in order (Sec. 151(f)(2); 19 U.S.C. 2191(f)(2)).
c. Motions to postpone the consideration of the resolution and motions to proceed to the consideration of other business are decided without debate. (Sec. 151(f)(3); 19 U.S.C. 2191(f)(3)).
d. All appeals from the decisions of the Chair relating to the application of the rules of the House of Representatives to the approval resolution are decided without debate (Sec. 151(f)(4); 19 U.S.C. 2191(f)(4)).
e. In all other respects, consideration of the approval resolution is governed by the rules of the House of Representatives applicable to other measures in similar circumstances (Sec. 151(f)(5); 19 U.S.C. 2191(f)(5)).
f. The vote (by simple majority) on the final passage of the approval resolution must be taken on or before the 15th day[11] after the Ways and Means Committee has reported the resolution, or has been discharged from its further consideration (Sec. 151(e)(1); 19 U.S.C. 2191(e)(1)).

---

[8] Committee consideration in the House as described in the body of this report, differs from that in the Senate (see item 9). This is due to the treatment, in this report, of the approval resolution as a "revenue" measure (an "implementing revenue resolution", which it is widely presumed to be, since it would affect-adversely-customs revenues due to the significantly lower NTR tariff rates assessed on imports from Vietnam after the agreement enters into force (cf. Sec. 151(b)(2)); 19 U.S.C. 2191 (b)(2); but see also footnote 11). As such, the resolution is required by the U.S. Constitution to originate in the House. This origination provision, however, does not mean that a companion resolution may not be introduced and considered in the Senate, but only that the measure eventually passed by both houses and submitted to the President for signature, has to be a House measure.

[9] In computing the number of days in either house, any day on which that house is not in session is excluded (Sec. 151(e)(3); 19 U.S.C. 2193(e)(3)). H.J.Res. 51 was reported favorably on September 5, 2001 (H.Rept. 107-189).

[10] This statutory deadline has in past practice often been reduced by floor action.

[11] Computed as in footnote 9 – H.J.Res. 51 passed House September 6, 2001.

(9) Committee Consideration in the Senate[12]

An approval resolution adopted by the House of Representatives and received in the Senate is referred to the Finance Committee (Sec. 151(c)(2) and (e)(2); 19 U.S.C. 2191(c)(2) and (e)(2)).[13] If the Finance Committee has not reported the resolution within 15 days after its receipt from the House or 45 days[14] after the introduction of its own corresponding resolution (whichever is later), the Committee is automatically discharged from further consideration of the resolution, and the resolution is placed on the appropriate calendar (Sec. 151(e)(1); 19 U.S.C. 2191(e)(1)).

(10) Floor Consideration in the Senate

a. A motion to proceed to the consideration of the approval resolution is privileged and non-debatable; an amendment to the motion, or a motion is reconsidered the note whereby the motion is agreed or disagreed to, is not in order (Sec. 151(g)(1); 19 U.S.C. 2191(g)(1)).
b. Debate on the approval resolution and on all debatable motions and appeals connected with it is limited to 20 hours, equally divided between and controlled by, the majority leader and the minority leader, or their designees (Sec. 151(g)(2); 19 U.S.C. 2191(g)(2)).
c. Debate on any debatable motion or appeal is limited to one hour, equally divided between, and controlled by, the mover and the manager of the resolution, except that if the manager of the resolution is in favor of any such motion or appeal, the time in opposition is controlled by the minority leader or his designee; such leaders may, from time under their control on the passage of the resolution, allot additional time to any Senator during the consideration of any debatable motion or appeal (Sec. 151(g)(3); 19 U.S.C. 2191(g)(3)).
d. A motion further to limit debate on the approval resolution is not debatable; a motion to recommit it is not in order (Sec. 151(g)(4); 19 U.S.C. 2191(g)(4)).
e. The vote (by simple majority) on the final passage of the approval resolution must be taken on or before the 15th day[15] after the Finance Committee has reported the resolution, or has been discharged from its further consideration (Sec. 151(e)(2); 19 U.S.C. 2191(e)(2)).
f. Although, unlike in the case of the House procedure[16] this is not specifically mentioned in Section 151, the Rules of the Senate govern the consideration of the

[12] This item describes the procedure for enacting "revenue" joint resolutions approving trade agreements with non-market economy countries. Ambiguity in the applicable statutory language, however, has engendered a controversy as to whether they are to be considered as "revenue" or "non-revenue" measures, which may eventually have to be resolved by a parliamentarian ruling.

[13] Although a joint resolution of approval must be introduced in both houses (see item 3)), Section 151 contains no specific provision regarding the consideration of a Senate "revenue" approval resolution (situation presumed in the procedure as described in this report). The reason for this omission appears to be in that a "revenue" measure can be enacted only as a House measure (see footnote __).

[14] Both computed as in footnote__. S.J.Res. 16 was reported favorably July 27, 2001 (S.Rept. 107-49).

[15] Computed as in footnote__. H.J. Res. 51 passed House October 3, 2001.

[16] See item (8)(e).

approval resolution in the Senate in all aspects not specifically addressed in Section 151.

g. If prior to the passage of its own approval resolution, the Senate receives the approval resolution already passed by the House, it continues the legislative procedure on its own resolution, but the vote on the final passage is on the House resolution.

(11) President's Implementing Authority

a. After the joint resolution approving the trade agreement with Vietnam is passed by both houses and signed by the President, it becomes public law, in effect, authorizing the President to put into effect the already issued proclamation[17] implementing the agreement extending nondiscriminatory treatment to Vietnam (Secs. 404(a) and 405(c); 19 U.S.C. 2434(a) and 2435(c).
b. Application of nondiscriminatory treatment is limited to the term during which the agreement remains in force (Sec. 404(b); 19 U.S.C. 2434(b)) (see also footnote 19 and text which it accompanies).
c. The President may at any time suspend or withdraw nondiscriminatory treatment of Vietnam (Sec. 404(c); 19 U.S.C. 2434(c)) and thereby subject all imports from that country to column 2 tariff rates (i.e., full rather than NTR rates).

(12) Approval by Vietnam

The agreement also must be approved by Vietnam.[18]

(13) Entry into Force

After the joint resolution of approval is enacted and the agreement is approved by Vietnam, the proclamation (see item (2) becomes effective, the agreement enters into force, and nondiscriminatory treatment is extended to Vietnam on the date of exchange f written notices of acceptance of the agreement by the United States and Vietnam. A notice of the effective date of the agreement is published by the U.S. Trade Representative in the *Federal Register.*[19]

[17] See footnote 4. Pres. Proc. 7449 (June 8, 2001; 66 F.R. 31375).

[18] A resolution approving the agreement was adopted by Vietnam's National Assembly on November 28 and signed by Vietnam's President on December 4, 2001.

[19] Notices of acceptance were exchanged on December 10, 2001 (66 F.R. 65019).

(14) Maintenance of Force

According to its own terms (Article 8 of Chapter VII – General Articles), the agreement with Vietnam remains in force for a period of three years and is automatically renewable for successive three-year terms unless either party to it, at least 30 days before the expiration of the then current term, gives notice of its intent to terminate the agreement. If either party ceases to have domestic legal authority to carry out its obligations under the agreement, it may suspend the application of the agreement, or, with the agreement of the other party, any part of the agreement.[20]

In addition, Section 405(b)(1) (19 U.S.C. 2435(b)(1)) limits the life of trade agreements restoring nondiscriminatory treatment to NME countries to an initial term of three years. Agreements may be renewable for additional three-year terms if a satisfactory balance of trade concessions has been maintained during the life of the agreement and the President determines that actual or foreseeable U.S. reductions of trade barriers resulting from multilateral negotiations are satisfactorily reciprocated by the other country.[21]

---

[20] One such circumstance would arise if Vietnam's waiver under the Jackson-Vanik amendment (see p__) were no longer in force either by President's failure to renew it annually or through the enactment of a joint resolution disapproving its annual extension. Enactment of such resolution (H.J.Res. 55) to disapprove the extension of Vietnam's waiver, introduced on June 1, 2001 (but defeated in the House on July 26, 2001) would have prevented the extension of nondiscriminatory treatment to Vietnam or, if already in force, nullified it.

[21] The latter provision reflects the fact that, by being granted nondiscriminatory treatment by the United States, an NME country would benefit from U.S. concessions extended to third countries, without itself, theoretically, having to extend any concessions that it has granted to third countries. In the case of Vietnam, however, the bilateral agreement does provide for comprehensive U.S.-specific concessions in addition to those applicable merely on MFN basis.

Chapter 5

THE VIETNAM-U.S. NORMALIZATION PROCESS

Mark E. Manyin

SUMMARY

U.S.-Vietnam diplomatic and economic relations remained essentially frozen for more than a decade after the 1975 communist victory in South Vietnam. Washington and Hanoi have incrementally normalized relations over the past decade. The pace has been relatively slow due to continued debates in the United States and Vietnam over improved relations. Congress has played a significant role in the normalization process.

Bilateral relations took a major step forward in February 1994, when President Clinton ordered an end to the 19-year old U.S. trade embargo on Vietnam. The following year, the United States and Vietnam settled diplomatic and private property claims and opened liaison offices in Washington and Hanoi. In April 1997, a U.S. Ambassador was approved by the Senate and took up his post in Hanoi. In March 1998, President Clinton granted a waiver from the Jackson-Vanik amendment that smoothed the way for Overseas Private Investment Corporation (OPIC) and Export-Import Bank support for U.S. business in Vietnam.

On July 13, 2000, the U.S. and Vietnam continued their normalization by signing a sweeping bilateral trade agreement (BTA), which was approved by Congress and signed by President Bush in 2001. Vietnam ratified the agreement shortly thereafter. Under the BTA, the U.S. extended normal trade relations to Vietnam. In return, Hanoi agreed to a range of trade liberalization measures and market-oriented reforms.

Each step in improving bilateral ties has brought controversy, albeit at diminishing levels. U.S. opponents in Congress and elsewhere have argued that Vietnam maintains a poor record on human, religious, and labor rights. Opposition has also come from groups arguing that Vietnam has not done enough to account for U.S. Prisoners of War/Missing in Action (POW/MIAs) from the Vietnam War, though this argument has diminished markedly in recent years.

Forces favoring normalization have included those in Congress and elsewhere reflecting a strong U.S. business interest in Vietnam's reforming economy and American strategic interests in working with U.S. friends and allies to promote stability and development by integrating Vietnam more fully into the existing East Asian order.

Within Vietnam, divisions over the course of the country's reforms have paralyzed Vietnamese leaders in recent years. Reformers in the Vietnamese government seek closer ties with the U.S., especially in economic relations. However, conservatives have resisted foreign influences that might undermine the Vietnamese Communist Party's monopoly of political power.

MOST RECENT DEVELOPMENTS

The U.S.-Vietnam bilateral trade agreement (BTA) entered into force on December 10, 2001, when the two countries formally exchanged letters implementing the agreement. Under the agreement, the U.S. extended temporary normal trade relations (NTR, also known as most-favored nation [MFN] status) to Vietnam. In return, Hanoi agreed to undertake a wide range of market-liberalization measures.

BACKGROUND AND ANALYSIS U.S.-VIETNAM RELATIONS, 1975-98

U.S.-Vietnam diplomatic and economic relations remained essentially frozen for over a decade after the 1975 communist victory in South Vietnam, despite a few U.S. overtures during the Carter Administration that were controversial domestically and were ultimately thwarted by Vietnamese actions.

Policy Initiatives During the Carter Administration

In March 1977, President Carter sent a commission to Vietnam. The United States no longer vetoed Vietnam's application for U.N. membership, paving the way for the July 20, 1977 U.N. Security Council recommendation – undertaken by consensus, without formal vote – that Vietnam be admitted to the United Nations. The United States proposed that diplomatic relations quickly be established between the United States and Vietnam, after which the United States would life export and asset controls on Vietnam. The Vietnamese responded that they would neither agree to establish relations nor furnish information on U.S. POW/MIAs until the United States pledged to provide several billion dollars in postwar reconstruction aid. Subsequently, they modified this position and provided some limited information on MIAs, even though the United States provided no aid.

The U.S. Congress responded unfavorably to the Carter Administration initiatives and the Vietnamese reaction. In 1977, both houses of Congress went on record as strongly opposing U.S. aid to Vietnam.

Vietnamese actions in 1978 in particular had a long-term negative effect on U.S.-Vietnamese relations. Vietnam expelled hundreds of thousands of its citizens (many of

Chinese origin) who then became refugees throughout Southeast Asia; aligned itself economically and militarily with the USSR; and invaded Cambodia, deposing the pro-Chinese Khmer Rouge regime and imposing a puppet Cambodian government backed by 200,000 Vietnamese troops. China conducted a one month military incursion along Vietnam's northern border in 1979 and kept strong military pressure on the North until 1990. In the face of these developments, the Carter Administration halted consideration of improved relations with Vietnam. It worked closely with the members of the Association of Southeast Asian Nations (ASEAN – then made up of Indonesia, Malaysia, the Philippines, Singapore and Thailand) to condemn and contain the Vietnamese expansion and to cope with the influx of refugees from Indochina.

Developments During the Reagan and Bush Administrations

The Reagan Administration opposed normal relations with Hanoi until there was a verified withdrawal of Vietnamese forces from Cambodia, a position amended in 1985 to include a verified withdrawal in the context of a comprehensive settlement. Administration officials also noted that progress toward normal relations depended on Vietnam fully cooperating in obtaining the fullest possible accounting for U.S. personnel listed as prisoners of war/missing in action (POW/MIAs).

As Vietnam withdrew forces from Cambodia in 1989 and sought a compromise peace settlement there, the Bush Administration decided on July 18, 1990, to seek contacts with Hanoi in order to assist international efforts to each a peace agreement in Cambodia.

Regarding the issue of the POW/MIAs, following a visit to Hanoi by a U.S. presidential delegation in 1987, Vietnam returned hundreds of sets of remains said to be those of U.S. MIAs. Some, but not most, were confirmed as American. Altogether, from 1974 to 1992, Vietnam returned the remains of over 300 Americans. Virtually all U.S. analysts agree that the Vietnamese "warehoused" several hundred remains and tactically released them in increments. The number of such remains and whether any are still held, is not known with any certainty.

In April 1991, the United States laid out a detailed "road map" for normalization with Vietnam, welcomed Vietnam's willingness to host a U.S. office in Hanoi to handle POW/MIA affairs, and pledged $1 million for humanitarian aid (mainly prosthetics) to Vietnam. The U.S. office began operation in mid-1991, and the aid was transferred by the end of FY1991. Also in 1991, the United States eased travel restrictions on Vietnamese diplomats stationed at the United Nations in New York and on U.S. organized travel to Vietnam.

In 1992, Vietnamese cooperation on POW/MIA matters improved, especially in the area of allowing U.S. investigators access to pursue "live sightings" reports. Important developments encouraged U.S. officials, armed with evidence (including photographs of extensive Vietnamese archival information on U.S. POW/MIAs) to request greater access to such data. Vietnamese representatives agreed. The United States pledged, and subsequently paid out, $3 million of humanitarian aid (mainly prosthetics and aid to abandoned or orphaned children) for Vietnam; agreed to restore direct telecommunications with Vietnam; agreed to allow U.S. commercial sales to meet basic human needs in Vietnam; and lifted restrictions on projects in Vietnam by U.S. nongovernmental organizations. The United States pledged and provided a disaster assistance grant to Vietnamese flood victims and provided additional aid to help Vietnam with malaria problems. In November 1992, the United States lifted restrictions on U.S. telephone service to Vietnam, allowing direct service between the two countries. In December, the United States eased some restrictions on U.S. companies doing businesses in Vietnam.

Coinciding with these developments, the Senate Select Committee on POW/MIA affairs conducted what many consider the most extensive independent investigation of the POW/MIA issue undertaken. The committee, chaired by John Kerry and vice-chaired by Bob Smith, operated from August 1991 – December 1992. In early 1993, the committee issued its report, which concluded that there was some evidence that POWs were alive after the U.S. withdrawal in 1973, and that although there was no "conspiracy" in Washington to cover up live POWs, the U.S. government had seriously neglected and mismanaged the issue, particularly in the 1970s. The committee's televised hearings played a major role in defusing much of the passion that had surrounded the POW issue.

Apart from Cambodia and the POW/MIA matter, the Reagan and Bush Administrations concerned themselves with a third problem – humanitarian issues. Major progress in negotiations with Vietnam resulted in plans to: facilitate emigration from Vietnam of relatives of Vietnamese-Americans or permanent Vietnamese residents of the United States; regulate the flow of Vietnamese immigrants to the United States and other countries under the so-called Orderly Departure Program managed by the U.N. High Commissioner for Refugees; resolve the issue of the estimated several thousand Amerasians (whose fathers are Americans and whose mothers are Vietnamese) who reportedly wish to emigrate from Vietnam to the United States; and obtain release from Vietnamese prison camps and the opportunity to immigrate to the United States of thousands of Vietnamese who worked for the United States in South Vietnam or were otherwise associated with the U.S. war effort there.

Meanwhile, U.S. officials in Congress and the Administration expressed repeatedly their concern about the large numbers of political prisoners said to be in Vietnam, warning that human rights is a central feature of U.S. foreign policy and could not but affect U.S. policy toward Vietnam.

Developments During the Clinton Administration

Early moves to improve relations during the Clinton Administration included the President's announcement on July 2, 1993, that the United States would no longer oppose arrangements supported by France, Japan, and others allowing for resumed international financial institution aid to Vietnam; however, he said the U.S. economic embargo on Vietnam would remain in effect. A high-level U.S. delegation visited Hanoi in mid-July to press for progress on POW/MIAs; the delegation gave the Vietnamese leaders U.S. documentary evidence that would help settle Vietnamese MIA cases; the delegation also disclosed that U.S. consular officials would henceforth be stationed in Hanoi. Individual Members of Congress played an important behind-the-scenes role in encouraging the Clinton Administration to take many of these, and subsequent, steps.

President Clinton's September 13, 1993, renewal of his authority to maintain trade embargoes included an eased version of the one on Vietnam that allowed U.S. companies to bid on development projects funded by international financial institutions in Vietnam. Also in September 1993, the Administration approved $3.5 million in U.S. aid to extend two humanitarian programs (prostheses and orphans) in Vietnam.

On February 3, 1994, President Clinton ordered an end to the U.S. trade embargo on Vietnam. The action came after many months of high-level U.S. interactions with Vietnam in resolving POW/MIA cases, and a January 27, 1994 vote in the Senate urging that the embargo be lifted, language that was attached to broad authorizing legislation (H.R. 2333). The language was controversial in the House, but H.R. 2333 passed Congress; it was signed into law (P.L. 103-236) on April 30, 1994.

On January 25, 1995, the United States and Vietnam settled bilateral diplomatic and property claims and opened liaison offices in Washington and Hanoi on February 1, and February 3, 1995, respectively. The Treasury Department announced on March 9, 1995, that it was unblocking accounts in which Vietnam or its nationals had an interest. On July 11, 1995, President Clinton announced that he would establish ambassadorial-level relations with Vietnam. The FY1996 State Department Appropriations bill (H.R. 2076) included language barring funding for full diplomatic relations with Vietnam until more progress was made on POW/MIA issues. President Clinton vetoed H.R. 2076 on December 19, 1995. On August 6, 1995, Secretary of State Christopher opened the U.S. Embassy in Hanoi, and Vietnam's embassy in Washington opened on August 5, 1995. An attempt in the Senate to restrict trade ties with Vietnam failed on September 20, 1995.

Controversy continued in 1995 and 1996 over provisions in legislation (H.R. 1561) that would place conditions on upgrading U.S. relations with Vietnam, and that would admit additional boat people from camps in Hong Kong and elsewhere to the United States. H.R. 1561 passed Congress in March 1996, but was vetoed by the President, and the veto was sustained on April 30, 1996. A modified version of the Vietnam provisions in H.R. 2076 was signed by President Clinton on April 26, 1996, as part of H.R. 3019, the Omnibus Appropriations bill (P.L. 104-134). To comply with the provisions, President Clinton issued Presidential Determination 96-28 on May 30, 1996, saying that Vietnam is cooperating in full faith with the United States on POW/MIA issues.

On April 10, 1997, the Senate approved former Vietnam War POW and Member of Congress Pete Peterson as U.S. Ambassador to Vietnam.

In Vietnam in late June 1997, Secretary of State Albright urged greater economic reform and better human rights; she signed a bilateral agreement on copyrights and said that the U.S. Trade and Development Program would conduct business in Vietnam.

On December 18, 1997, National Security Adviser Sandy Berger said the Administration was consulting with Congress on granting Vietnam a waiver from the Jackson-Vanik amendment that would smooth the way for Overseas Private Investment Corporation (OPIC) and Export-Import Bank to support U.S. business activities in Vietnam. On March 11, 1998, President Clinton granted the waiver, and a formal agreement on OPIC was signed eight days later. On November 31, 1999, OPIC signed its first financing agreement – a $2.3 million loan to Caterpillar Inc.'s authorized dealership in Vietnam – for American business in Vietnam since the end of the Vietnam War. The U.S. Export-Import Bank announced on April 10, 1998 that it was ready to finance sales to Vietnam. On December 9, 1999, the Ex-Im Bank signed two framework agreements with the State Bank of Vietnam to facilitate project-financing cooperation between the two agencies.

On June 3, 1998, President Clinton issued a required annual waiver on Jackson-Vanik amendment restrictions regarding Vietnam, China, and other countries. Joint disapproval resolutions were introduced in the Senate (S.J.Res. 47) and the House (H.J. Res. 120) on June 4, 1998. They were reported adversely by the Senate Finance Committee and the House Ways and Means Committee. H.J.Res. 120 was defeated in the House on July 30, 1998, roll call #356 (163-260).

On June 3, 1999, President Clinton again issued an annual waiver on Jackson-Vanik amendment restrictions on U.S. interactions with Vietnam. Joint resolutions disapproving the President's action were introduced in the Senate (S.J. Res. 28, June 7) and the House (H.J.Res. 58, June 9). On July 20, the Senate rejected a motion to discharge S.J.Res. 28 from committee, effectively defeating the measure, roll call #214 (5-94). On August 3, the House voted down H.J.Res. 58, roll call #365 (130-297). The measure received 33 fewer votes than it had the previous year.

On June 2, 2000, President Clinton announced his third annual waiver of Jackson-Vanik amendment restrictions for Vietnam. Joint resolutions disapproving the President's action were introduced in the Senate (S.J.Res. 47) and the House (H.J.Res. 99). On July 26, 2000, the House voted down H.J.Res. 99, roll call 441 (91-332). The measure received 39 fewer votes that it had in 1999, and 72 fewer votes than it had in 1998. Until the U.S.-Vietnam bilateral trade agreement – which was signed on July 13, 2000 – goes in to effect the waiver does not change Vietnam's current, non-most-favored-nation (MFN), trade status with the United States. Instead, in the absence of an approved trade agreement, the wavier only allows OPIC and Export-Import Bank support for U.S. business in Vietnam. In order for the agreement to go into effect, it must be approved by Congress and the Vietnamese National Assembly.

RECENT U.S.-VIETNAM RELATIONS

Economic Ties – The Bilateral Trade Agreement

On December 10, 2001, a sweeping bilateral trade agreement (BRA) between the United States and Vietnam entered into force. The two sides had signed the deal, which by law required congressional approval, in July 2000, but it had taken over a year to complete the ratification process. Under the BTA, which the U.S. and Vietnam spent five years negotiation, the U.S. will extend temporary normal trade relations status (NTR, formerly most-favored-nation [MFN]) to Vietnam, a move that would significantly reduce U.S. tariffs on most imports from Vietnam. In return, Hanoi agreed to undertake a wide range of market-liberalization measures, including extending NTR treatment to U.S. exports, reducing tariffs on goods, easing barriers to U.S. services (such as banking and telecommunications), committing to protect certain intellectual property rights, and providing additional inducements and protections for inward foreign direct investment.

The agreement paves the way for President Bush to extend *temporary* NTR treatment to Vietnam. NTR treatment would be temporary because Vietnam's trade status would still be subject to annual Congressional review under the U.S. Trade Act of 1974's Jackson-Vanik provisions, which govern trade with non-market economies.

Implementation of the BTA

Vietnam's implementation of the BTA is likely to be closely monitored by Congress, particularly during the annual debate over whether to extend Vietnam's NTR status. Most of Vietnam's concessions are doe to be phased in within three to five years. However, a number of reforms took effect upon the BTA's entry into force on December 10, 2001. These include according national treatment (i.e., not discriminating between foreign and domestic enterprises) business activities, allowing all enterprises to import and export, eliminating most non-tariff barriers, streamlining the process for foreign investors to obtain licenses and approval, and publicizing laws, regulations and administrative procedures pertaining to any matter covered by the Trade Agreement. Hanoi appears to have taken steps to implement nearly all of these initial commitments.

U.S.-Vietnam Trade Flows

In 2001, U.S.-Vietnam trade was worth $1.4 billion, a 20% increase from 2000. As shown in Table 1 below, since 1997 the U.S. has run a trade deficit with Vietnam. Imports from Vietnam are concentrated in a handful of products. Shrimp, fuel products and footwear accounted for nearly two-thirds of total imports from Vietnam in 2001. Major U.S. exports to Vietnam in 2001 included aircraft, heavy and electrical machinery, raw cotton, footwear parts, and fertilizer. Nearly all of the $60 million rise in U.S. exports from 2000 to 2001 is explained by the increase in sales of two items: aircraft ($50 million) and cotton ($13 million).

U.S. Textile Imports from Vietnam

Vietnam's clothing exports are expected to increase dramatically now that the country's exports are entering the United States under MFN tariff rates. Vietnam currently exports relatively few apparel products to the U.S. – just over $47 million in 2000 and 2001 – because of the higher, non-MFN, tariff rates it faced. In contrast, Vietnamese garment exports to Japan and the 15 countries of the European Union in 1999 totaled more than $500 million and $640 million, respectively. The country's largest textile producer, state-run Vietnam Textiles and Garment Corporation (VINATEX), estimates in the first quarter of 2002 it will export $30 million to the U.S., roughly the same as its exports to the U.S. for all of 2001.

A Bilateral Textile Agreement

The BTA contains no provisions on Vietnamese textile exports to the U.S., but the safeguard provision would allow the U.S. to impose quotas on textile imports in the event of a surge of imports. During the congressional debate over the BTA, many Members urged the Bush Administration to negotiate a bilateral textile agreement soon after the BTA came into effect. Such an agreement would set quotas for Vietnamese textile exports to the U.S. Additionally, some Members have pressed for a commitment that a bilateral textile accord include provisions that would link the size of Vietnam's quotas to progress in its labor rights, similar to the U.S.-Cambodia textile agreement. The preliminary stage of the negotiations began in late February 2002. The Vietnamese government reportedly has been reluctant to enter into negotiations at an early date, arguing that the two sides should not set quotas until the pattern of U.S.-Vietnam textile trade under NTR rates becomes apparent. The U.S. has significant leverage on the textile issue, however. Not only does Vietnam's textile industry – which employs approximately 25% of the country's industrial workforce – need access to the U.S. market, but also the U.S. could unilaterally impose quotas on Vietnam at any time because Hanoi is not a member of the World Trade Organization.

Table 1. U.S.-Vietnam Trade, 1994-2001 (millions of dollars)

	U.S. Imports from Vietnam	U.S. Exports to Vietnam	Total Trade	Trade Balance
1994	50.5	172.2	222.7	121.7
1995	199.0	252.9	451.9	53.9
1996	319.0	616.1	935.1	297.1
1997	388.2	277.8	666.0	-110.4
1998	553.4	274.2	827.6	-279.2
1999	601.9	277.3	879.2	-324.6
2000	827.4	330.5	1,157.9	-496.9
2001	1,026.4	393.8	1,420.2	-632.6
Major Imports from Vietnam	Frozen shrimp, coffee, footwear, petroleum products, cashews			
Major Exports to Vietnam	Raw cotton, footwear parts, electronic machinery, fertilizer, aircraft			

Source: U.S. Department of Commerce. Data are for merchandise trade on a customs basis.

"Catfish"

In the first potential post-BTA trade dispute, section 755 of the 2002 Food and Drug Agency appropriations act passed by Congress and signed into law by President Bush (P.L. 107-76) prohibits the labeling of certain fish – primarily those imported from Vietnam – as catfish. An attempt by Senators John McCain and John Kerry to repeal the catfish clause was defeated on December 18, 2002, by a 68-27 vote. Vietnamese exports of basa and tra "catfish" have increased sharply in recent years. American catfish farmers have argued that the Vietnamese fish were improperly labeled as catfish.

Other Commercial Agreements

As part of its efforts to fully normalize commercial relations with Vietnam, since the beginning of 2000 the U.S. has completed or initiated negotiations over agreements covering investment, anti-narcotics measures, labor, scientific cooperation, airline code-sharing, and weather forecasting.

U.S. Bilateral Economic Assistance to Vietnam

U.S. aid to Vietnam has increased sharply in recent years. Programs administered by the United States Agency for International Development (USAID), for instance, rose from under $2 million in 1996 to over $8 million in 2001. For fiscal 2002, USAID has budgeted for over $12 million for its assistance program to Vietnam. In FY2002, total U.S. assistance to Vietnam – which includes USAID programs – is expected to exceed $30 million, which includes funds budgeted for food assistance ($11 million), the Fulbright exchange program ($4 million), HIV/AIDS programs ($8.5 million), land mine victims and orphans ($3 million), a dialog on labor issues ($1.5 million), and technical assistance to help Vietnam understand, develop, and implement trade reforms ($4.6 million). This total includes $5 million that is budgeted for a new educational exchange program – the Vietnam Education Foundation – that Congress authorized in 2000 but has yet to be implemented. In November 2000, USAID officially opened an office in Hanoi, it first presence in Vietnam since the end of the Vietnam War.

Political Ties

President Clinton visited Vietnam from November 16-20, 2000, the first trip by a U.S. President since Richard Nixon went to Saigon (now Ho Chi Minh City) in July 1969. The purpose of the trip was largely symbolic, to highlight the degree to which the U.S. and Vietnam have normalized their relations since the Vietnam War. The visit was notable for the unexpected enthusiasm expressed by ordinary Vietnamese, who thronged by the thousands to greet or catch a glimpse of the President and the First Lady. These spontaneous outbursts, combined with the President's public and private remarks about human rights and democratization, triggered rhetorical responses from conservative Vietnamese leaders.

Throughout his three-day visit, President Clinton spoke to the Vietnamese about the benefits of economic globalization (including implementing the bilateral trade agreement), the rule of law, efforts to locate and repatriate the remains of U.S. soldiers, and Vietnam's record on human rights and religious freedom. His speech at Vietnam National University was televised live, although the portions mentioning human rights and religious freedom were not mentioned in subsequent Vietnamese press reports. The President also spent the better part of a day dealing with Vietnam War-related issues, including traveling to a site where Vietnamese workers were digging for the suspected remains of a fallen U.S. pilot.

Vietnamese leaders pressed the U.S. for compensation for Agent Orange victims, for assistance locating the remains of Vietnam's soldiers who are still missing from fighting with the U.S., and for an increase in the U.S.' bilateral economic assistance program (the U.S. pledged $21.9 million in bilateral aid to Vietnam in 2000). During Clinton's trip, the U.S. took some small steps toward meeting these demands, including the following: U.S. and Vietnamese officials agreed to meet later in 2000 to discuss joint research on the effects of dioxin/Agent Orange; bilateral de-mining efforts were expanded; a science and technology agreement was signed; a bilateral labor cooperation agreement was signed; the U.S. provided materials to help locate the estimated 300,000 Vietnamese troops missing from the Vietnam War; OPIC opened a $200 million line of credit to help U.S. companies finance projects in Vietnam; and the U.S. announced that it would double its aid for HIV/AIDS prevention in Vietnam.

Secretary of State Colin Powell visited Hanoi from July 24-26, 2001 to attend the ASEAN Regional Forum (ARF). While in Vietnam, Powell held meetings with senior Vietnamese leaders.

Human Rights

On humanitarian issues, U.S. law (P.L. 105-277, signed October 21, 1998), requires the Administration to report annually on:

- Vietnam's release of political and religious prisoners;
- Vietnam's cooperation with the United States to obtain full and free access to persons of humanitarian interest to the United States for interviews and possible transfer to the United States.

In its review of Vietnam's human rights situation in 2001, the U.S. State Department reported that Hanoi's "poor human rights record worsened in some respects" in that the government increased its repression of most religious and political organizational activities, on the grounds of preserving national security and societal stability. Human rights groups reported that over the past year the Vietnamese government has tried to clamp down on political and religious dissidents by isolating and intimidating them – through such means as house arrest and constant surveillance – rather than imprisoning them, in order to avoid international criticism. Hanoi also retains strict controls over the Vietnamese press. During his July 2001 trip to Vietnam, Secretary of State Powell reportedly raised the issues of human and religious rights in his conversations with Vietnamese leaders, though he refrained from raising the issue in his public appearances. In August 2001, during the annual "human rights dialogue" with Vietnam, U.S. officials reportedly raised a number of specific issues of concern, while Vietnam urged the U.S. to do more to alleviate the continued suffering caused during the Vietnam War.

On the matter of religious freedom, U.S. law (P.L. 105-292, signed October 27, 1998) requires the State Department to report to Congress annually on the state of religious freedom in other countries. In its 2000 report, the State Department noted that Vietnam's respect for the freedom of worship varies by region. In some areas – particularly around Ho Chi Minh City, where there is a large concentration of Roman Catholics – local officials are relatively tolerant, and Vietnamese religious officials have reported an increase in religious activity and observance. In August 1999, for example, authorities allowed approximately 200,000 Catholics to attend a special Mass in central Vietnam, in what was thought to be the largest event not arranged by the Communist Party in its 24 years in power. The Catholic Church claims eight million followers out of Vietnam's 76 million, predominantly Buddhist, population.

However, the State Department report noted that in other regions – particularly those populated by ethnic minorities – authorities allow Vietnamese little discretion in practicing their faith. Indeed, according to Western human rights watch groups and State Department officials, over the past several months the government has increased its repression of unofficial religious organizations, particularly those in rural areas populated by ethnic minorities. Throughout the country, the government requires religious groups to register, and uses this process to monitor and restrict the operations of religious groups. Local officials reportedly continue to detain and imprison Vietnamese citizens for their religious beliefs. Recently, Western news sources have uncovered evidence of police raids on unofficial Christian groups, and in October 2001, a prominent Catholic priest, Father Nguyen Van Ly, was sentenced to 15 years in prison for anti-government activities. On September 6, 2001, the House passed the Vietnam Human Rights Act (H.R. 2833, by a vote of 410-1), which would ban increases (over FY2001 levels) in non-humanitarian aid to the Vietnamese government if the President does not certify that Vietnam is making "substantial progress" in human rights. The act allows the President to waive the cap on aid increases. Vietnamese officials harshly criticized the bill, arguing that U.S.-Vietnam ties must be based upon non-interference in each other's affairs.

Security Issues

Bilateral security ties have slowly been improving in recent years. Most recently, the commander-in-chief of the U.S. Pacific Command, Admiral Dennis Blair, visited Vietnam in February 2002. While in Hanoi, Blair invited Vietnam to send military personnel to observe the annual U.S.-Thailand-Singapore "Cobra Gold" military exercises. Blair also reportedly discussed Vietnam's plans for the Cam Ranh Bay military base, which will be abandoned by Russia when its lease expires in 2004.

In Mid-March 2000, U.S. Defense Secretary William Cohen visited Vietnam, the first trip by a U.S. defense secretary in nearly 30 years. During his three-day visit, which the Vietnamese government had postponed twice in 1999, Cohen met with Vietnam's top leadership, visited crash sites of U.S. fighter pilots, accepted the remains of two missing U.S. servicemen, and discussed the establishment of low-level military ties in areas such as flood control and military medicine.

The U.S. has also begun to cooperate with Vietnam on combating trade in illicit drugs. Drug trafficking through Vietnam has risen dramatically in recent years, due to the country's proximity to heroin-producing areas in Laos and Burma, and to methyl-amphetamine producing regions in southern China. In February 2000, the U.S. Drug Enforcement Agency opened an office in Hanoi in February 2000. On June 22, 2000, U.S. "drug czar" Barry McCaffrey visited Vietnam to expand bilateral anti-narcotics efforts.

POW/MIA Issues

President Clinton's receipt of the presumed remains of U.S. servicemen during his trip to Vietnam was a symbol of the increased resources devoted by Vietnam to POW/MIA research and analysis in recent years. By 1998 a substantial permanent staff in Vietnam was deeply involved in frequent searches of aircraft crash sites and discussions with local Vietnamese witnesses throughout the country. The Vietnamese authorities also had allowed U.S. analysts access to numerous POW/MIA-related archives and records. The U.S. Defense Department has reciprocated by allowing Vietnamese officials access to U.S. records and maps to assist their search for Vietnamese MIAs.

The increased efforts have led to substantial understanding about the fate of several hundred of the over 2,000 Americans still unaccounted for in Indochina. On September 21, 1998, U.S. Ambassador to Vietnam Peterson told the media in reference to Americans still listed as missing from the Vietnam War that "...it is very, very, very unlikely that you would expect to see any live Americans discovered in Vietnam, Cambodia, or Laos." He noted that investigations of 121 reported sightings of missing Americans have ended in "zero outcome, not even a trace." Official U.S. policy, however, does not "remove a name from the rolls" of those unaccounted for unless remains are identified.

VIETNAM'S SITUATION

Ever since communist North Vietnamese forces defeated U.S.-backed South Vietnam in 1975, reunified Vietnam has been struggling with how to maintain a balance between two often contradictory goals – maintaining ideological purity and promoting economic development. For the first decade after reunification, the emphasis was on the former. By the mid-1980s, disastrous economic conditions led the country to adopt a more pragmatic line, enshrined in the *doi moi* (renovation) economic reforms of 1986. Under *doi moi*, the government gave farmers greater control over what they produce, abandoned central state planning, cut subsidies to state enterprises, reformed the price system, and opened the country to foreign direct investment.

Economic Development

For first decade after the *doi moi* reforms were launched, Vietnam became one of the world's fastest growing countries, averaging around 8% annual GDP growth from 1990 to 1997. Agricultural production doubled, transforming Vietnam from a net food importer into the world's second-largest exporter of rice and third-largest producer of coffee. The move away from a command economy also helped reduce poverty levels from 58% of the population in 1992 to 37% in 1997.[1] A substantial portion of the country's growth was driven by foreign investment, primarily from Southeast Asian sources, most of which the government channeled into the country's state-owned sector.

By the mid-1990s, however, the economic reform movement had stalled, as disagreement between reformers and conservatives paralyzed economic decision-making. The economy staggered after the 1997 Asian financial crisis, as real GDP growth fell to 5.8% in 1998, and 4.8% in 1999, though it did rebound to 6.7% in 2000 and 6.8% in 2001. Foreign direct investment plummeted to $600 million in 1999, the lowest level since 1992. Observers have cited Vietnam's failure to tackle its remaining structural economic problems – including unprofitable state-owned enterprises, a weak banking sector, massive red tape, and bureaucratic corruption – as major impediments to continued growth. Vietnam remains an overwhelmingly poor country; about one-third of Vietnamese children under 5 years of age suffer malnutrition. Per capita domestic product (GDP) is estimated at $370, equivalent to $1,850 when measured on a purchasing power parity basis.

Rapid growth has transformed Vietnam's economy, which has come to be loosely divided into three sectors: the state-owned, the foreign-invested, and the privately owned, which makes up roughly 50%, 30%, and 20% of industrial output, respectively. For much of

[1] *Vietnam Development Report 2000: Attacking Poverty* (Draft), Joint Report of the Vietnam Government-Donor-NGO Working Group, November 15, 1999, p. ii.

the 1990s, Vietnam's foreign-invested enterprises (FIEs) were among the country's most dynamic. Since the 1997 Asian financial crisis, the private sector has also made impressive gains, to the point where privately owned firms employ nearly a quarter of the workforce. Most of the giant state-owned enterprises (SOEs), meanwhile, are functionally bankrupt, and require significant government subsidies and assistance to continue operating. In 1990, 2.5 million people were employed by state firms. In 2001, this figure was down to 1.6 million.

Overseas Vietnamese

In an effort to boost its economy, Hanoi in late October 1999 announced that overseas Vietnamese (*Viet Kieu*) will be allowed to travel to Vietnam without visas. The program is designed to encourage the estimated 2.5 million Vietnamese living abroad to visit and work in their home country. Remittance from overseas Vietnamese totaled an estimated $1.2 billion in 1999; nearly 10% of Vietnam's export earnings that year.

Political Trends

Vietnam's experiments with political reform have lagged behind its economic changes. A new constitution promulgated in 1992, for instance, reaffirmed the central role of the Communist Party in politics and society, and Vietnam remains a one-party state. Although personal freedoms have increased dramatically, Hanoi still does not tolerate signs of organized political dissent. In subtle ways, however, the decision to prioritize economic development above ideological orthodoxy has led the Party to slowly loosen its former stranglehold on political power. Recognizing that Party cadres often were ill suited to administering its own policy directives, for instance, the Party created a more powerful and professionalized executive branch in the 1992 constitution. The new constitution also gave more influence to the legislative branch, the National Assembly, in part because the Party realized it needed to make the organs of government more responsive at the grass roots level. Over the past decade, the Assembly has slowly and subtly increased its influence. In December 2001, constitutional amendments were passed allowing the Assembly to hold no-confidence votes against the government, and to dismiss the president and prime minister (though not the general secretary of the Party).

Rapid economic growth, increased integration with the global economy, and weak domestic institutions have caused a rise in corruption and a decline in the Vietnamese Communist Party's (VCP) authority, alarming many Party hard-liners. As a result, Vietnamese policymaking in recent years has been virtually paralyzed, as reformist and conservative elements within the Party have battled to a stalemate over how to deal with the major economic and demographic forces transforming the country. The former group calls for a steady rollout of new reforms and increased integration into the global economy. The latter feats that economic reform will lead to the loss of government control over the economic means of production and financial and monetary levers; they also fear the possible infiltration of heterodox outside ideas. Vietnam's consensus-based decision-making style, combined with the absence of any paramount leader, has meant that these divisions have produced only piecemeal economic reforms, though implementing the BTA may force more significant changes.

The 9th Party Congress

Vietnamese Communist Party Congresses, which are held every five years, often are occasions for major leadership realignments and set the direction for Vietnam's economic, diplomatic, and social policies. At its ninth Party Congress that ended on April 22, 2001, Vietnam's Communist Party selected **Nong Duc Manh** as its Secretary General, the Party's top post. Manh (60) is generally considered to be more moderate than his predecessor, **Le Ka Phieu** (69), a conservative who was ousted after a heated struggle. Significantly, Manh's selection was made possible when the Party's Central Committee rejected – an unprecedented move – the Politburo's decision to endorse Phieu for another term. Manh, the former speaker of Vietnam's National Assembly, is an ethnic Tay, making him the first member of an ethnic minority to head Vietnam's Communist Party. In other significant moves, the 9th Party Congress reduced the size of the Politburo (from 19 to 15 members), retired seven Politburo members, and shrunk the Central Committee from 170 to 150 members.

Manh's selection as Secretary General is but the latest in a long string of seemingly contradictory personnel shifts and policy moves that Vietnam-watchers have been struggling to interpret for signs that the economic reformers or hard-liners have gained the upper hand. Manh's selection has not yet resulted in the expected acceleration of reforms, as he has devoted most of his attention to an anti-corruption campaign that features greater local supervision of local authorities. A sign that Manh may have begun to try to revive the *doi moi* (economic renovation) process occurred in January 2000, when he directed the Party to begin considering how to develop the private sector and whether Party members should be allowed to start their own businesses.

Vietnam's new leadership will have to confront the problem of how to reverse the Communist Party's declining legitimacy. Attracting new recruits into the Party has become increasingly difficult, particularly among young Vietnamese – a major problem since more than half of the population is under the age of 25. Some prominent retired military leaders, including war hero General Vo Nguyen Giap, have publicly called for the Party to become more democratic.

Unrest in the Central Highlands Region

Additionally, over the past several years, there have been reports of protests and riots by peasants in the Central Highlands provinces against local government corruption and by ethnic minorities against encroachment on their ancestral lands by recent settlers; in February 2001, thousands of minorities, primarily from Montagnard groups, protested in the Central Highlands, the largest-scale social unrest in years. The Vietnamese government dispatched military troops and local police to quell the unrest, and in the spring of 2001 launched a crackdown against the protesters. Vietnam has accused U.S. groups of providing financial and logistical support to the protestors. Hanoi has also criticized the United States for granting asylum to 24 Vietnamese refugees, all members of the Central Highlands minority groups that protested, who fled into Cambodia following the unrest. Some refugees reported that the Vietnamese government has imprisoned the tortured many protestors. Hundreds of asylum seekers from Vietnam remain in Cambodia. A repatriation agreement signed in January 2002 by Vietnam, Cambodia, and the United Nations High Commissioner for Refugees (UNHCR) crumbled after Vietnam refused to abide by its agreement to allow the UNHCR access to the Central Highlands to monitor refugee returns. To settle the dispute, Cambodia in late March 2001 accepted an offer from the United States to resettle the more than 900 Montagnards that remained in Cambodia. There is speculation that Vietnam's acquiescence to the plan was obtained by Cambodia's pledge to close its borders to future asylum-seekers from Vietnam.

Foreign and Defense Policy

For many years, a major impediment to Vietnam's development was the strong international sanctions imposed in response to Vietnam's 1978 invasion and subsequent 11-year occupation of Cambodia. Faced with a cutoff of much aid from the Soviet bloc, the Vietnamese in the early 1990s increased their flexibility on a Cambodian settlement, moved to accommodate China on sensitive issues, and stepped up action on the POW/MIA and other humanitarian issues with the United States. In the mid-1990s, Hanoi continued the process of rejoining the world political community by joining the regional political group, the Association of Southeast Asian Nations (ASEAN), the regional security forum, the SEAN Regional Forum (ARF), and the regional economic group, the Asian Pacific Economic Cooperation (APEC) forum.

Vietnam has had periodic spats with its neighbors over the islands in the South China Sea. In 1974, China seized the Paracel Island chain from Vietnam. In 1988, the Vietnamese and Chinese navies clashed over conflicting claims to the Spratly Islands, parts or all of which are also claimed by Taiwan, Malaysia, the Philippines, and Brunei. Although most of the Spratlys are low-lying reefs and rocky outcrops, the sea bed beneath them is thought to contain massive oil and gas reserves, and the 155,000 square miles of surrounding waters are home to rich fishing grounds. Hanoi's latest flare-up in the Spratlys occurred in October 1999, when Vietnamese troops on Tennent Reef fired at a Filipino reconnaissance plane flying low over a suspected Vietnamese military installation.

In recent years, Hanoi has improved ties with many of its neighbors, the October 1999 incident with Manila notwithstanding. Most significantly, Vietnam has moved to fully normalize relations with Mainland China. Following Chinese Prime Minister Zhu Rongji's four-day visit to Vietnam in early December, for instance, the two sides signed a long-elusive land border treaty on December 30, 1999. In late December 2000, Vietnamese President Tran Duc Long traveled to Beijing, where he signed an agreement establishing the two countries' sea border in the Gulf of Tonkin. The two countries, however, still have overlapping claims to the Spratly Island chain in the South China Sea, differences that led to military clashes in the late 1980s. Along with other Southeast Asian nations, Vietnam has tried – thus fare unsuccessfully – to convince China to agree to a multilateral code of conduct for the South China Sea. Vietnam did not push the issue in 2001 during its tenure as chair of the standing committee of the Association of Southeast Asian Nations (ASEAN).

Shortly after assuming the ASEAN chair, Vietnam rebuffed United Nations Secretary General Kofi Annan's suggestion that it convene a troika of ASEAN ministers to help start a dialogue between Myanmar's military government and dissident Aung San Suu Kyi. A

Vietnamese official said that Hanoi had rejected the idea because it constituted an unwarranted "interference" in Myanmar's affairs. During the 2000 annual meeting of ASEAN Foreign Ministers, participants had agreed that the organization should form a troika of officials to resolve political and security problems of common concern in the region.

In 1999 and 2000, Vietnam improved its historically troubled relations with Cambodia, sending a high-level delegation to Phnom Penh, strongly supporting Cambodia's entry into ASEAN in early 1999, and pledging to resolve outstanding border disagreements with Laos and Thailand to harmonize and simplify regulations governing flows of good, vehicles, and people. The deal is part of the proposed $350 million, 240 mile East-West Transport Corridor highway project designed to link areas of Laos and Thailand to the port of Da Nang in central Vietnam. There have been reports that Vietnamese troops have assisted the Laotian regime in combating an insurgency by ethnic minorities. In March 2001, Russian President Vladimir Putin visited Vietnam, where the two countries signed a new strategic partnership agreement, and restructured Vietnam's Soviet-era debt to Russia. In the summer of 2001, the Russian Defense Minister announced that Moscow would not renew its lease of the Cam Ranh Bay military base in Vietnam's southeast coast. That lease, which the Soviet Union and Russia had held since the late 1970s, is due to expire in 2004.

Issues for Congress

If past events are any guide, future steps to improve U.S.-Vietnam relations are likely to remain controversial in the United States and Vietnam. Potential issues of concern to the U.S. Congress should include:

- Consideration of a Presidential waiver of Jackson-Vanik restrictions;
- Calling attention to Vietnam's record on human, religious, and labor rights, and possibly linking these issues to the Jackson-Vanik waiver or to U.S. non-humanitarian assistance to Vietnam;
- Pushing for the U.S. and Vietnam to negotiate a bilateral agreement on trade in textiles;
- Granting of Generalized System of Preference (GSP) status to a range of Vietnamese imports,
- Increase of U.S. foreign assistance.

Congress plays a funding, authorizing, or oversight role in each of these issues. Congressional supporters of warmer U.S. relations with Vietnam include Members who support growing U.S. business interests in Vietnam. Many Members also supported Clinton Administration arguments that improved relations with Vietnam help U.S. strategic interests in working closely with friends and allies to promote stability and development by integrating Vietnam more fully into the East Asian regional order. The Clinton Administration contended that increasing U.S. economic, political, and other interaction with Vietnam is a good way to promote political liberalization in the country. Finally, there are Members who believe that the United States is more likely to elicit Vietnamese cooperation on POW/MIA, human rights, or other sensitive issues through a policy of closer "engagement," rather than one that restricts ties until Vietnam meets firm U.S. conditions.

Against these advocates are those Members who are sharply critical of the Vietnamese government's repressive political regime and human rights violations, including suppression of religious freedom; those who represent U.S. constituencies concerned with poor labor conditions in many industries in Vietnam; those who see no significant U.S. interest in stimulating the economic development of this regime; and those who represent some Vietnamese-American constituencies that strongly oppose the current Hanoi government.

LEGISLATION

H.R. 2833 (Christopher Smith)

Withholds bilateral non-humanitarian unless Vietnam receives a Presidential certification that it is meeting certain human rights conditions. Introduced September 5, 2001; referred to Committee on International Relations and Financial Services. Passed by the House, 410-1 (roll call 335) on September 6, 2001.

Chapter 6

VIETNAM: HISTORICAL BACKGROUND*

Ronald J. Cima (Editor)

GEOGRAPHY

Size

Approximately 331,688 square kilometers.

Topography

Hills and densely forested mountains, with level land covering no more than 20 percent. Mountains account for 40 percent, hills 40 percent, and forests 75 percent. North consists of highlands and the Red River Delta; south divided into coastal lowlands, Giai Truong Son (central mountains) with high plateaus, and Mekong River Delta.

Climate

Tropical and monsoonal; humidity averages 84 percent throughout year. Annual rainfall ranges from 120 to 300 centimeters, and annual temperatures vary between 5°C and 37°C.

---

* This chapter has been excerpted from *Vietnam: A Country Study* edited by Ronald J. Cima, which is available from the Federal Research Division of the Library of Congress.

SOCIETY

Population

64,411,668 (1989 census); 2.1 percent average annual population growth rate. Nineteen percent urban; 81 percent rural. Population centers Hanoi and Ho Chi Minh City (formerly Saigon).

Languages

Vietnamese official language; also French, various Chinese dialects, tribal languages, and English.

Ethnic Groups

Vietnamese account for 87.5 percent of population (1979 figures). Fifty-three minorities account for remainder, including Hoa (Chinese, comprising approximately 1.8 percent), Tay, Thai, Khmer, Muong, Nung, Hmong, and numerous mountain tribes.

Religion

Mahayana Buddhism, Theravada Buddhism, Cao Dai, Hoa Hao, Roman Catholicism, Protestantism, Islam, Hinduism, and animism.

Education and Literacy

Nine years of primary and junior high school, three years of secondary school. First nine years compulsory. Manual labor comprises 15 percent of primary curriculum and 17 percent of secondary. Ninety-three colleges and universities, with close to 130,000 students enrolled, able to admit only 10 percent of applicants. Education emphasizes training of skilled workers, technicians, and managers. Students nevertheless tend to avoid vocational schools and specialized middle schools because they are believed to preclude entry to high-status occupations. Literacy 78 percent (for all age groups).

Health

Total of approximately 11,000 hospitals, medical aid stations, public health stations, and village maternity clinics, staffed by 240,000 medical personnel. Approximately 1 physician per 1,000 persons. Life expectancy sixty-three years. Malaria, tuberculosis, and other communicable diseases prevalent. Government undertaken a campaign to improve cleanliness by launching "Three Cleans Movement" (clean food, water, and living conditions) and "Three Exterminations Movement" (exterminate flies, mosquitos, and rats).

ECONOMY

Salient Features

In 1984 gross domestic product (GDP-- see Glossary) stood at US$18.1 billion, US$300 per capita at official exchange rate of 12.1 dong to US$1 (actual per capita income is closer to US$200). Produced National Income (PNI--see Glossary) grew by 2.1 percent in 1987, down from 3.3 percent in 1986.

Agriculture

Major agricultural products produced in 1985: grain (18.2 million tons), sugar (434,000 tons), tea (26,000 tons), coffee (6,000 tons), and rubber (52,000 tons). Agriculture represented 51 percent of PNI.

Industry

Thirty-two percent of PNI in 1985; major industries included electricity (5.4 billion kilowatt hours), coal (60 million tons), steel (57,000 tons), cement (1.4 million tons), cloth (80 million square meters), paper (75,000 tons), fish sauce (174 million liters), and processed sea fish (550,000 tons). Mineral resources included iron ore, tin, copper, lead, zinc, nickel, manganese, titanium, chromite, tungsten, bauxite, apatite, graphite, mica, silica sand, and limestone.

Energy Sources

Timber, coal, offshore oil deposits.

Foreign Trade

Exports totaled US$739.5 million in 1986. Principal exports consisted of coal, rubber, rice, tea, coffee, wood, and marine products. Imports totaled US$2.5 billion in 1986. Principal imports consisted of petroleum products, fertilizers, rice, and steel. In 1986 total debt estimated at nearly US$7.7 billion. According to figures given to International Monetary Fund by Hanoi, from 1981-85 Vietnam's debt to communist bloc countries rose from US$3 billion to more than US$6 billion. Trade deficit with the Soviet Union grew from US$224 million in 1976 to US$1.5 billion in 1986.

Transportation and Communications

Railroads

Total of 4,250 kilometers of track. Most important section connects Hanoi and Ho Chi Minh City.

Roads

Some 85,000 kilometers of road; of which 9,400 kilometers paved, 48,700 kilometers gravel or improved earth, and 26,900 kilometers unimproved.

Maritime Shipping

125 vessels, including 80 coastal freighters, 12 oil tankers, and 15 ocean-going freighters. Total of thirty-two ports, of which nine major ports. Three largest located at Da Nang, Haiphong, and Ho Chi Minh City.

Civil Aviation

Controlled by military. Domestic air service connects Hanoi with Ho Chi Minh City, Da Nang, Pleiku, Da Lat, Buon Me Thuot, Phu Bai and Nha Trang. Ho Chi Minh City also connected to Rach Gia, Phu Quoc and Con Son Island. International air service connects Hanoi with Vientiane, Phnom Penh, Moscow, and Bangkok. Total of 128 usable airfields, 46 with surfaced runways.

Telecommunications

Two satellite-ground communications stations linking Hanoi, Ho Chi Minh City, and Moscow, and integrating Vietnam into Soviet Intersputnik Communication Satellite Organization.

Government and Politics

Party and Government

Democratic Republic of (North) and former Republic of (South) Vietnam united to form Socialist Republic of Vietnam on July 2, 1976. Constitution adapted in 1980 stipulates National Assembly as highest governing body. Members serve five-year terms and nominally directly elected by electorate. Council of State, which serves as collective presidency, and Council of Ministers, which manages governmental activities, nominally accountable to, and elected by, National Assembly. Political power effectively in hands of Vietnamese Communist Party (VCP, Viet Nam Cong San Dang). Most government positions filled by party members, who act at direction of party. Party led by National Party Congress, which meets infrequently. Congress elects Central Committee, which in turn elects Political Bureau, party's highest policy-making body.

Administrative Divisions

Country divided into thirty-six provinces, three autonomous municipalities, and one special zone. Provinces divided into districts, towns, and capitals.

Judicial System

Supreme People's Court; local People's Courts at provincial, district, and city levels; military tribunals; and People's Supreme Organ of Control. National Assembly elects Procurator General, who heads People's Supreme Organ of Control and performs overall administration of justice.

Foreign Affairs

Vietnam dominated Laos through numerous Hanoi-dictated cooperation agreements; most important-- Treaty of Friendship and Cooperation signed in 1977. Occupied Cambodia as result of military conquest in January 1979 and subsequently negotiated Treaty of Friendship and Cooperation. Relations with China marked by China's limited invasion in 1979 and frequent border skirmishes. Formally aligned with Soviet Union through Treaty of Friendship and Cooperation signed in November 1978. Both countries shared membership in Council for Mutual Economic Assistance (Comecon--see Glossary); Soviet Union largest donor of economic and military aid. Limited governmental and commercial ties established with all Association for Southeast Asian Nations (ASEAN) members but prevented from developing further by ASEAN's opposition to Vietnam's Cambodia policy. In 1988 no diplomatic relations with United States, which maintained economic boycott against Vietnam and stressed Vietnam's cooperation in accounting for servicemen missing in action as prerequisite to normal relations. Admitted to membership in United Nations in 1977.

NATIONAL SECURITY

Armed Forces

Largest military force in Southeast Asia and third largest force in the world after China and the Soviet Union. Estimated in 1987 to total over 5 million: army, 1.2 million; navy, 15,000; air force, 20,000; Regional Force, 500,000; Militia-Self Defense Force, 1.2 million; Armed Youth Assault Force, 1,500,000; and Tactical Rear Force, 500,000.

Combat Units and Major Equipment

Command structure divided geographically into military theaters and military regions or zones. Tactically divided into corps, divisions, brigades, regiments, and battalions, companies, platoons, and squads. Army comprised eight corps (each numbering 30,000 to 50,000 troops). In 1986 total of thirty-eight regular infantry divisions: nineteen in Cambodia, ten in northern Vietnam, six in central and southern Vietnam, and three in Laos. Thirteen economic construction divisions, which carried burden of 1979 war with China, deployed in China border region. Army equipped with 1,600 Soviet-made T-34 -54 -55 -62, Type-59 tanks and 450 PT-76 and type 60 63 light tanks; 2,700 reconnaissance vehicles; some 600 artillery guns and howitzers, unspecified number of multiple rocket launchers, mortars, and antitank weapons; and 3,000 air defense weapons. Navy, with Soviet assistance, largest naval force in Southeast Asia in 1986. Five naval regions, headquartered at Da Nang, Haiphong, Vinh, Vung Tau, and Rach Gia. Navy equipped with 2 principal combat vessels, 192 patrol boats, 51 amphibious warfare ships, 104 landing ships, and 133 auxiliary craft. Approximately 1,300 ex-United States, South Vietnamese naval vessels, naval and civilian junks and coasters augment this force. Air Force divided into seventeen air regiments, (seven attack fighter plane regiments, four basic and advanced training regiments, three cargo transport regiments, three helicopter regiments, and one light bomber force), headquartered at Noi Bai (Hanoi), Da Nang, Tho Xuan, and Tan Son Nhut (Ho Chi Minh City). Air Force equipped with some 450 combat aircraft (including 225 MiG-21s), 225 trainers, 350 cargo-transport planes, 600 helicopters, and 60 light bombers.

Military Budget

No expenditure estimates available. Military aid from Soviet Union estimated about US$1.5 billion annually beginning in 1986.

Police Agencies and Paramilitary

Police functions vested in People's Security Force (PSF), People's Public Security Force (PPSF), and People's Armed Security Force (PASF). PSF strictly law enforcement agency operating chiefly in urban rather than rural areas. PASF composed of party security cadres and PAVN personnel concerned with illegal political acts and insurgency movements as well as criminal activity.

Foreign Military Alliances

Friendship and cooperation treaties signed with Laos in 1977, Soviet Union in 1978, and Cambodia in 1979.

INTRODUCTION

The victory of communist forces in Vietnam in April 1975 ranks as one of the most politically significant occurrences of the post-World War II era in Asia. The speed with which the North finally seized the South, and the almost simultaneous communist victories in Laos and Cambodia, were stunning achievements. The collapse of the three Indochinese noncommunist governments brought under communist control a region that, over the course of four decades of war, had become the focus of United States policy for the containment of communism in Asia. The achievement was even more phenomenal for having been accomplished in the face of determined United States opposition and for having called into question the very policy of containing communism.

The events of April 1975 prepared the way for the official reunification of North and South in 1976, some three decades after Ho Chi Minh first proclaimed Vietnam's independence under one government in September 1945 and more than a century after France divided Vietnam in order to rule its regions separately. The departure of defeated Japanese troops, who had occupied Vietnam during World War II, had created the opportunity for Vietnamese communists to seize power in August 1945, before French authorities were able to return to reclaim control of the government. Communist rule was cut short, however, by nationalist Chinese and British occupation forces whose presence tended to support the Communist Party's political opponents. Between 1945 and 1975, the generation of communists responsible for victory in the South pursued a lengthy war for independence from the French, acquiesced temporarily to division of the country into a communist North and noncommunist South, and engaged in a subsequent war for control of the South against a southern regime supported by the United States. Reunification and independence, however, were goals that predated the communists. They were the long-established objectives of Ho Chi Minh's nationalist and anticolonialist predecessors, who had resisted Chinese rule for 1,000 years and French domination for a century.

Indeed, Vietnam's unrelenting resistance to foreign intervention remains a dominant Vietnamese historical theme, manifested in the repeated waging of *dau tranh*, or struggle to gain a long-term objective through total effort, and motivated by *chinh nghia*, or just cause. Vietnam's communist leaders claim that every Vietnamese has been a soldier in this struggle. Paradoxically, Vietnam's fierce determination to remain free of foreign domination has often been combined with an equally strong willingness to accept foreign influence. Historically, the pattern has been to adopt foreign ideas to indigenous conditions whenever they applied.

China was the chief source of Vietnam's foreign ideas and the earliest threat to its national sovereignty. Beginning in the first century B.C., China's Han dynasty (206 B.C.-A.D. 220) imposed Chinese rule that endured for ten centuries despite repeated Vietnamese uprisings and acts of rebellion. Only the collapse of the Tang dynasty (618-907) in the early tenth century enabled Vietnamese national hero Ngo Quyen to reestablish Vietnam's independence a generation later. The Vietnamese subsequently were able to fend off further invasion attempts for 900 years (see The Chinese Millennium; Nine Centuries of Independence).

Whether ruled by China or independent, the Vietnamese elite consistently modeled Vietnamese cultural institutions on those of the Chinese. Foremost among such Chinese institutions was Confucianism, after which Vietnamese family, bureaucratic, and social structures were patterned. The Vietnamese upper classes tended also to study Chinese classical literature and to use the Chinese system of ideographs in writing. Emperor Gia Long, in a particularly obvious act of imitation in the early nineteenth century, even modeled his new capital at Hue after the Chinese capital at Beijing. The process of sinicization, however, tended to coexist with, rather than to replace, traditional Vietnamese culture and language. Imitation of the Chinese was largely confined to the elite classes. Traditional Vietnamese society, on the other hand, was sustained by the large peasant class, which was less exposed to Chinese influence.

Vietnam's lengthy period of independence ended in 1862, when Emperor Tu Duc, agreeing to French demands, ceded three provinces surrounding Saigon to France. During the colonial period, from 1862 to 1954, resistance to French rule was led by members of the scholar-official class, whose political activities did not involve the peasantry and hence failed. The success of the communists, on the other hand, was derived from their ability to organize and retain the peasantry's support. The Vietnamese Communist Party (VCP--Viet Nam Cong San Dang) and its various communist antecedents presented Marxism-Leninism as an effective means of recovering the independence that was Vietnam's tradition. Belief in this ideal was instrumental in sustaining Northern and Southern peasant-based communist forces during the lengthy Second Indochina War, which lasted from 1954 to 1975.

In the post-1975 period, however, it was immediately apparent that the popularity and effectiveness of the communist party's wartime policies did not necessarily extend to its peacetime nation-building plans. Having unified the North and South politically, the VCP still had to integrate them socially and economically. In this task, VCP policy-makers were confronted with Southern resistance to change, as well as traditional animosities arising from cultural and historical differences between the North and South. The situation was further complicated by a deterioration in economic conditions that ignited an unprecedented level of discontent among low-level VCP members and open criticism of VCP policies. The party appeared to be in a state of transition, wavering over the pace and manner of the South's integration with the North and debating the place of reform in development strategy. The first generation communist leaders, co-founders of the party together with Ho Chi Minh, were aging and were beginning to step down in favor of younger, often reform-minded technocrats. The Sixth National Party Congress held in December 1986 was a milestone; it marked the end of the party's revolutionary period, when social welfare and modernization were subordinate to security concerns, and the beginning of a time when experimentation and reform were encouraged to stimulate development.

In the 1980s, Vietnam ranked third in population--60 million--and first in population density--an average of 182 persons per square kilometer--among the world's communist nations. A 2 percent annual population growth rate and uneven population distribution adversely affected resource allocation, work force composition, and land use. Population projections indicated a population of 80 million by the year 2000, if the growth rate remained unchanged. The Fourth National Party Congress in December 1976 stressed the need to curtail the population growth rate and introduced a plan to relocate 54 million people to 1 million hectares of previously uncultivated land, now organized into "new economic zones," by the mid-1990s. As of 1988, however, progress toward the plan's fulfillment was considerably behind schedule (see Population).

A predominantly rural society with more than half of its work force committed to agriculture, Vietnam's standard of living remained one of the poorest in the world. A series of harvest shortfalls that reduced food supplies and a scarcity of foreign exchange that made it difficult to replenish food reserves contributed to this condition. Shortages of raw materials and energy forced production facilities to operate at considerably less than full capacity, and the party bureaucracy remained incapable of acting quickly enough to reduce shortages.

Economic development prospects for the 1980s and 1990s were tied to party economic policy in critical ways. Party leaders, in establishing economic policy at the Fourth National Party Congress, envisioned Vietnam's post-reunification economy to be in a "period of transition to socialism." The plan, or series of plans, called for the economy to evolve through three phases: The first, outlining the objectives of the Second Five-Year Plan (1976-80), set extremely high goals for industrial and agricultural production while also giving high priority to construction, reconstruction, and the integration of the North and the South. The second, entitled "socialist industrialization," was divided into two stages--from 1981 to 1990 and from 1991 to 2005. During these stages, the material and technical foundations of communism were to be constructed, and development plans were to focus equally on agriculture and industry. The third and final phase, covering the years from 2006 to 2010; was to be a time set aside to "perfect the transitional period."

By 1979, however, it was obvious to Vietnam's leaders that the Second Five-Year Plan would fail to meet its goals and that the long-range goals established for the transition period were unrealistic. The economy continued to be dominated by small-scale production, low productivity, high unemployment, material and technological shortages, and insufficient food and consumer goods.

The Fifth National Party Congress, held in March 1982, approved the economic goals of the Third Five-Year Plan (1981- 85). The policies introduced were comparatively liberal and called for the temporary retention of private capitalist activities in the South, in order to spur economic growth. By sanctioning free enterprise, the congress ended the nationalization of small business concerns and reversed former policies that sought the immediate transformation of the South to communism. The July 1984 Sixth Plenum of the Fifth National Party Congress' Central Committee confirmed the party's earlier decision, recognizing that the private sector's domination over wholesale and retail trade in the South could not be eliminated until the state was capable of assuming that responsibility. Proposals subsequently were made to upgrade the state's economic sophistication by decentralizing planning procedures and improving the managerial skills of government and party officials. To attract foreign currency and expertise, the government approved a new foreign investment code in December 1987.

Vietnam's security considerations in the 1980s also represented a new set of challenges to the party. Until the fall of the South Vietnamese government in 1975, the party had relegated foreign policy to a secondary position behind the more immediate concerns of national liberation and reunification. Once the Second Indochina War had ended, however, the party needed to look outward and reevaluate foreign policy, particularly as it applied to Cambodia, China, the Soviet Union, member nations of the Association of Southeast Asian Nations (ASEAN), and the United States and other Western nations (see Foreign Relations).

By the end of the 1970s, the Vietnamese were threatened on two fronts, a condition which Vietnam had not faced previously, even at the height of the Second Indochina War. Conflict between Vietnamese and Cambodian communists on their common border began almost immediately after their respective victories in 1975. To neutralize the threat, Vietnam invaded Cambodia in December 1978 and overran Phnom Penh, the Cambodian capital, driving out the incumbent Khmer Rouge communist regime and initiating a prolonged military occupation of the country. Vietnam's relations with China, a seemingly staunch ally during the Second Indochina War, subsequently reached their nadir, when China retaliated against Vietnam's incursion into Cambodia by launching a limited invasion of Vietnam in February and March 1979. Relations between the two countries had actually been deteriorating for some time. Territorial disagreements, which had remained dormant during the war against the South, were revived at the war's end, and a postwar campaign engineered by Hanoi to limit the role of Vietnam's ethnic Chinese (Hoa) community in domestic commerce elicited a strong Chinese protest. China was displeased with Vietnam primarily, however, because of its rapidly improving relationship with the Soviet Union.

A new era in Vietnamese foreign relations began in 1978, when Hanoi joined the Soviet-led Council for Mutual Economic Assistance (Comecon) and signed the Soviet-Vietnamese Treaty of Friendship and Cooperation with Moscow. The agreement called for mutual assistance and consultation in the event either was threatened by a third country. A secret protocol accompanying the treaty also permitted Soviet use of Vietnamese airport and harbor facilities, particularly the former United States military complex at Cam Ranh Bay. In return, Vietnam acquired military and economic aid needed to undertake an invasion of Cambodia and was able to exploit Soviet influence as a deterrent to Chinese intervention (see Foreign Relations).

After China had cut off military assistance to Vietnam, such aid--amounting to US$200 to $300 million annually--was almost exclusively Soviet in origin during the 1980s. As Vietnam's primary source of economic aid as well, the Soviet Union during this period provided close to US$1 billion annually in balance- of-payments aid, project assistance, and oil price subsidies.

Vietnam's growing dependence on the Soviet Union concerned Hanoi's Southeast Asian neighbors. As did China, the ASEAN nations thought that the relationship provided a springboard for Soviet influence in the region and that Soviet support provided a critical underpinning for Vietnam's Cambodia policy. The ASEAN nations assumed a key role in rallying United Nations (UN) General Assembly opposition to Vietnam's interference in Cambodia and led the UN in preventing the Vietnamese-supported regime in Phnom Penh from assuming Cambodia's General Assembly seat. ASEAN members were instrumental in combining--at least on paper--the various Cambodian communist and noncommunist factions opposing the Vietnamese into a single resistance coalition.

The decision to intervene militarily in Cambodia further isolated Vietnam from the international community. The United States, in addition to citing Vietnam's minimal cooperation in accounting for Americans who were missing in action (MIAs) as an obstacle to normal relations, barred normal ties as long as Vietnamese troops occupied Cambodia. In 1987 Washington also continued to enforce the trade embargo imposed on Hanoi at the conclusion of the war in 1975.

Normalization of diplomatic relations with the United States, however, was not a primary Vietnamese foreign policy objective in 1987. The sizable economic benefits it would yield, plus its strategic value remained secondary to other more immediate security concerns, although the potential economic benefits were judged sizable. Instead, Vietnam prepared to enter the 1990s with foreign relations priorities that stressed extrication from the military stalemate in Cambodia in a manner consistent with security needs, repair of ties with China to alleviate Chinese military pressure on Vietnam's northern border, and reduction of military and economic dependence on the Soviet Union.

Domestic and foreign policy in 1987 reflected changes initiated by the elevation of reformer Nguyen Van Linh to VCP general secretary at the Sixth National Party Congress. Policies were characterized by a program of political and economic experimentation that was similar to contemporary reform agendas undertaken in China and the Soviet Union. The goal of all three nations was to pursue economic development at the cost of some compromise of communist ideological orthodoxy. In the case of Vietnam, however, the conservative members of the leadership continued to view orthodoxy as an ultimate goal. According to their plan, the stress on economic development was only a momentary emphasis; the real goal remained the perfection of Vietnam's communist society.

* * *

In 1988 and 1989, the years immediately following the completion of research and writing on this book, Vietnam's foreign and domestic policy was increasingly determined by economic considerations. The mood of dramatic economic and political reform, inspired by the Sixth National Party Congress and Linh's appointment to party leadership, however, appeared to have dissipated, and the mood of confidence that had prevailed in 1987 gradually evaporated as disagreement among Political Bureau members over the pace of change stymied the implementation of many policy innovations.

A campaign for political and economic renewal (*doi moi*) was launched by Linh immediately following the congress, but the progress of change, particularly economic change, failed to meet expectations. Linh was strongly opposed within the party's leadership, and his economic reforms were initially stalled or blocked by the resistance efforts of a strong conservative coalition of party leaders, made up of ideological conservatives, bureaucrats, and members of the military establishment.

Linh's initiatives for dealing with the country's economic problems were bold, but the coalition of conservative party leaders opposing his policies effectively denied him the consensus he needed to implement his plans. Consequently, his powers to effect change appeared to wane as the severity of the country's economic crisis deepened.

Despite their opposition to reform policy, reform, per se, was viewed as "correct" by most, if not all, members of Vietnam's Political Bureau. A member's position on the subject, however, was probably determined less by his view of the process in the abstract than by his willingness to undertake risk, and in 1988 and 1989 the non-risk takers appeared to have the upper hand.

In March 1988 Prime Minister Pham Hung died, and Linh's choice of conservative Do Muoi over fellow reformer Vo Van Kiet to replace him was viewed as a clear concession to the non-risk takers. National Assembly members, however, for the first time challenged the central committee's nominee for a key government post by demanding that two candidates be permitted to run. Muoi, the party's choice, was required to face Vo Van Kiet, the nominee of delegates from the south.

The dissent displayed in the debate leading to Muoi's selection was not isolated, but mirrored a dramatic increase in all political debate and discussion in 1988. The October 1988 meeting of the Congress of National Trade Unions, for example, was extremely critical of the government's economic failures. Similarly, the Fourth Session of the 8th National Assembly, held in December 1988, heatedly debated the issues. It was conducted without the customary Central Committee meeting beforehand and, on the surface, appeared to be acting without Central Committee guidance.

Lastly, a campaign against corruption, initiated by Nguyen Van Linh in 1987, invited private and official criticism of public policy and encouraged the press to take the lead in uncovering corruption. By early 1988, the campaign had resulted in the replacement of almost all of the country's 40 province secretaries and 80 percent of the 400 or so district party chiefs. Eleven-hundred party cadres were tried for corruption in the first six months of the year, and the press was credited with the party's removal of Ha Truong Hoa, the party Provincial Secretary of Thanh Hoa, whose position was widely regarded as impregnable despite his well publicized abuses of office. The policy of encouraging criticism, however, was mysteriously reversed in early 1989 when the press was urged to moderate its criticism of the Party. It was speculated that the reversal was meant to appease conservatives within the Political Bureau who were concerned about the erosion of party authority caused by public criticism.

Party leaders themselves, however, continued to be critical of party policy. Nguyen The Phan, the head of the theoretical department of the Marxist-Leninist Institute, for example, told a January 1989 meeting of high-ranking officials that by following the Soviet economic model, Vietnam had developed a centralized and subsidized economic system "inferior to capitalism," and "had abolished motivation in people and society." He called on party leaders to learn about marketplace competition from capitalist countries.

Goals established and reinforced at the December 1988 meeting of the Eighth National Assembly were consistent with this theme. The primary goal was described as development of an economy that was less controlled by the government and more subject to the rules of the marketplace. This was to be achieved by subjecting all economic transactions to the standards of basic business accountability and by expanding the private sector. Centralized bureaucratism was to be abolished, and some state-run economic establishments were to be guaranteed autonomy in their business practices. Lastly, the system of state subsidies for food, import-export operations, or for losses incurred by state-run enterprises was scheduled to be eliminated.

Beginning in 1988, individual farmers were given more responsibility for the rice growing process in order to increase their incentive to produce higher yields. Land tenure laws were modified to guarantee farmers a ten-year tenure on the land, and the contract system between peasants and the government was revised to permit peasants to keep 45 to 50 percent of their output rather than the 25 percent previously allowed. Other reforms removed restrictions on private-production enterprises in Hanoi and introduced the concept of developing industry outside the state-run sector. A law passed in January 1989 helped free the economy from central control by granting entrepreneurs the right to pool their capital and set up their own business organizations. Such concessions were of particular assistance to entrepreneurs in the South, where the economy in 1988 and 1989 was more or less directed by its own momentum, and where it had become increasingly evident that Vietnam's economic planners had opted to exploit the region's economic potential rather than stifle it by employing rigid controls.

The sixth plenum of the party central committee (Sixth Party Congress), held in late March 1989, concluded, however, that despite the establishment of goals and the introduction of some new policies little was actually being accomplished because local cadres were failing to implement reform plans or institutionalize party resolutions in a timely manner. The plenum, therefore, resolved to emphasize the implementation and institutionalization of reforms and resolutions already introduced in order to accelerate the process.

Chinese student pro-democracy demonstrations in Beijing a few months later were watched very closely by Vietnam's leaders. In their view, the disaffection demonstrated by Chinese students had resulted directly from China's experimentation with political and economic reforms. Having undertaken similar changes, they were concerned that Vietnam was equally vulnerable to displays of unrest. To avoid China's experience, the government reportedly dealt with student protesters in Hanoi in May 1989 by acceding to their demands for improved conditions. Progress toward greater political liberalization, however, was subsequently checked.

Vietnam's world view noticeably altered in the closing years of the 1980s, moving from an ideologically dominated perspective, stressing Vietnam's independence and the division of the world into communist and noncommunist camps, to a non-ideological view emphasizing Vietnam's role in a complex world of economic interdependence. The most significant example of a foreign policy initiative motivated by this view was the decision, announced in early 1989, to remove all Vietnamese troops from Cambodia by the end of September 1989. By disengaging from Cambodia, Vietnam hoped to remove the single largest obstacle to gaining admission to the regional and world economic community and to convince its non-communist neighbors, the West and China, that it was ready to end its diplomatic and economic isolation.

Ending the Cambodian conflict itself, however, was another matter, and as events unfolded in 1988 and 1989 it was not clear whether Vietnam's withdrawal would expedite or prolong a resolution. Initially, the possibility of ending the stalemate appeared to improve. Acting entirely on his own initiative, resistance leader Prince Norodom Sihanouk, in December 1987, arranged unprecedented direct dialogues between himself and Hun Sen, the premier of the People's Republic of Kampuchea. Although they failed to yield major results, the talks nevertheless initiated valuable face-to-face discussions between representatives of both sides and introduced diplomacy as a means of ending the conflict.

In May 1988, eleven days after the Soviets began their troop withdrawal from Afghanistan and three days before a Moscow summit between President Reagan and Soviet Secretary Gorbachev was to convene, Vietnam announced plans to withdraw 50,000 troops by the end of the year. The withdrawal, commencing in June and ending in December as promised, involved not only the removal of troops, but also the dismantling of Vietnam's military high command in Cambodia and the reassignment of remaining troops to Cambodian commands.

In July 1988, Hanoi participated in the first meeting of all parties in the Cambodia conflict. The "cocktail party" meeting, or Jakarta Informal Meeting (JIM), convened in Bogor, Indonesia, was termed a limited success because, if nothing more, it established a negotiating framework and set the agenda for future discussion. However, it also shifted the emphasis of the search for a conflict resolution away from Vietnam and to the question of how to prevent the Khmer Rouge from seizing power once a political agreement was reached. At the meeting, Vietnam linked a total withdrawal of its troops to the elimination of the Khmer Rouge and won the support of the ASEAN nations and the non- communist factions of the Cambodian resistance coalition, who also feared that Pol Pot would return to power in the absence of Vietnamese forces.

A second "informal" meeting of the four Cambodian factions, held in February 1989 ended inconclusively, deadlocked on fundamental issues such as the shape of the international force that was to supervise an agreement and the manner in which a quadripartite authority to rule in Phnom Penh would be established. The February meeting was followed by a month-long international conference, held in Paris in August 1989 and attended by twenty nations, which also ended short of a comprehensive agreement. Although the conference had been called to help mediate a settlement between the Vietnamese-backed government in Phnom Penh and the three-member resistance coalition, it foundered over finding an appropriate place for the Khmer Rouge once Vietnam's troop withdrawal was complete. Thus in September 1989, on the eve of the withdrawal, the promise of an impending political settlement in Cambodia remained unfulfilled. Instead, the inability of the four factions to arrive at a compromise renewed prospects for an escalation of conflict on the battlefield.

In 1988 one of Vietnam's top foreign policy priorities was finding a way to cut China's support for the Khmer Rouge. China, Hanoi argued, was the key to a Cambodian resolution because, as Pol Pot's chief source of supply, Beijing alone had the power to defuse the Khmer Rouge threat. As the year progressed, it became increasingly evident that Beijing was more interested in a settlement than in prolonging the conflict and that its position on Cambodia was shifting to facilitate settlement. This fact was evidenced in July 1988 when a Chinese proposal, repeating long standing demands for a complete withdrawal of all Vietnamese troops and a quadripartite government led by Sihanouk, surprisingly ruled out a personal role for Pol Pot in any post- settlement government. The proposal was also novel because it intimated that Beijing, for the first time, was willing to discuss a provisional coalition government before the departure of all Vietnamese troops. At the International Conference on the conflict held in August 1989, the Chinese appeared to be undercutting their support for the Khmer Rouge by arguing that civil war was to be avoided at all costs and promising to cut off military aid once a settlement was reached. China's position on the Khmer Rouge, nevertheless, remained ambiguous.

In a 1988 incident, possibly related to Cambodia because it potentially strengthened China's position at a future bargaining table, the ongoing dispute between China and Vietnam over sovereignty to the Spratly Islands erupted into an unprecedented exchange of hostilities. The situation was reduced to an exchange of accusations following the armed encounter. Vietnam's repeated calls for China to settle the dispute diplomatically won rare support for Vietnam from the international community, but elicited little response from Beijing.

A conciliatory mood developed on both sides of the Sino- Vietnamese border in 1989, partly because Vietnam's proposal to withdraw completely from Cambodia responded to a basic Chinese condition for improved relations. Formal talks at the deputy foreign minister level were initiated, and a cross-border trade in Chinese and Vietnamese goods flourished in the Vietnamese border town of Lang Son. The internal turmoil experienced by China in May and June 1989 may have actually benefited the relationship from Vietnam's point of view. Historically, whenever Beijing had been forced to turn its attention inwardly to quell internal dissension, Vietnam's security situation had correspondingly improved.

Beijing's interest in improving ties with Moscow in 1988 and 1989, however, complicated the situation and put Vietnam increasingly at odds with the Soviet Union. As the reality of an eventual Sino-Soviet reconciliation approached, it became increasingly clear that Vietnamese and Soviet strategic interests did not always coincide. The presence of Vietnamese troops in Cambodia, for example, was the leading obstacle to Sino-Soviet reconciliation. Accordingly, the most significant development to occur in Soviet-Vietnamese relations in 1988 and 1989 was the application of increased Soviet pressure on Vietnam to resolve the Cambodian situation, a pressure that undoubtedly helped prompt Vietnam's policy of withdrawal.

Hanoi was naturally wary of any talks between the Soviet Union and China, fearing that a deal would be made on Cambodia at Vietnam's expense. The two powers convened bilateral discussions in Beijing in August 1988 and proceeded to normalize relations at a summit meeting in Beijing in May 1989. Very little with regard to Cambodia was actually accomplished, however, and the summit resulted simply in the two sides agreeing to "disagree" on the mechanics of a political solution.

By actively pursuing an end to the Cambodian conflict, Vietnam acted also to further the chances of normalizing its relations with the United States. Both sides in 1988 appeared particularly receptive to improving relations, and Vietnam's troop withdrawal as well as its participation in the JIM were interpreted by the United States as positive gestures directed toward Vietnam's disengagement from Cambodia, a requirement imposed by Washington for diplomatic recognition. Hanoi also acted, in the early part of the year, to remove other obstacles to recognition by agreeing in principle to resettlement in the United States of thousands of former political prisoners and by consenting to cooperate in joint excavations of United States military aircraft crash sites in an attempt to locate the remains of Americans missing in action (MIAs). Some remains were returned. In 1989, additional sets of MIA remains were returned, and an accord was reached between Vietnam and the United States granting re-education camp inmates who had worked for the United States permission to emigrate.

Finally, Vietnam sought to improve its regional relations in 1988 and 1989 by extending a conciliatory gesture to its Asian neighbors. In response to a rise in the number of Vietnamese refugees, Vietnam assured its neighbors that it would ease their burdens as countries of first asylum by reversing a policy that forbade refugees to return home. Hanoi also proposed to open discussions with Southeast Asian officials on ending the refugee exodus. In 1989, however, Vietnam permitted only those refugees who "voluntarily" sought repatriation to return to Vietnam. Because genuine volunteers were few in number, the policy was regarded as inadequate by countries with Vietnamese refugee populations. More boat people departed Vietnam in 1989 than in any single year since the beginning of the decade, and their numbers were no longer limited to southerners fleeing political persecution but included northerners seeking economic opportunity. The willingness of countries of first asylum to accept Vietnamese refugees had lessened considerably since 1979, however, and many were seriously considering policies advocating forced repatriation.

Vietnam's relationship with the Association of Southeast Asian Nations (ASEAN), nevertheless, showed dramatic improvement during this two-year period, and Thailand, in particular, was singled out by Hanoi as critically important to Vietnam's economic future. The success of a January 1989 official visit to Hanoi by Thai Foreign Minister Sitthi Sawetsila surpassed all expectations and led Thai Prime Minister Chatchai Chunhawan to encourage Thai businessmen to expand trade relations with the Indochinese countries. According to Thai Prime Minister Chatichai Choonhavan, the Thai goal was to turn the Southeast Asian peninsula into an economic "Golden Land" (*Suwannaphume* in Thai) with Thailand as its center and Indochina, transformed from "a battlefield into a trading market," as its cornerstone. Although the plan was controversial, it appeared to reflect the shift of regional priorities from security to economic concerns.

Vietnam still lacked an adequate foreign investment structure in 1989, although a Foreign Trade Office and a Central Office to Supervise Foreign Investment had been established along with a State Commission for Cooperation and Investment to draft investment policies. The Ministry of Foreign Economic Relations convened a three-day conference in February 1989, attended by 500 delegates associated with foreign trade, to discuss modifying Vietnam's existing foreign economic policies and mechanisms in order to more effectively attract foreign investors. Ho Chi Minh City also authorized the establishment of a "Zone of Fabrication and Exportation" where foreign companies would be free to import commodities, assemble products, use low cost local labor, and reexport final products. Ho Chi Minh City, followed by Vung Tau- Con Dao Special Zone, led all other localities in number of foreign investment projects and joint ventures initiated, and a large proportion of the investors were identified as overseas Vietnamese.

Although changes introduced in the closing years of the 1980s stopped short of systemic reform, they demonstrated a new level of commitment on the part of Vietnam's leaders to resolve the country's peacetime economic problems. Having known great success in warfare, the government appeared to have accepted that yet another struggle was underway that would require the kind of focused resolve previously displayed in wartime. The process was marked both by the possibility for change and by inertia. Political and foreign policy agendas were opened to redefinition, and strategic goals were re-evaluated to emphasize economic rather than military strength. The process, however, was slowed considerably by party conservatives, who stressed the danger of political liberalization and questioned the pace of economic reform. Change, nevertheless, was evident. In foreign policy, Vietnam moved to attract foreign investment and to end its international isolation by disengaging from Cambodia. Likewise, in the economic sphere at home, where the need for change was determined to be particularly critical, market forces assumed a larger role in Vietnam's controlled economy then they had previously. In undertaking such changes, Vietnam seemed on the verge of joining the geopolitical trend observed in the late 1980s, in which the behavior of socialist and capitalist systems alike appeared to favor economic over military development. The Vietnamese leadership, however, was not prepared to move quickly. Although committed to the process of change, the Political Bureau's ability to act was constricted by internal differences over how to proceed and how much to risk. As the country approached the 1990s, the question of whether the need to develop economically was worth the political risk had yet to be fully resolved.

HISTORICAL SETTING

The Vietnamese trace the origins of their culture and nation to the fertile plains of the Red River Delta in northern Vietnam. After centuries of developing a civilization and economy based on the cultivation of irrigated rice, the Vietnamese began expanding southward in search of new ricelands. Moving down the narrow coastal plain of the Indochina Peninsula, through conquest and pioneering settlement they eventually reached and occupied the broad Mekong River Delta. Vietnamese history is the story of the struggle to develop a sense of nationhood throughout this narrow 1,500-kilometer stretch of land and to maintain it against internal and external pressures.

Hanoi temple dedicated to King An Duong Vuong
(ruler of Kingdom of Au Lac, third century B.C.)

The first major threat to Vietnam's existence as a separate people and nation was the conquest of the Red River Delta by the Chinese, under the mighty Han dynasty (206 B.C.-A.D. 220), in the first century B.C. At that time, and in later centuries, the expanding Chinese empire assimilated a number of small bordering nations politically and culturally. Although Vietnam spent 1,000 years under Chinese rule, it succeeded in throwing off the yoke of its powerful neighbor in the tenth century.

The Vietnamese did not, however, emerge unchanged by their millennium under Chinese rule. Although they were unsuccessful in assimilating the Vietnamese totally, the Chinese did exert a permanent influence on Vietnamese administration, law, education, literature, language, and culture. Their greatest impact was on the Vietnamese elite, with whom the Chinese administrators had the most contact. The effects of this Sinicization (*Hanhwa*) were much less intensive among the common people, who retained a large part of their pre-Han culture and language.

China's cultural influence increased in the centuries following the expulsion of its officials, as Vietnamese monarchs and aristocrats strove to emulate the cultural ideal established by the Middle Kingdom. Even for the Vietnamese elite, however, admiration for Chinese culture did not include any desire for Chinese political control. In the almost uninterrupted 900 years of independence that followed China's domination, the Vietnamese thwarted a number of Chinese attempts at military reconquest, accepting a tributary relationship instead. During this period, learning and literature flourished as the Vietnamese expressed themselves both in classical Chinese written in Chinese characters and in Vietnamese written in *chu nom*, a script derived from Chinese ideographs.

During the Chinese millennium, other cultural influences also reached the shores of the Red River Delta. A thriving maritime trade among China, India, and Indonesia used the delta as a convenient stopover. Among the array of goods and ideas thus brought to Vietnam was Buddhism from India. While the Vietnamese aristocracy clung to Chinese Confucianism, during most periods the common people embraced Buddhism, adapting it to fit their own indigenous religions and world view.

As the Red River Delta prospered, its population began expanding southward along the narrow coastal plains. The period from the twelfth century to the eighteenth century was marked by warfare with both the Cham and Khmer, the peoples of the Indianized kingdoms of Champa and Cambodia, who controlled lands in the Vietnamese line of march to the south. The Cham were finally defeated in 1471, and the Khmer were forced out of the Mekong Delta by 1749. Vietnamese settlers flooded into the largely untilled lands, turning them to rice cultivation. The southward expansion severely taxed the ability of the Vietnamese monarchy, ruling from the Red River Delta, to maintain control over a people spread over such a distance.

The inability of the ruling Le dynasty to deal with this and other problems led to the partition of the country by the nobility in the sixteenth century. After two hundred years of warfare between competing noble families, a peasant rebellion reunified the country in the late eighteenth century. The rebels, however, were unable to solve the problems of a country ravaged by war, famine, and natural disasters and lost control to a surviving member of the Nguyen noble family. Nguyen Anh took the reign name Gia Long (a composite derived from the Vietnamese names for the northern and southern capitals of the country during partition) and established a new centrally located capital at Hue in 1802.

Gia Long and his successors also were unable or unwilling to solve the persisting problems of the country, particularly the age-old dilemma of land alienation, the concentration of large tracts of land in the hands of a few and the resulting creation of vast numbers of landless peasants. The monarchy and aristocracy grew more and more removed from the people by the mid-nineteenth century. This period also climaxed the growth of European expansionism, as Western nations sought to carve out colonies in Asia and other parts of the non-Western world. Between 1858 and 1873, the French conquered Vietnam, dividing it into three parts--Cochinchina, Annam, and Tonkin--roughly corresponding to the areas referred to bt the Vietnamese as Nam Bo (southern Vietnam), Trung Bo (central Vietnam), and Bac Bo (northern Vietnam). To the Vietnamese, however, these were geographical terms, and the use of them to imply a political division of their homeland was as odious as the loss of their independence.

French colonial rule was, for the most part, politically repressive and economically exploitative. Vietnamese resistance in the early years was led by members of the scholar-official class, many of whom refused to cooperate with the French and left their positions in the bureaucracy. The early nationalists involved themselves in study groups, demonstrations, production and dissemination of anticolonialist literature, and acts of terrorism. Differences in approach among the groups were exemplified by Phan Boi Chau, who favored using the Vietnamese monarchy as a rallying point for driving out the French, and Phan Chu Trinh, who favored abolishing the monarchy and using Western democratic ideas as a force for gradual reform and independence. The success of these early nationalists was limited both by their inability to agree on a strategy and their failure to involve the Vietnamese peasantry, who made up the vast majority of the population. After World War I, another Vietnamese independence leader arose who understood the need to involve the masses in order to stage a successful anticolonial revolt. Ho Chi Minh, schooled in Confucianism, Vietnamese nationalism, and MarxismLeninism , patiently set about organizing the Vietnamese peasantry according to Communist theories, particularly those of Chinese leader Mao Zedong.

The defeat of the Japanese, who had occupied Vietnam during World War II, left a power vacuum, which the Communists rushed to fill. Their initial success in staging uprisings and in seizing control of most of the country by September 1945 was partially undone, however, by the return of the French a few months later. Only after nine years of armed struggle was France finally persuaded to relinquish its colonies in Indochina. The 1954 Geneva Conference left Vietnam a divided nation, however, with Ho Chi Minh's communist government ruling the northern half from Hanoi and Ngo Dinh Diem's regime, supported by the United States, ruling the south from Saigon (later Ho Chi Minh City). Another two decades of bitter conflict ensued before Vietnam was again reunified as one independent nation.

EARLY HISTORY

The Vietnamese people represent a fusion of races, languages, and cultures, the elements of which are still being sorted out by ethnologists, linguists, and archaeologists. As was true for most areas of Southeast Asia, the Indochina Peninsula was a crossroads for many migrations of peoples, including speakers of Austronesian, Mon-Khmer, and Tai languages. The Vietnamese language provides some clues to the cultural mixture of the Vietnamese people. Although a separate and distinct language, Vietnamese borrows much of its basic vocabulary from Mon-Khmer, tonality from the Tai languages, and some grammatical features from both Mon-Khmer and Tai. Vietnamese also exhibits some influence from Austronesian languages, as well as large infusions of Chinese literary, political, and philosophical terminology of a later period.

The area now known as Vietnam has been inhabited since Paleolithic times, with some archaeological sites in Thanh Hoa Province reportedly dating back several thousand years. Archaeologists link the beginnings of Vietnamese civilization to the late Neolithic, early Bronze Age, Phung-nguyen culture, which was centered in Vinh Phu Province of contemporary Vietnam from about 2000 to 1400 B.C. By about 1200 B.C., the development of wet-rice cultivation and bronze casting in the Ma River and Red River plains led to the development of the Dong Son culture, notable for its elaborate bronze drums. The bronze weapons, tools, and drums of Dong Sonian sites show a Southeast Asian influence that indicates an indigenous origin for the bronze-casting technology. Many small, ancient copper mine sites have been found in northern Vietnam. Some of the similarities between the Dong Sonian sites and other Southeast Asian sites include the presence of boat-shaped coffins and burial jars, stilt dwellings, and evidence of the customs of betel-nut-chewing and teeth-blackening.

According to the earliest Vietnamese traditions, the founder of the Vietnamese nation was Hung Vuong, the first ruler of the semilegendary Hung dynasty (2879-258 B.C., mythological dates) of the kingdom of Van Lang. Hung Vuong, in Vietnamese mythology, was the oldest son of Lac Long Quan (Lac Dragon Lord), who came to the Red River Delta from his home in the sea, and Au Co, a Chinese immortal. Lac Long Quan, a Vietnamese cultural hero, is credited with teaching the people how to cultivate rice. The Hung dynasty, which according to tradition ruled Van Lang for eighteen generations, is associated by Vietnamese scholars with Dong Sonian culture. An important aspect of this culture by the sixth century B.C. was the tidal irrigation of rice fields through an elaborate system of canals and dikes. The fields were called Lac fields, and Lac, mentioned in Chinese annals, is the earliest recorded name for the Vietnamese people.

The Hung kings ruled Van Lang in feudal fashion with the aid of the Lac lords, who controlled the communal settlements around each irrigated area, organized construction and maintenance of the dikes, and regulated the supply of water. Besides cultivating rice, the people of Van Lang grew other grains and beans and raised stock, mainly buffaloes, chickens, and pigs. Potterymaking and bamboo-working were highly developed crafts, as were basketry, leather-working, and the weaving of hemp, jute, and silk. Both transport and communication were provided by dugout canoes, which plied the network of rivers and canals.

The last Hung king was overthrown in the third century B.C. by An Duong Vuong, the ruler of the neighboring upland kingdom of Thuc. An Duong Vuong united Van Lang with Thuc to form Au Lac, building his capital and citadel at Co Loa, thirty-five kilometers north of present-day Hanoi. An Duong's kingdom was short-lived, however, being conquered in 208 B.C. by the army of the Chinese Qin dynasty (221-207 B.C.) military commander Trieu Da (Zhao Tuo in Chinese). Reluctant to accept the rule of the Qin dynasty's successor, the new Han dynasty (206 B.C.-A.D. 220), Trieu Da combined the territories under his control in southern China and northern Vietnam and established the kingdom of Nam Viet (Nan Yue in Chinese), meaning Southern Viet. Viet (Yue) was the term applied by the Chinese to the various peoples on the southern fringes of the Han empire, including the people of the Red River Delta. Trieu Da divided his kingdom of Nam Viet into nine military districts; the southern three (Giao Chi, Cuu Chan, and Nhat Nam) included the northern part of present-day Vietnam. The Lac lords continued to rule in the Red River Delta, but as vassals of Nam Viet.

The Chinese Millennium

Vietnamese historians regard Trieu Da as a defender of their homeland against an expanding Han empire. In 111 B.C., however, the Chinese armies of Emperor Wu Di defeated the successors of Trieu Da and incorporated Nam Viet into the Han empire. The

Chinese were anxious to extend their control over the fertile Red River Delta, in part to serve as a convenient supply point for Han ships engaged in the growing maritime trade with India and Indonesia. During the first century or so of Chinese rule, Vietnam was governed leniently, and the Lac lords maintained their feudal offices. In the first century A.D., however, China intensified its efforts to assimilate its new territories by raising taxes and instituting marriage reforms aimed at turning Vietnam into a patriarchal society more amenable to political authority. In response to increased Chinese domination, a revolt broke out in Giao Chi, Cuu Chan, and Nhat Nam in A.D. 39, led by Trung Trac, the wife of a Lac lord who had been put to death by the Chinese, and her sister Trung Nhi. The insurrection was put down within two years by the Han general Ma Yuan, and the Trung sisters drowned themselves to avoid capture by the Chinese. Still celebrated as heroines by the Vietnamese, the Trung sisters exemplify the relatively high status of women in Vietnamese society as well as the importance to Vietnamese of resistance to foreign rule.

Saigon scholar-official, late nineteenth century
Courtesy Library of Congress

Following the ill-fated revolt, Chinese rule became more direct, and the feudal Lac lords faded into history. Ma Yuan established a Chinese-style administrative system of three prefectures and fifty-six districts ruled by scholar-officials sent by the Han court. Although Chinese administrators replaced most former local officials, some members of the Vietnamese aristocracy were allowed to fill lower positions in the bureaucracy. The Vietnamese elite in particular received a thorough indoctrination in Chinese cultural, religious, and political traditions. One result of Sinicization, however, was the creation of a Confucian bureaucratic, family, and social structure that gave the Vietnamese the strength to resist Chinese political domination in later centuries, unlike most of the other Yue peoples who were sooner or later assimilated into the Chinese cultural and political world. Nor was Sinicization so total as to erase the memory of pre-Han Vietnamese culture, especially among the peasant class, which retained the Vietnamese language and many Southeast Asian customs. Chinese rule had the dual effect of making the Vietnamese aristocracy more receptive to Chinese culture and cultural leadership while at the same time instilling resistance and hostility toward Chinese political domination throughout Vietnamese society.

Chinese Cultural Impact

In order to facilitate administration of their new territories, the Chinese built roads, waterways, and harbors, largely with corvee labor (unpaid labor exacted by government authorities, particularly for public works projects). Agriculture was improved with better irrigation methods and the use of ploughs and draft animals, innovations which may have already been in use by the Vietnamese on a lesser scale. New lands were opened up for agriculture, and settlers were brought in from China. After a few generations, most of the Chinese settlers probably intermarried with the Vietnamese and identified with their new homeland.

The first and second centuries A.D. saw the rise of a HanViet ruling class owning large tracts of rice lands. More than 120 brick Han tombs have been excavated in northern Vietnam, indicating Han families that, rather than returning to China, had become members of their adopted society and were no longer, strictly speaking, Chinese. Although they brought Chinese vocabulary and technical terms into their new culture, after a generation or two, they probably spoke Vietnamese.

The second century A.D. was a time of rebellion in Giao Chi, Cuu Chan, and Nhat Nam, largely due to the declining quality of the Han administrators, who concentrated their energies on making their fortunes and returning north as soon as possible. Revolts against corrupt and repressive Chinese officials were often led by the Han-Viet families. The fall of the Han dynasty in China in 220 A.D. further strengthened the allegiance of the Han-Viet ruling elite to their new society and gave them a sense of their own independent political power. Meanwhile, among the peasant class there was also a heightened sense of identity fostered by the spread of Buddhism by sea from India to Vietnam by the early third century. The new religion was often adapted to blend with indigenous religions. Buddhist temples were sometimes dedicated to the monsoon season, for example, or identified with the guardian spirit of agricultural fertility. Although ruling-class Vietnamese tended to cling to

Confucianism, various local rulers patronized the Buddhist religion, thus helping to legitimize their own rule in the eyes of the common people.

After the demise of the Han dynasty, the period of the third to the sixth century was a time of turbulence in China, with six different dynasties in succession coming to power. The periods between dynasties or the periods when dynasties were weak in China were usually the most peaceful in Vietnam. When dynasties were strong and interfered with local rule, the Vietnamese aristocracy engaged in a series of violent revolts that weakened China's control over its southern territory. A rebellion led by the noblewoman Trieu Au (Lady Trieu) in A.D. 248 was suppressed after about six months, but its leader earned a place in the hearts and history of the Vietnamese people. Despite pressure to accept Chinese patriarchal values, Vietnamese women continued to play an important role and to enjoy considerably more freedom than their northern counterparts.

Political Resistance to the Chinese

The sixth century was an important stage in the Vietnamese political evolution toward independence. During this period, the Vietnamese aristocracy became increasingly independent of Chinese authority, while retaining Chinese political and cultural forms. At the same time, indigenous leaders arose who claimed power based on Vietnamese traditions of kingship. A series of failed revolts in the late sixth and early seventh centuries increased the Vietnamese national consciousness. Ly Bi, the leader of a successful revolt in 543 against the Liang dynasty (502-556), was himself descended from a Chinese family that had fled to the Red River Delta during a period of dynastic turbulence in the first century A.D. Ly Bi declared himself emperor of Nam Viet in the tradition of Trieu Da and organized an imperial court at Long Bien. Ly Bi was killed in 547, but his followers kept the revolt alive for another fifty years, establishing what is sometimes referred to in Vietnamese history as the Earlier Ly dynasty.

While the Ly family retreated to the mountains and attempted to rule in the style of their Chinese overlords, a rebel leader who based his rule on an indigenous form of kingship arose in the Red River Delta. Trieu Quang Phuc made his headquarters on an island in a vast swamp. From this refuge, he could strike without warning, seizing supplies from the Liang army and then slipping back into the labyrinthine channels of the swamp. Despite the initial success of such guerrilla tactics, by which he gained control over the Red River Delta, Trieu Quang Phuc was defeated by 570. According to a much later Vietnamese revolutionary, General Vo Nguyen Giap, Vietnamese concepts of protracted warfare were born in the surprise offensives, night attacks, and hit-and- run tactics employed by Trieu Quang Phuc.

The Chinese Tang dynasty (618-907) instituted a series of administrative reforms culminating in 679 in the reorganization of Vietnamese territory as the Protectorate of Annam (or Pacified South), a name later used by the French to refer to central Vietnam. The Tang dynastic period was a time of heavy Chinese influence, particularly in Giao Chau Province (in 203 the district of Giao Chi, had been elevated to provincial status and was renamed Giao Chou), which included the densely populated Red River plain. The children of ambitious, aristocratic families acquired a classical Confucian education, as increased emphasis was placed on the Chinese examination system for training local administrators. As a result, literary terms dating from the Tang dynasty constitute the largest category of Chinese loan words in modern Vietnamese. Despite the stress placed on Chinese literature and learning, Vietnamese, enriched with Chinese literary terms, remained the language of the people, while Chinese was used primarily as an administrative language by a small elite. During the Tang era, Giao Chau Province also became the center of a popular style of Buddhism based on spirit cults, which evolved as the dominant religion of Vietnam after the tenth century. Buddhism, along with an expanding sea trade, linked Vietnam more closely with South and Southeast Asia as Buddhist pilgrims traveled to India, Sumatra, and Java aboard merchant vessels laden with silk, cotton, paper, ivory, pearls, and incense.

As Tang imperial power became more corrupt and oppressive during the latter part of the dynasty, rebellion flared increasingly, particularly among the minority peoples in the mountain and border regions. Although the Viet culture of Giao Chau Province, as it developed under Tang hegemony, depended upon Chinese administration to maintain order, there was growing cultural resistance to the Tang in the border regions. A revolt among the Muong people, who are closely related to the central Vietnamese, broke out in the early eighth century. The rebels occupied the capital at Tong Binh (Hanoi), driving out the Tang governor and garrison, before being defeated by reinforcements from China. Some scholars mark this as the period of final separation of the Muong peoples from the central.

Vietnamese, which linguistic evidence indicates took place near the end of the Tang dynasty. In the mid-ninth century, Tai minority rebels in the border regions recruited the assistance of Nan-chao, a Tai mountain kingdom in the southern Chinese province of Yunnan, which seized control of Annam in 862. Although the Tang succeeded in defeating the Nan-chao forces and restoring Chinese administration, the dynasty was in decline and no longer able to dominate the increasingly autonomous Vietnamese. The Tang finally collapsed in 907 and by 939 Ngo Quyen, a Vietnamese general, had established himself as king of an independent Vietnam.

NINE CENTURIES OF INDEPENDENCE

Having driven out the Chinese, Ngo Quyen defeated a series of local rival chiefs and, seeking to identify his rule with traditional Vietnamese kingship, established his capital at Co Loa, the third century B.C. citadel of An Duong Vuong. The dynasty established by Ngo Quyen lasted fewer than thirty years, however, and was overthrown in 968 by a local chieftain, Dinh Bo Linh, who reigned under the name Dinh Tien Hoang. He brought political unity to the country, which he renamed Dai Co Viet (Great Viet). The major accomplishments of Dinh Bo Linh's reign were the establishment of a diplomatic basis for Vietnamese independence and the institution of universal military mobilization. He organized a 100,000-man peasant militia called the Ten Circuit Army, comprising ten circuits (geographical districts). Each circuit was defended by ten armies and each army was composed of ten brigades. Brigades in turn were made up of ten companies with ten ten-member squads a piece. After uniting the Vietnamese and establishing his kingdom, Dinh Bo Linh sent a tributary mission to the newly-established Chinese Northern Song dynasty (A.D. 960-1125). This diplomatic maneuver was a successful attempt to stave off China's reconquest of its former vassal. The Song emperor gave his recognition to Dinh Bo Linh, but only as "King of

Giao Chi Prefecture," a state within the Chinese empire. Not until the rise of the Ly dynasty (1009-1225), however, did the Vietnamese monarchy consolidate its control over the country.

A gate to the "Imperial City" of Hue, constructed by Emperor Gia Long in the early nineteenth century. Courtesy New York Times, Paris Collection, National Archives

The Great Ly Dynasty and the Flowering of Buddhism

Following the death of Dinh Bo Linh in 979, the Song rulers attempted to reassert Chinese control over Vietnam. Le Hoan, the commander in chief of Dinh Bo Linh's army, seized the throne and successfully repulsed the Chinese army in 981. Ly Cong Uan, a former temple orphan who had risen to commander of the palace guard, succeeded Le Hoan in 1009, thereby founding the great Ly dynasty that lasted until 1225. Taking the reign name Ly Thai To, he moved his capital to Dai La (modern Hanoi). The early Ly kings established a prosperous state with a stable monarchy at the head of a centralized administration. The name of the country was changed to Dai Viet by Emperor Ly Thanh Tong in 1054.

Magistrate supervising punishment, late nineteenth century
Courtesy Library of Congress

The first century of Ly rule was marked by warfare with China and the two Indianized kingdoms to the south, Cambodia and Champa. After these threats were dealt with successfully, the second century of Ly rule was relatively peaceful enabling the Ly kings to establish a Buddhist ruling tradition closely related to the other Southeast Asian Buddhist kingdoms of that period. Buddhism became a kind of state religion as members of the royal family and the nobility made pilgrimages, supported the building of pagodas, sometimes even entered monastic life, and otherwise took an active part in Buddhist practices. Bonzes (see Glossary) became a privileged landed class, exempt from taxes and military duty. At the same time, Buddhism, in an increasingly Vietnamized form associated with magic, spirits, and medicine, grew in popularity with the people (see Religion).

During the Ly dynasty, the Vietnamese began their long march to the south (*nam tien*) at the expense of the Cham and the Khmer. Le Hoan had sacked the Cham capital of Indrapura in 982, whereupon the Cham established a new capital at Vijaya. This was captured twice by the Vietnamese, however, and in 1079 the Cham were forced to cede to the Ly rulers their three northern provinces. Soon afterwards, Vietnamese peasants began moving into the untilled former Cham lands, turning them into rice fields and moving relentlessly southward, delta by delta, along the narrow coastal plain. The Ly kings supported the improvement of Vietnam's agricultural system by constructing and repairing dikes and canals and by allowing soldiers to return to their villages to work for six months of each year. As their territory and population expanded, the Ly kings looked to China as a model for organizing a strong, centrally administered state. Minor officials were chosen by examination for the first time in 1075, and a civil service training institute and an imperial academy were set up in 1076. In 1089 a fixed hierarchy of state officials was established, with nine degrees of civil and military scholarofficials . Examinations for public office were made compulsory, and literary competitions were held to determine the grades of officials.

The Tran Dynasty and the Defeat of the Mongols

In 1225 the Tran family, which had effectively controlled the Vietnamese throne for many years, replaced the Ly dynasty by arranging a marriage between one of its members and the last Ly monarch, an eight-year-old princess. Under the Tran dynasty (1225-1400), the country prospered and flourished as the Tran rulers carried out extensive land reform, improved public administration, and encouraged the study of Chinese literature. The Tran, however, are best remembered for their defense of the country against the Mongols and the Cham. By 1225, the Mongols controlled most of northern China and Manchuria and were eyeing southern China, Vietnam, and Champa. In 1257, 1284, and 1287, the Mongol armies of Kublai Khan invaded Vietnam, sacking the capital at Thang Long (renamed Hanoi in 1831) on each occasion, only to find that the Vietnamese had anticipated their attacks and evacuated the city beforehand. Disease, shortage of supplies, the climate, and the Vietnamese strategy of harassment and scorchedearth tactics foiled the first two invasions. The third Mongol invasion, of 300,000 men and a vast fleet, was also defeated by the Vietnamese under the leadership of General Tran Hung Dao. Borrowing a tactic used by Ngo Quyen in 938 to defeat an invading Chinese fleet, the Vietnamese drove iron-tipped stakes into the bed of the Bach Dang River (located in northern Vietnam in present-day Ha Bac, Hai Hung, and Quang Ninh provinces), and then, with a small Vietnamese flotilla, lured the Mongol fleet into the river just as the tide was starting to ebb. Trapped or impaled by the iron-tipped stakes, the entire Mongol fleet of 400 craft was sunk, captured, or burned by Vietnamese fire arrows. The Mongol army retreated to China, harassed enroute by Tran Hung Dao's troops.

The fourteenth century was marked by wars with Champa, which the Tran reduced to a feudatory state by 1312. Champa freed itself again by 1326 and, under the leadership of Cham hero Che Bong Nga, staged a series of attacks on Vietnam between 1360 and 1390, sacking Thang Long in 1371. The Vietnamese again gained the upper hand following the death of Che Bong Nga and resumed their southward advance at Champa's expense. Despite their earlier success, the quality of the Tran rulers had declined markedly by the end of the fourteenth century, opening the way for exploitation of the peasantry by the feudal landlord class, which caused a number of insurrections. In 1400 General Ho Quy-ly seized the throne and proclaimed himself founder of the short-lived Ho dynasty (1400-07). He instituted a number of reforms that were unpopular with the feudal landlords, including a limit on the amount of land a family could hold and the rental of excess land by the state to landless peasants; proclamations printed in Vietnamese, rather than Chinese; and free schools in provincial capitals. Threatened by the reforms, some of the landowners appealed to China's Ming Dynasty (1368-1644) to intervene. Using reinstatement of the Tran dynasty as an excuse, the Ming reasserted Chinese control in 1407.

Renewed Chinese Influence

The Ming administered the country as if it were a province of China and ruled it harshly for the next twenty years. The forced labor of its people was used to exploit Vietnam's mines and forests solely for China's enrichment. Taxes were levied on all products including salt a dietary staple. Under the Ming, Vietnamese cultural traditions, including the chewing of betel nut, were forbidden, men were required to wear their hair long and women to dress in the Chinese style. Vietnamese Buddhism was replaced at court by Ming-sponsored neo-Confucianism, but Ming attempts to supplant popular Vietnamese religious traditions with an officially sponsored form of Buddhism were less successful.

The Chinese impact on Vietnamese culture was probably as great, or greater, in the centuries following independence as it was during the 1,000 years of Chinese political domination. Much of China's cultural and governmental influence on Vietnam dates from the Ming period. Other aspects of Chinese culture were introduced later by Vietnamese kings struggling to bring a Confucian order to their unruly kingdom. Chinese administrative reforms and traditions, when sponsored by Vietnamese kings and aristocracy, tended to be more palatable and hence more readily assimilated than those imposed by Chinese officials. Although the Vietnamese upper classes during the Ming period studied Chinese classical literature and subscribed to the Chinese patriarchal family system, the majority of the Vietnamese people recognized these aspects of Chinese culture mainly as ideals. Less exposed to Chinese influence, the peasantry retained the Vietnamese language and many cultural traditions that predated Chinese rule. Other factors also encouraged the preservation of Vietnamese culture during the periods of Chinese rule. Contact with the Indianized Cham and Khmer civilizations, for example, widened the Vietnamese perspective and served as a counterweight to Chinese influence. Vietnam's location on the South China Sea and the comings and goings of merchants and Buddhists encouraged contact with other cultures of South and Southeast Asia. China, itself, once it developed the port of Guangzhou (Canton), had less need to control Vietnam politically in order to control the South China Sea. Moreover, the Vietnamese who moved southward into lands formerly occupied by the Cham and the Khmer became less concerned about the threat from China.

The Le Dynasty and Southward Expansion

Le Loi, one of Vietnam's most celebrated heroes, is credited with rescuing the country from Ming domination in 1428. Born of a wealthy landowning family, he served as a senior scholar-official until the advent of the Ming, whom he refused to serve. After a decade of gathering a resistance movement around him, Le Loi and his forces finally defeated the Chinese army in 1428. Rather than putting to death the captured Chinese soldiers and administrators, he magnanimously provided ships and supplies to send them back to China. Le Loi then ascended the Vietnamese throne, taking the reign name Le Thai To and establishing the Le dynasty (1428-1788).

The greatest of the Le dynasty rulers was Le Thanh Tong (1460-97), who reorganized the administrative divisions of the country and upgraded the civil service system. He ordered a census of people and landholdings to be taken every six years, revised the tax system, and commissioned the writing of a national history. During his reign he accomplished the conquest of Champa in 1471, the suppression of Lao-led insurrections in the western border area, and the continuation of diplomatic relations with China through tribute missions established under Le Thai To. Le Thanh Tong also ordered the formulation of the Hong Duc legal code, which was based on Chinese law but included distinctly Vietnamese features, such as recognition of the higher position of women in Vietnamese society than in Chinese society. Under the new code, parental consent was not required for marriage, and daughters were granted equal inheritance rights with sons. Le Thanh Tong also initiated the construction and repair of granaries, dispatched his troops to rebuild irrigation works following floods, and provided for medical aid during epidemics. A noted writer and poet himself, he encouraged and emphasized of the Confucian examination system.

A great period of southward expansion also began under Le Thanh Tong. The *don dien* system of land settlement, borrowed from the Chinese, was used extensively to occupy and develop territory wrested from Champa. Under this system, military colonies were established in which soldiers and landless peasants cleared a new area, began rice production on the new land, established a village, and served as a militia to defend it After three years, the village was incorporated into the Vietnamese administrative system, a communal village meeting house (*dinh*) was built, and the workers were given an opportunity to share in the communal lands given by the state to each village. The remainder of the land belonged to the state. As each area was cleared and a village established, the soldiers of the *don dien* would move on to clear more land. This method contributed greatly to the success of Vietnam's southward expansion.

Although the Le rulers had ordered widespread land distribution, many peasants remained landless, while the nobility, government officials, and military leaders continued to acquire vast tracts. The final conquest of Champa in 1471 eased the situation somewhat as peasants advanced steadily southward along the coast into state-owned communal lands. However, most of the new land was set aside for government officials and, although the country grew wealthier, the social structure remained the same. Following the decline of the Le dynasty, landlessness was a major factor leading to a turbulent period during which the peasantry questioned the mandate of their rulers.

In the Confucian world view, emperors were said to have the "mandate of heaven" to rule their people, who, in turn, owed the emperor total allegiance. Although his power was absolute, an emperor was responsible for the prosperity of his people and the maintenance of justice and order. An emperor who did not fulfill his Confucian responsibilities could, in theory, lose his mandate. In practice, the Vietnamese people endured many poor emperors, weak and strong. Counterbalancing the power of the emperor was the power of the village, illustrated by the Vietnamese proverb, "The laws of the emperor yield to the customs of the village." Village institutions served both to restrain the power of the emperor and to provide a buffer between central authority and the individual villager. Each village had its council of notables, which was responsible for the obligations of the village to the state. When the central government imposed levies for taxes, for corvee labor for public projects, or for soldiers for defense, these levies were based on the council of notables' report of the resources of the villages, which was often underestimated to protect the village. Moreover, there was a division between state and local responsibilities. The central government assumed responsibility for military, judicial, and religious functions, while village authorities oversaw the construction of public works projects such as roads, dikes, and bridges, which were centrally planned. The autonomy of the villages, however, contributed to the weakness of the Vietnamese political system. If the ruling dynasty could no longer protect a village, the village would often opt for the protection of political movements in opposition to the dynasty. These movements, in turn, would have difficulty maintaining the allegiance of the villages unless they were able both to provide security and to institutionalize their political power. Although it insured the preservation of a sense of national and cultural identity, the strength of the villages was a factor contributing to the political instability of the society as it expanded southward.

Partition and the Advent of the Europeans

The degenerated Le dynasty, which endured under ten rulers between 1497 and 1527, in the end was no longer able to maintain control over the northern part of the country, much less the new territories to the south. The weakening of the monarchy created a vacuum that the various noble families of the aristocracy were eager to fill. In 1527 Mac Dang Dung, a scholar-official who had effectively controlled the Le for a decade, seized the throne, prompting other families of the aristocracy, notably the Nguyen and Trinh, to rush to the support of the Le. An attack on the Mac forces led by the Le general Nguyen Kim resulted in the partition of Vietnam in 1545, with the Nguyen family seizing control of the southern part of the country as far north as what is now Thanh Hoa Province. The Nguyen, who took the hereditary title *chua* (see Glossary), continued to profess loyalty to the Le dynasty. By the late sixteenth century the Trinh family had ousted the Mac family and had begun to rule the northern half of the country also in the name of the Le dynasty. The Trinh, who, like the Nyuyen, took the title *chua*, spent most of the seventeenth century attempting to depose the Nguyen. In order to repulse invading Trinh forces, the Nguyen in 1631 completed the building of two great walls, six meters high and eighteen kilometers long, on their northern frontier. The Trinh, with 100,000 troops, 500 elephants, and 500 large junks, were numerically far superior to their southern foe. The Nguyen, however, were better equipped, having by this time acquired Portuguese weapons and gunpowder, and, as the defending force, had the support of the local people. In addition, the Nguyen had the advantage of controlling vast open lands in the Mekong Delta, wrested from the Khmer, with which to attract immigrants and refugees from the north. Among those who took up residence in the delta were an estimated 3,000 Chinese, supporters of the defunct Ming dynasty, who arrived in 1679 aboard fifty junks and set about becoming farmers and traders. The Nguyen, aided by the Chinese settlers, succeeded in forcing the Khmer completely out of the Mekong Delta by 1749.

After major offensives by the Trinh in 1661 and 1672 foundered on the walls built by the Nguyen, a truce in the fighting ensued that lasted nearly 100 years. During that time, the Nguyen continued its southward expansion into lands held, or formerly held, by the Cham and the Khmer. The Trinh, meanwhile, consolidated its authority in the north, instituting administrative reforms and supporting scholarship. The nobility and scholar-officials of both north and south, however, continued to block the development of manufacturing and trade, preferring to retain a feudal, peasant society, which they could control.

The seventeenth century was also a period in which European missionaries and merchants became a serious factor in Vietnamese court life and politics. Although both had arrived by the early sixteenth century, neither foreign merchants nor missionaries had much impact on Vietnam before the seventeenth century. The Portuguese, Dutch, English, and French had all established trading posts in Pho Hien by 1680. Fighting among the Europeans and opposition by the Vietnamese made the enterprises unprofitable, however, and all of the foreign trading posts were closed by 1700.

European missionaries had occasionally visited Vietnam for short periods of time, with little impact, beginning in the early sixteenth century. The best known of the early missionaries was Alexandre de Rhodes, a French Jesuit who was sent to Hanoi in 1627, where he quickly learned the language and began preaching in Vietnamese. Initially, Rhodes was well-received by the Trinh court, and he reportedly baptized more than 6,000 converts; however, his success probably led to his expulsion in 1630. He is credited with perfecting a romanized system of writing the Vietnamese language (*quoc ngu*), which was probably developed as the joint effort of several missionaries, including Rhodes. He wrote the first catechism in Vietnamese and published a Vietnamese-Latin-Portuguese dictionary; these works were the first books printed in *quoc ngu*. *Quoc ngu* was used initially only by missionaries; classical Chinese or *chu nom* continued to be used by the court and the bureaucracy. The French later supported the use of *quoc ngu*, which, because of its simplicity, led to a high degree of literacy and a flourishing of Vietnamese literature. After being expelled from Vietnam, Rhodes spent the next thirty years seeking support for his missionary work from the Vatican and the French Roman Catholic hierarchy as well as making several more trips to Vietnam.

The stalemate between the Trinh and the Nguyen families that began at the end of the seventeenth century did not, however, mark the beginning of a period of peace and prosperity. Instead the decades of continual warfare between the two families had left the peasantry in a weakened state, the victim of taxes levied to support the courts and their military adventures. Having to meet their tax obligations had forced many peasants off the land and facilitated the acquisition of large tracts by a few wealthy landowners, nobles, and scholar--officials. Because scholar--officials were exempted from having to pay a land tax, the more land they acquired, the greater was the burden that fell on those peasants who had been able to retain their land. In addition, the peasantry faced new taxes on staple items such as charcoal, salt, silk, and cinnamon, and on commercial activities such as fishing and mining. The disparate condition of the economy led to neglect of the extensive network of irrigation systems as well. As they fell into disrepair, disastrous flooding and famine resulted, unleashing great numbers of starving and landless people to wander aimlessly about the countryside. The widespread suffering in both north and south led to numerous peasant revolts between 1730 and 1770. Although the uprisings took place throughout the country, they were essentially local phenomena, breaking out spontaneously from similar local causes. The occasional coordination between and among local movements did not result in any national organization or leadership. Moreover, most of the uprisings were conservative, in that the leaders supported the restoration of the Le dynasty. They did, however, put forward demands for land reform, more equitable taxes, and rice for all. Landless peasants accounted for most of the initial support for the various rebellions, but they were often joined later by craftsmen, fishermen, miners, and traders, who had been taxed out of their occupations. Some of these movements enjoyed limited success for a short time, but it was not until 1771 that any of the peasant revolts had a lasting national impact.

The Tay Son Rebellion

The Tay Son Rebellion (1771-1802), which ended the Le and Trinh dynasties, was led by three brothers from the village of Tay Son in Binh Dinh Province. The brothers, who were of the Ho clan (to which Ho Quy Ly had belonged), adopted the name Nguyen. The eldest brother, Nguyen Nhac, began an attack on the ruling Nguyen family by capturing Quang Nam and Binh Dinh provinces in 1772. The chief principle and main slogan of the Tay Son was "seize the property of the rich and distribute it to the poor." In each village the Tay Son controlled, oppressive landlords and scholar-officials were punished and their property redistributed. The Tay Son also abolished taxes, burned the tax and land registers, freed prisoners from local jails, and distributed the food from storehouses to the hungry. As the rebellion gathered momentum, it gained the support of army deserters, merchants, scholars, local officials, and bonzes.

In 1773 Nguyen Nhac seized Qui Nhon, which became the Tay Son capital. By 1778 the Tay Son had effective control over the southern part of the country, including Gia Dinh (later Saigon). The ruling Nguyen family were all killed by the Tay Son rebels, with the exception of Nguyen Anh, the sixteen-year-old nephew of the last Nguyen lord, who escaped to the Mekong Delta. There he was able to gather a body of supporters and retake Gia Dinh. The city changed hands several times until 1783, when the Tay Son brothers destroyed Nguyen Anh's fleet and drove him to take refuge on Phu Quoc Island. Soon thereafter, he met with French missionary bishop Pigneau de Behaine and asked him to be his emissary in obtaining French support to defeat the Tay Son. Pigneau de Behaine took Nguyen Anh's five-year-old son, Prince Canh, and departed for Pondichery in French India to plead for support for the restoration of the Nguyen. Finding none there, he went to Paris in 1786 to lobby on Nguyen Anh's behalf. Louis XVI ostensibly agreed to provide four ships, 1,650 men, and supplies in exchange for Nguyen Anh's promise to cede to France the port of Tourane (Da Nang) and the island of Poulo Condore. However, the local French authorities in India, under secret orders from the king, refused to supply the promised ships and men. Determined to see French military intervention in Vietnam, Pigneau de Behaine himself raised funds for two ships and supplies from among the French merchant community in India, hired deserters from the French navy to man them, and sailed back to Vietnam in 1789.

In the meantime, by 1786 the Tay Son had overcome the crumbling Trinh dynasty and seized all of the north, thus uniting the country for the first time in 200 years. The Tay Son made good their promise to restore the Le dynasty, at least for ceremonial purposes. The three Nguyen brothers installed themselves as kings of the north, central, and southern sections of the country respectively, while continuing to acknowledge the Le emperor in Thang Long. In 1788, however, the reigning Le emperor fled north to seek Chinese assistance in defeating the Tay Son. Eager to comply, a Chinese army of the Qing dynasty (1644-1911) invaded Vietnam, seized Thang Long, and invested the Le ruler as "King of Annam." That same year, the second eldest Tay Son brother, Nguyen Hue, proclaimed himself Emperor Quang Trung. Marching north with 100,000 men and 100 elephants, Quang Trung attacked Thang Long at night and routed the Chinese army of 200,000, which retreated in disarray. Immediately following his victory, the Tay Son leader sought to reestablish friendly relations with China, requesting recognition of his rule and sending the usual tributary mission.

Quang Trung stimulated Vietnam's war-ravaged economy by encouraging trade and crafts, ordering the recultivation of fallow lands, reducing or abolishing taxes on local products, and resettling landless peasants on communal lands in their own villages. Quang Trung also established a new capital at Phu Xuan (near modern Hue), a more central location from which to administer the country. He reorganized the government along military lines, giving key posts to generals, with the result that military officials for the first time outranked civilian officials. Vietnamese was substituted for Chinese as the official national language, and candidates for the bureaucracy were required to submit prose and verse compositions in *chu nom* rather than in classical Chinese.

Quang Trung died in 1792, without leaving a successor strong enough to assume leadership of the country, and the usual factionalism ensued. By this time, Nguyen Anh and his supporters had won back much of the south from Nguyen Lu, the youngest and least capable of the Tay Son brothers. When Pigneau de Behaine returned to Vietnam in 1789, Nguyen Anh was in control of Gia Dinh. In the succeeding years, the bishop brought Nguyen Anh a steady flow of ships, arms, and European advisers, who supervised the building of forts, shipyards, cannon foundries and bomb factories, and instructed the Vietnamese in the manufacture and use of modern armaments. Nguyen's cause was also greatly aided by divisions within the Tay Son leadership, following the death of Quang Trung, and the inability of the new leaders to deal with the problems of famine and natural disasters that wracked the war-torn country. After a steady assault on the north, Nguyen Anh's forces took Phu Xuan in June 1801 and Thang Long a year later.

The Nguyen Dynasty and Expanding French Influence

In June 1802, Nguyen Anh adopted the reign name Gia Long to express the unifying of the country--Gia from Gia Dinh (Saigon) and Long from Thang Long (Hanoi). As a symbol of this unity, Gia Long changed the name of the country from Dai Viet to Nam Viet. For the Chinese, however, this was too reminiscent of the wayward General Trieu Da. In conferring investiture on the new government, the Chinese inverted the name to Viet Nam, the first use of that name for the country. Acting as a typical counterrevolutionary government, the Gia Long regime harshly suppressed any forces opposing it or the interests of the bureaucracy and the landowners. In his drive for control and order, Gia Long adopted the Chinese bureaucratic model to a greater degree than any previous Vietnamese ruler. The new capital at Hue, two kilometers northeast of Phu Xuan, was patterned after the Chinese model in Beijing, complete with a Forbidden City, an Imperial City, and a Capital City. Vietnamese bureaucrats were required to wear Chinese-style gowns and even adopt Chinese-style houses and sedan chairs. Vietnamese women, in turn, were compelled to wear Chinese-style trousers. Gia Long instituted a law code, which followed very closely the Chinese Qing dynasty (1644-1911) model. Under the Gia Long code, severe punishment was meted out for any form of resistance to the absolute power of the government. Buddhism, Taoism, and indigenous religions were forbidden under the Confucianist administration. Traditional Vietnamese laws and customs, such as the provisions of the Hong Duc law code protecting the rights and status of women, were swept away by the new code. Taxes that had been reduced or abolished under the Tay Son were levied again under the restored Nguyen dynasty. These included taxes on mining, forestry, fisheries, crafts, and on various domestic products, such as salt, honey, and incense. Another heavy burden on the peasantry was the increased use of corvee labor to build not only roads, bridges, ports, and irrigation works but also palaces, fortresses, shipyards, and arsenals. All but the privileged classes were required to work on such projects at least sixty days a year, with no pay but a rice ration. The great Mandarin Road, used by couriers and scholar-officials as a link between Gia Dinh, Hue, and Thang Long, was started during this period in order to strengthen the control of the central government. Military service was another burden on the peasantry; in some areas one out of every three men was required to serve in the Vietnamese Imperial Army. Land reforms instituted under the Tay Son were soon lost under the restored Nguyen dynasty, and the proportion of communal lands dwindled to less than 20 percent of the total. Although *chu nom* was retained as the national script by Gia Long, his son and successor Minh Mang, who gained the throne upon his father's death in 1820, ordered a return to the use of Chinese ideographs.

Peasant rebellion flared from time to time throughout the first half of the nineteenth century, fueled by government repression and such calamities as floods, droughts, epidemics, and famines. Minority groups, including the Tay-Nung, Muong, and Cham, were also in revolt. Although they were primarily peasant rebellions, some of these movements found support from, or were led by, disaffected scholars or some of the surviving pretenders to the Le throne. Vietnam's foreign relations were also a drain on the central government during this period. Tributary missions were sent biennially to the Qing court in Beijing, bearing the requisite 600 pieces of silk, 200 pieces of cotton, 1,200 ounces of perfume, 600 ounces of aloes wood, 90 pounds of betel nuts, 4 elephant tusks, and 4 rhinoceros horns. Other missions to pay homage (also bearing presents) were sent every four years. At the same time, Vietnam endeavored to enforce tributary relations with Cambodia and Laos. In 1834, attempts to make Cambodia a Vietnamese province led to a Cambodian revolt and to Siamese intervention, with the result that a joint Vietnamese-Siamese protectorate was established over Cambodia in 1847. Other foreign adventures included Vietnamese support for a Laotian rebellion against Siamese overlordship in 1826-27.

The most serious foreign policy problem for the Nguyen rulers, however, was dealing with France through the French traders, missionaries, diplomats, and naval personnel who came in increasing numbers to Vietnam. The influnce of missionaries was perceived as the most critical issue by the court and scholar-officials. The French Societe des Missions Etrangeres reported 450,000 Christian converts in Vietnam in 1841. The Vietnamese Christians were for the most part organized into villages that included all strata of society, from peasants to landowners. The Christian villages, with their own separate customs, schools, and hierarchy, as well as their disdain for Confucianism, were viewed by the government as breeding grounds for rebellion--and in fact they often were. The French presence did, however, enjoy some support at high levels. Gia Long felt a special debt to Pigneau de Behaine and to his two chief French naval advisers, Jean-Baptiste Chaigneau and Philippe Vannier, both of whom remained in the country until 1824. There were also members of the Vietnamese court who urged the monarchy to undertake a certain degree of westernization and reform in order to strengthen itself in the areas of administration, education, and defense. In the southern part of the country, Christians enjoyed the protection of Viceroy Le Van Duyet until his death in 1832. Soon thereafter the Nguyen government began a serious attempt to rid itself of French missionaries and their influence. A series of edicts forbade the practice of Christianity, forcing the Christian communities underground. An estimated ninety-five priests and members of the laity were executed by the Vietnamese during the following quarter of a century.

In response, the missionaries stepped up their pressure on the French government to intervene militarily and to establish a French protectorate over Vietnam. During this period, French traders became interested in Vietnam once more, and French diplomats in China began to express the view that France was falling behind the rest of Europe in gaining a foothold in Asia. Commanders of a French naval squadron, permanently deployed in the South China Sea after 1841, also began to agitate for a stronger role in protecting the lives and interests of the missionaries. Given tacit approval by Paris, naval intervention grew steadily. In 1847 two French warships bombarded Tourane (Da Nang), destroying five Vietnamese ships and killing an estimated 10,000 Vietnamese. The purpose of the attack was to gain the release of a missionary, who had, in fact, already been released. In the following decade, persecution of missionaries continued under Emperor Tu Duc, who came to the throne in 1848. While the missionaries stepped up pressure on the government of Louis Napoleon (later Napoleon III), which was sympathetic to their cause, a Commission on Cochinchina made the convincing argument that France risked becoming a second-class power by not intervening.

UNDER FRENCH RULE

By 1857 Louis-Napoleon had been persuaded that invasion was the best course of action, and French warships were instructed to take Tourane without any further efforts to negotiate with the Vietnamese. Tourane was captured in late 1858 and Gia Dinh (Saigon and later Ho Chi Minh City) in early 1859. In both cases Vietnamese Christian support for the French, predicted by the missionaries, failed to materialize. Vietnamese resistance and outbreaks of cholera and typhoid forced the French to abandon Tourane in early 1860. Meanwhile, fear was growing in Paris that if France withdrew the British would move in. Also current in Paris at that time was the rationalization that France had a civilizing mission--a duty to bring the benefits of its superior culture to the less fortunate lands of Asia and Africa. (This was a common justification for the colonial policies of most of the Western countries.) Meanwhile, French business and military interests increased their pressure on the government for decisive action. Thus in early 1861, a French fleet of 70 ships and 3,500 men reinforced Gia Dinh and, in a series of bloody battles, gained control of the surrounding provinces. In June 1862, Emperor Tu Duc, signed the Treaty of Saigon agreeing to French demands for the cession of three provinces around Gia Dinh (which the French had renamed Saigon) and Poulo Condore, as well as for the opening of three ports to trade, free passage of French warships up the Mekong to Cambodia, freedom of action for the missionaries, and payment of a large indemnity to France for its losses in attacking Vietnam.

Even the French were surprised by the ease with which the Vietnamese agreed to the humiliating treaty. Why, after successfully resisting invasions by the Chinese for the previous 900 years, did the monarchy give in so readily to French demands? Aside from the seriousness of the loss of Saigon and the possible overestimation of French strength, it appears that the isolation of the monarchy from the people created by decades of repression prevented Tu Duc and his court from attempting to rally the necessary popular support to drive out the French. In fact, by placating the French in the south, Tu Duc hoped to free his forces to put down a widespread Christian-supported rebellion in Bac Bo, which he indeed crushed by 1865. French missionaries, who had urged their government to support this rebellion, were disillusioned when it did not, especially after thousands of Christians were slaughtered by Tu Duc's forces following the rebellion. The missionaries, however, had served only as an initial excuse for French intervention in Vietnam; military and economic interests soon became the primary reasons for remaining there.

The French navy was in the forefront of the conquest of Indochina. In 1863 Admiral de la Grandiere, the governor of Cochinchina (as the French renamed Nam Bo), forced the Cambodian king to accept a French protectorate over that country, claiming that the Treaty of Saigon had made France heir to Vietnamese claims in Cambodia. In June 1867, the admiral completed the annexation of Cochinchina by seizing the remaining three western provinces. The following month, the Siamese government agreed to recognize a French protectorate over Cambodia in return for the cession of two Cambodian provinces, Angkor and Battambang, to Siam. With Cochinchina secured, French naval and mercantile interests turned to Tonkin (as the French referred to Bac Bo). The 1873 storming of the citadel of Hanoi, led by French naval officer Francis Garnier, had the desired effect of forcing Tu Duc to sign a treaty with France in March 1874 that recognized France's "full and entire sovereignty" over Cochinchina, and opened the Red River to commerce. In an attempt to secure Tonkin, Garnier was killed and his forces defeated in a battle with Vietnamese regulars and *Black Flag forces* (see Glossary). The latter were Chinese soldiers, who had fled south following the Taiping Rebellion in that country and had been hired by the Hue court to keep order in Tonkin.

In April 1882, a French force again stormed the citadel of Hanoi, under the leadership of naval officer Henri Riviere. Riviere and part of his forces were wiped out in a battle with a Vietnamese-Black Flag army, a reminder of Garnier's fate a decade earlier. While Garnier's defeat had led to a partial French withdrawal from Tonkin, Riviere's loss strengthened the resolve of the French government to establish a protectorate by military force. Accordingly, additional funds were appropriated by the French Parliament to support further military operations, and Hue fell to the French in August 1883, following the death of Tu Duc the previous month. A Treaty of Protectorate, signed at the August 1883 Harmand Convention, established a French protectorate over North and Central Vietnam and formally ended Vietnam's independence. In June 1884, Vietnamese scholar-officials were forced to sign the Treaty of Hue, which confirmed the Harmand Convention agreement. By the end of 1884, there were 16,500 French troops in Vietnam. Resistance to French control, however, continued. A rebellion known as the Can Vuong (Loyalty to the King) movement formed in 1885 around the deposed Emperor Ham Nghi and attracted support from both scholars and peasants. The rebellion was essentially subdued with the capture and exile of Ham Nghi in 1888. Scholar and patriot Phan Dinh Phung continued to lead the resistance until his death in 1895. Although unsuccessful in driving out the French, the Can Vuong movement, with its heroes and patriots, laid important groundwork for future Vietnamese independence movements.

Colonial Administration

Not all Vietnamese resisted the French conquest, and some even welcomed it. The monarchy, through decades of repression, had lost the support of the people; and Tu Duc, in the eyes of large segments of the peasantry, had lost his mandate to rule. He had been able to protect his people neither from foreign aggression nor from an unusually high incidence of natural disasters such as floods, famines, locusts, droughts, and a cholera epidemic in 1865 that killed more than 1 million people. Tu Duc's repression of Catholics also created a large opposition group ready to cooperate with the French, and those who did were often rewarded with lands vacated during the French invasion. Much of this land, however, was given to French *colons* (colonial settlers), often in sizable holdings of 4,000 hectares or more. Gradually a French-Vietnamese landholding class developed in Cochinchina. Vietnamese, however, were appointed only to the lower levels of the bureaucracy established to administer the new colony. Seeking to finance the growing bureaucracy, the early admiral-governors of Vietnam viewed the colony as the source of the necessary revenue. Rice exports, forbidden under the monarchy, reached 229,000 tons annually in 1870. Taxes extracted from Cochinchina increased tenfold in the first decade of French control. State monopolies and excise taxes on opium, salt, and alcohol eventually came to provide 70 percent of the government's operating revenue.

In 1887 France formally established the Indochinese Union, comprising the colony of Cochinchina and the protectorates of Annam, Tonkin, and Cambodia, with Laos being added as a protectorate in 1893. There was a rapid turnover among governorsgeneral of the Indochinese Union, and few served a full five-year term. One who did, Paul Doumer (1897-1902), is considered to have been the architect of a colonial system under which Vietnam was politically dominated and economically exploited. Following the partitioning of Vietnam into three parts, the emperor was stripped of the last vestiges of his authority. In 1897 the powers of the *kinh luoc* (emperor's viceroy) were transferred to the Resident Superieur at Hanoi, who governed in the name of the emperor. That same year, the Privy Council or *Co Mat Vien* (see Glossary) in Annam was replaced with a French-controlled Council of Ministers. The following year in Annam, the French took over tax collection and payment of officials. Most of the Vietnamese scholar-officials had refused to cooperate with the French, but those who did were restricted to minor or ceremonial positions. Consequently, Frenchmen were recruited to staff a new, continually expanding bureaucracy. By 1925 there were 5,000 European administrators ruling an Indochinese population of 30 million, roughly the same number used to administer British India, which had a population more than ten times as large. Under the French laws applicable to individuals, Vietnamese were prohibited from traveling outside their districts without identity papers; and they were not allowed to publish, meet, or organize. They were subject to corvee, and they could be imprisoned at the whim of any French magistrate. The colonial police enforced the law through a network of French and Vietnamese agents.

Land alienation was the cornerstone of economic exploitation under the colonial government. By 1930 more than 80 percent of the riceland in Cochinchina was owned by 25 percent of the landowners, and 57 percent of the rural population were landless peasants working on large estates. Although the situation was somewhat better in the north, landless peasants in Annam totaled 800,000 and in Tonkin nearly 1 million. Heavy taxes and usurious interest rates on loans were added burdens on the peasants. More than ninety percent of rubber plantations were French owned. Twothirds of the coal mined in Vietnam (nearly two million tons in 1927) was exported. Manufacturing was limited to cement and textiles, partly to placate French industrialists who saw Indochina as a market for their own goods. Naval shipyards and armament factories built under the Nguyen dynasty were dismantled under the French. Much of the craft industry survived, however, because it produced affordable consumer goods in contrast to imported French goods, which only the French colons or wealthy Vietnamese could afford.

French efforts at education in the early decades of colonial rule were negligible. A few government *quoc ngu* schools were established along with an Ecole Normale to train Vietnamese clerks and interpreters. A few Vietnamese from wealthy families, their numbers rising to about ninety by 1870, were sent to France to study. Three *lycees* (secondary schools), located in Hanoi, Hue, and Saigon, were opened in the early 1900s, using French as the language of instruction. The number of *quoc ngu* elementary schools was gradually increased, but even by 1925 it was estimated that no more than one school-age child in ten was receiving schooling. As a result, Vietnam's high degree of literacy declined precipitously during the colonial period. The University of Hanoi, founded in 1907 to provide an alternative for Vietnamese students beginning to flock to Japan, was closed for a decade the following year because of fear of student involvement in a 1908 uprising in Hanoi. In Tonkin and Annam, traditional education based on Chinese classical literature continued to flourish well into the twentieth century despite French efforts to discourage it. The triennial examinations were abolished in 1915 in Tonkin and in 1918 in Annam. China, which had always served as a source of teaching materials and texts, by the turn of century was beginning to be a source of reformist literature and revolutionary ideas. Materials filtering in from China included both Chinese texts and translations of Western classics, which were copied and spread from province to province.

Phan Boi Chau and the Rise of Nationalism

By the turn of the century, a whole generation of Vietnamese had grown up under French control. The people continued, as in precolonial times, to look to the scholar-gentry class for guidance in dealing with French imperialism and the loss of their country's independence. A few scholar-officials collaborated with the French, but most did not. Among those who refused was a group of several hundred scholars who became actively involved in the anticolonial movement. The best known among them was Phan Boi Chau, a scholar from Nghe An Province, trained in the Confucian tradition under his father and other local teachers. In 1885 Phan Boi Chau observed at close range the actions of French troops in crushing scholar-gentry resistance to the colonial overlords. For the next decade he devoted himself to his studies and finally passed the regional examination with highest honors in 1905. During the following five years, he traveled about the country making contacts with other anticolonial scholars and seeking out in particular the survivors of the Can Vuong movement, with whom he hoped to launch a rebellion against the French. He also sought to identify a member of the Nguyen ruling family sympathetic to the cause, who would serve as titular head of the independence movement and as a rallying point for both moral and financial support. Chosen to fill this role was Cuong De, a direct descendant of Gia Long.

In 1904 Phan Boi Chau and about twenty others met in Quang Nam to form the Duy Tan Hoi (Reformation Society), the first of a number of revolutionary societies he organized. The following year, he went to Japan to meet with Japanese and Chinese revolutionaries and seek financial support for the Vietnamese cause. The Japanese defeat of the Russian fleet at Tsushima the month before his arrival had caused great excitement among the various Asian anticolonialist movements. Phan Boi Chau brought Cuong De, along with several Vietnamese students, to Japan in 1906. That same year he convinced the other great Vietnamese nationalist leader of the period, Phan Chu Trinh, to visit him in Tokyo. After two weeks of discussions, however, they were unable to resolve their basic tactical differences. Whereas Phan Boi Chau favored retaining the monarchy as a popular ideological symbol and a means of attracting financial support, Phan Chu Trinh wanted primarily to abolish the monarchy in order to create a base on which to build national sovereignty. Furthermore, he was greatly influenced by the writings of French political philosophers Rousseau and Montesquieu, and he believed that the French colonial administration could serve as a progressive force to establish a Western democratic political structure through peaceful reform. Phan Boi Chau, conversely, wanted to drive out the French immediately through armed resistance and restore Vietnamese independence.

In 1907 Phan Boi Chau organized the Viet Nam Cong Hien Hoi (Vietnam Public Offering Society) to unite the 100 or so Vietnamese then studying in Japan. The organization was important because of the opportunity it provided for the students to think and work together as Vietnamese, rather than as Cochinchinese, Annamese, or Tonkinese, as the French called them. The following year, however, the Japanese, under pressure from the French, expelled the students, forcing most of them to return home. In March 1909, Phan Boi Chau was also deported by the Japanese. He went first to Hong Kong, later to Bangkok and Guangzhou. Even during his years abroad, his writings served to influence nationalist activities in Vietnam. In 1907 the Dong Kinh Nghia Thuc (Free School of the Eastern Capital [Hanoi]) was founded to educate nationalist political activists. Phan Boi Chau's writings were studied and Phan Chu Trinh gave lectures at the school. Suspecting that Phan Boi Chau was associated with the school, however, the French closed it in less than a year. The French also blamed Phan Boi Chau for instigating antitax demonstrations in Quang Nam and Quang Ngai provinces and in Hue in early 1908. As a symbol of the movement, the demonstrators forcibly cut off men's traditional long hair. An abortive Hanoi uprising and poison plot in June 1908 was also blamed on Phan Boi Chau. In response to the uprising, the French executed thirteen of the participants and initiated a crackdown on Vietnamese political activists, sending hundreds of scholar-patriots, including Phan Chu Trinh, to prison on Poulo Condore (now Con Dao). A major expedition was also launched in 1909 against De Tham, a resistance leader who was involved in the Hanoi uprising. De Tham, who had led a thirty-year campaign against the French in the mountains around Yen The in the northeastern part of Tonkin, managed to hold out until he was assassinated in 1913.

Stimulated by the Chinese Revolution led by Sun Yat-sen in 1911, Phan Boi Chau and the other Vietnamese nationalists in exile in Guangzhou formed a new organization in 1912 to replace the moribund Duy Tan Hoi. The main goals of the newly organized Viet Nam Quang Phuc Hoi (Vietnam Restoration Society) included expulsion of the French, recovery of Vietnamese independence, and establishment of a "Vietnamese democratic republic." Phan

Boi Chau had by this time given up his monarchist position, although Cuong De was accorded presidential status within the organization's provisional government. In order to gain support and financial backing for the new organization, Phan Boi Chau organized a number of terrorist bombings and assassinations in 1913, to which the French responded harshly. By 1914 the counterrevolutionary government of Yuan Shi-kai was in charge in China, and, by French request, Phan Boi Chau and other Vietnamese exiles in that country were imprisoned.

World War I began shortly thereafter, and some 50,000 Vietnamese troops and 50,000 Vietnamese workers were sent to Europe. The Vietnamese also endured additional heavy taxes to help pay for France's war efforts. Numerous anticolonial revolts occurred in Vietnam during the war, all easily suppressed by the French. In May 1916, the sixteen-year-old king, Duy Tan, escaped from his palace in order to take part in an uprising of Vietnamese troops. The French were informed of the plan and the leaders arrested and executed. Duy Tan was deposed and exiled to Reunion in the Indian Ocean. One of the most effective uprisings during this period was in the northern Vietnamese province of Thai Nguyen. Some 300 Vietnamese soldiers revolted and released 200 political prisoners, whom, in addition to several hundred local people, they armed. The rebels held the town of Thai Nguyen for several days, hoping for help from Chinese nationalists. None arrived, however, and the French retook the town and hunted down most of the rebels.

In 1917, Phan Boi Chau was released from prison. He spent the next eight years in exile in China, studying and writing but exerting little direct influence on the Vietnamese nationalist movement. In 1925 he was kidnaped by the French in Shanghai and returned to Hanoi, where he was tried and sentenced to hard labor for life. The sentence was later changed to house arrest until his death in 1940. Vietnamese historians view Phan Boi Chau's contribution to the country's independence as immeasurable. He advocated forcibly expelling the French, although he was not able to solve the problems involved in actually doing it. He suggested learning from other Asian independence movements and leaders, while realizing that in the end only the Vietnamese could win their own independence. His greatest weakness, according to many historians, was his failure to involve the Vietnamese peasantry, who composed 80 percent of the population, in his drive for independence. Rather than recruiting support at the village level, Phan Boi Chau and his followers concentrated on recruiting the elite, in the belief that the peasant masses would automatically rally around the scholar-gentry. Future Vietnamese independence leaders took inspiration from the efforts of the early nationalists and learned from their mistakes the importance of winning support at the local level.

An important development in the early part of the twentieth century was the increased use of *quoc ngu* in the northern part of the country through a proliferation of new journals printed in that script. There had been *quoc ngu* publications in Cochinchina since 1865, but in 1898 a decree of the colonial government prohibited publication without permission, in the protectorate areas, of periodicals in *quoc ngu* or Chinese that were not published by a French citizen. In 1913 Nguyen Van Vinh succeeded in publishing *Dong Duong Tap Chi* (Indochinese Review), a strongly antitraditional but pro- French journal. He also founded a publishing house that translated such Vietnamese classics as the early nineteenth century poem *Kim Van Kieu* as well as Chinese classics into *quoc ngu*. Nguyen Van Vinh's publications, while largely pro-Western, were the major impetus for the increasing popularity of *quoc ngu* in Annam and Tonkin. In 1917 the moderate reformist journalist Pham Quynh began publishing in Hanoi the *quoc ngu* journal *Nam Phong*, which addressed the problem of adopting modern Western values without destroying the cultural essence of the Vietnamese nation. By World War I, *quoc ngu* had become the vehicle for the dissemination of not only Vietnamese, Chinese, and French literary and philosophical classics but also a new body of Vietnamese nationalist literature emphasizing social comment and criticism.

In the years immediately following World War I, the scholar-led Vietnamese independence movement in Cochinchina began a temporary decline as a result, in part, of tighter French control and increased activity by the French-educated Vietnamese elite. The decrease of both French investments in and imports to Vietnam during the war had opened opportunities to entrepreneurial Vietnamese, who began to be active in light industries such as rice milling, printing, and textile weaving. The sale of large tracts of land in the Mekong Delta by the colonial government to speculators at cheap prices resulted in the expansion of the Vietnamese landed aristocracy. These factors in combination led to the rise of a wealthy Vietnamese elite in Cochinchina that was pro-French but was frustrated by its own lack of political power and status.

Prominent among this group was Bui Quang Chieu, a French- trained agricultural engineer, who helped organize the Constitutionalist Party in 1917. Founded with the hope that it would be able to exert pressure on the Colonial Council of Cochinchina, the governing body of the colony, the party drew its support from Vietnamese who were large landowners, wealthy merchants, industrialists, and senior civil servants. The Colonial Council, established in 1880, was controlled by French interests, having only ten Vietnamese members out of twenty-four by 1922. The demands of the party included increased Vietnamese representation on the Colonial Council, higher salaries for Vietnamese officials, replacement of the scholar-official administration system with a modern bureaucracy, and reform of the naturalization law to make it easier for Vietnamese to become French citizens.

When the party failed to gain acceptance of any of these demands, it turned to its most pressing economic grievance, the ethnic Chinese domination of the Cochinchinese economy. While French investors exercised almost exclusive control over industry and shared control of agriculture with the Vietnamese, the ethnic Chinese were sought out by the French to act as middlemen and came to dominate rice trade and retail business in both urban and rural areas. A boycott of Chinese goods organized by the party, however, was largely unsuccessful. By the mid 1920s, the Vietnamese entrepreneurial elite and the Constitutionalist Party had grown increasingly critical of the French. However, more progressive groups had displaced them in the Vietnamese nationalist movement.

The mid 1920s brought a period of increased activity among the growing Vietnamese worker class, and pedicab drivers, dye workers, and textile workers launched strikes with some success. In August 1925, workers belonging to an underground union struck at the Ba Son naval arsenal in Saigon-Cholon, ostensibly for higher pay but in actuality to block two French naval ships from being sent to Shanghai to pressure striking Chinese workers. The strikers were successful in their demands and, in November, held massive demonstrations in Saigon to protest the arrest of Phan Boi Chau in Shanghai.

Ho Chi Minh and the Communist Movement

The year 1925 also marked the founding of the Viet Nam Thanh Nien Cach Menh Dong Chi Hoi (Revolutionary Youth League) in Guangzhou by Ho Chi Minh. Born Nguyen Sinh Cung in Kim Lien village, Nghe An Province in May 1890, Ho was the son of Nguyen Sinh Sac (or Huy), a scholar from a poor peasant family. Following a common custom, Ho's father renamed him Nhuyen Tat Thanh at about age ten. Ho was trained in the classical Confucian tradition and was sent to secondary school in Hue. After working for a short time as a teacher, he went to Saigon where he took a course in navigation and in 1911 joined the crew of a French ship. Working as a kitchen hand, Ho traveled to North America, Africa, and Europe. While in Paris from 1919-23, he took the name Nguyen Ai Quoc (Nguyen the Patriot). In 1919 he attempted to meet with United States President Woodrow Wilson at the Versailles Peace Conference in order to present a proposal for Vietnam's independence, but he was turned away and the proposal was never officially acknowledged. During his stay in Paris, Ho was greatly influenced by Marxist-Leninist literature, particularly Lenin's *Theses on the National and Colonial Questions* (1920), and in 1920 he became a founding member of the French Communist Party. He read, wrote, and spoke widely on Indochina's problems before moving to Moscow in 1923 and attending the Fifth Congress of the *Communist International* (see Glossary), also called the Comintern, in 1924. In late 1924, Ho arrived in Guangzhou, where he spent the next two years training more than 200 Vietnamese cadres in revolutionary techniques. His course of instruction included study of Marxism-Leninism, Vietnamese and Asian revolutionary history, Asian leaders such as Gandhi and Sun Yat- sen, and the problem of organizing the masses. As a training manual, Ho used his own publication *Duong Cach Menh* (The Revolutionary Path), written in 1926 and considered his primer on revolution. Going by the name Ly Thuy, he formed an inner communist group, Thanh Nien Cong San Doan (Communist Youth League), within the larger Thanh Nien (Youth) organization. The major activity of Thanh Nien was the production of a journal, *Thanh Nien*, distributed clandestinely in Vietnam, Siam, and Laos, which introduced communist theory into the Vietnamese independence movement. Following Chiang Kai-shek's April 1927 coup and the subsequent suppression of the Communists in southern China, Ho fled to Moscow.

In December of that year, a teacher from a Vietnamese peasant family, Nguyen Thai Hoc, founded Viet Nam Quoc Dan Dang, (VNQDD, Vietnamese Nationalist Party), in Hanoi. With a membership largely of students, low-ranking government employees, soldiers, and a few landlords and rich peasants, VNQDD was patterned after the Chinese Nationalist Party (Kuomintang), from which it received financial support in the 1930s. Another source of funds for the VNQDD was the Vietnam Hotel in Hanoi, which it opened in 1928 as both a commercial enterprise and the party headquarters. The hotel restaurant, however, provided French agents with an easy means of penetrating the party and monitoring its activities. At various times, the VNQDD attempted, without success, to form a united front with Thanh Nien and other independence organizations. Thanh Nien, being two years older, however, had had a head start over VNQDD in organizing in schools, factories, and local government, which it had done with patience and planning. The VNQDD therefore concentrated instead on recruitment of Vietnamese soldiers and the overthrow of French rule through putschist-style activities.

In February 1929, the French official in charge of recruiting coolie labor was killed by an assassin connected with the VNQDD. The French immediately arrested several hundred VNQDD leaders and imprisoned seventy-eight. VNQDD leaders Nguyen Thai Hoc and Nguyen Khac Nhu escaped, but most members of the Central Committee were captured. The remaining leadership under Nguyen Thai Hoc decided to stage a general uprising as soon as possible. All dissent to the plan was overridden, and the party began manufacturing and stockpiling weapons. On February 9, 1930, a revolt instigated by the VNQDD broke out at Yen Bai among the Vietnamese garrison, but it was quickly suppressed. Simultaneous attacks on other key targets, including Son Tay and Lam Thu, were also unsuccessful because of poor preparation and communication. The Yen Bai uprising was disastrous for the VNQDD. Most of the organization's top leaders were executed, and villages that had given refuge to the party were shelled and bombed by the French. After Yen Bai, the VNQDD ceased to be of importance in the anticolonial struggle. Although more modernist and less bound by tradition than the scholar-patriots of the Phan Boi Chau era, the VNQDD had remained a movement of urban intellectuals who were unable to involve the masses in their struggle and too often favored reckless exploits over slow and careful planning.

On June 17, 1929, the founding conference of the first Indochinese Communist Party (ICP--Dang Cong San Dong Duong) was held in Hanoi under the leadership of a breakaway faction of Thanh Nien radicals. The party immediately began to publish several journals and to send out representatives to all parts of the country for the purpose of setting up branches. A series of strikes supported by the party broke out at this time, and their success led to the convening of the first National Congress of Red Trade Unions the following month in Hanoi. Other communist parties were founded at this time by both supporting members of Thanh Nien and radical members of yet another party revolutionary with Marxist leavings but no direct tie with the Comintern, called the New Revolutinary Party or Tan Viet Party. At the beginning of 1930, there were actually three communist parties in French Indochina competing for members. The establishment of the ICP prompted remaining Thanh Nien members to transform the Communist Youth Leaque into a communist party - the Annam Communist Party (ACP, Annam Cong San Dang), and Tan Viet Party members followed suit by renaming their organization the Indochinese Communist League (Dong Duong Cong San Lien Doan). As a result, the Comintern issued a highly critical indictment of the factionalism in the Vietnamese revolutionary movement and urged the Vietnamese to form a united communist party. Consequently, the Comintern leadership sent a message to Ho Chi Minh, then living in Siam, asking him to come to Hong Kong to unify the groups. On February 3, 1930, in Hong Kong, Ho presided over a conference of representatives of the two factions derived from Thanh Nien (members of the Indochinese Communist League were not represented but were to be permitted membership in the newly formed party as individuals) at which a unified Vietnamese Communist Party (VCP) was founded, the Viet Nam Cong San Dang. At the Comintern's request, the name was changed later that year at the first Party Plenum to the Indochinese Communist Party, thus reclaiming the name of the first party of that named founded in 1929. At the founding meeting, it was agreed that a provisional Central Committee of nine members (three from Bac Bo, two from Trung Bo, two from Nam Bo, and two from the overseas Chinese community) should be formed and that recognition should be sought from the Comintern. Various mass organizations including unions, a peasants' association, a women's association, a relief society, and a youth league were to be organized under the new party. Ho drew up a program of party objectives, which were approved by the conference. The main points included overthrow of the French; establishment of Vietnamese independence; establishment of a workers', peasants', and soldiers' government; organization of a workers' militia; cancellation of public debts; confiscation of means of production and their transfer to the proletarian government; distribution of French-owned lands to the peasants; suppression of taxes; establishment of an eight-hour work day; development of crafts and agriculture; institution of freedom of organization; and establishment of education for all.

The formation of the ICP came at a time of general unrest in the country, caused in part by a global worsening of economic conditions. Although the size of the Vietnamese urban proletariat had increased four times, to about 200,000, since the beginning of the century, working conditions and salaries had improved little. The number of strikes rose from seven in 1927 to ninety- eight in 1930. As the effects of the worldwide depression began to be felt, French investors withdrew their money from Vietnam. Salaries dropped 30 to 50 percent, and employment, approximately 33 percent. Between 1928 and 1932, the price of rice on the world market decreased by more than half. Rice exports totaling nearly 2 million tons in 1928 fell to less than 1 million tons in 1931. Although both French colons and wealthy Vietnamese landowners were hit by the crisis, it was the peasant who bore most of the burden because he was forced to sell at least twice as much rice to pay the same amount in taxes or other debts. Floods, famine, and food riots plagued the countryside. By 1930 rubber prices had plummeted to less than one-fourth their 1928 value. Coal production was cut, creating more layoffs. Even the colonial government cut its staff by one-seventh and salaries by one-quarter.

The Nghe-Tinh Revolt

Strikes grew more frequent in Nam Bo in early 1930 and led to peasant demonstrations in May and June of that year. The focus of reaction to the worsening economic conditions, however, was Nghe An Province, which had a long history of support for peasant revolts. Plagued by floods, drought, scarcity of land, and colonial exploitation, the people of Nghe An had been supporters of the Can Vuong movement and the activities of Phan Boi Chau. By late 1929, the ICP had begun organizing party cells, trade unions, and peasant associations in the province. By early 1930, it had established a provincial committee in the provincial capital of Vinh and had begun to found mass organizations throughout Nghe An. French sources reported that by mid-summer 1930 there were about 300 Communist activists in Nghe An and the neighboring province of Ha Tinh. This figure rose to 1,800 a few months later. The communists helped to mobilize the workers and peasants of Nghe-Tinh, as the two-province area was known, to protest the worsening conditions. Peasant demonstrators demanded a moratorium on the payment of the personal tax and a return of village communal lands that were in the hands of wealthy landowners. When the demands were ignored, demonstrations turned to riots; government buildings, manor houses, and markets were looted and burned, and tax rolls were destroyed. Some village notables joined in the uprisings or refused to suppress them. Local officials fled, and government authority rapidly disintegrated. In some of the districts, the communists helped organize the people into local village associations called soviets (using the Bolshevik term). The soviets, formed by calling a meeting of village residents at the local *dinh*, elected a ruling committee to annul taxes, lower rents, distribute excess rice to the needy, and organize the seizure of communal land confiscated by the wealthy. Village militias were formed, usually armed only with sticks, spears, and knives.

By September the French had realized the seriousness of the situation and brought in Foreign Legion troops to suppress the rebellion. On September 9, French planes bombed a column of thousands of peasants headed toward the provincial capital. Security forces rounded up all those suspected of being communists or of being involved in the rebellion, staged executions, and conducted punitive raids on rebellious villages. By early 1931, all of the soviets had been forced to surrender. Of the more than 1,000 arrested, 400 were given long prison sentences, and 80, including some of the party leaders, were executed. With the aid of other Asian colonial authorities, Vietnamese communists in Singapore, China, and Hong Kong were also arrested.

The early 1930s was a period of recovery and rebuilding for the ICP in Vietnam. Reorganization and recruitment were carried on even among political prisoners, of whom there were more than 10,000 by 1932. In the prison of Poulo Condore, Marxist literature circulated secretly, an underground journal was published, and party members (among them future party leaders Pham Van Dong and Le Duan) organized a university, teaching courses in sciences, literature, languages, geography, and Marxism-Leninism. The party also began to recruit increasingly from among Vietnamese minorities, particularly the Tay-Nung ethnic groups living in the Viet Bac. Located along Vietnam's northern border with China, this remote mountainous region includes the modern provinces of Lang Son, Cao Bang, Bac Thai, and Ha Tuyen.

This period also marked the rise of a Trotskyite faction within the communist movement, which in 1933 began publishing a widely read journal called *La Lutte* (Struggle). The Comintern's hostility toward Trotskyites prevented their formal alliance with the ICP, although. informal cooperation did exist. In 1935 a combined slate of ICP members and Trotskyites managed to elect four candidates to the Saigon municipal council. Cooperation between the two groups began to break down, however, when a Popular Front government led by the French Socialist Party under Leon Blum was elected in Paris. The Trotskyites complained that, despite the change of leadership in France, nothing had changed in Indochina. From the communist viewpoint, the major contribution to Vietnamese independence made by the Popular Front government was an amnesty declared in 1936 under which 1,532 Vietnamese political prisoners were freed.

WORLD WAR II AND JAPANESE OCCUPATION

The signing of the Nazi-Soviet Non-Agression pact in August 1939, caused France immediately to ban the French Communist Party and, soon afterwards, to declare illegal all Vietnamese political parties including the ICP. The colonial authorities began a crack down on communists, arresting an estimated 2,000 and closing down all communist and radical journals. The party consequently was forced to shift its activities to the countryside, where French control was weaker--a move that was to benefit the communists in the long run. In November the ICP Central Committee held its Sixth Plenum with the goal of mapping out a new united front strategy, the chief task of which was national liberation. According to the new strategy, support would now be welcomed from the middle class and even the landlord class, although the foundation of the party continued to be the proletarian-peasant alliance.

After the fall of France to the Nazis in June 1940, Japan demanded that the French colonial government close the HanoiKunming railway to shipments of war-related goods to China. In an agreement with the Vichy government in France in August, Japan formally recognized French sovereignty in Indochina in return for access to military facilities, transit rights, and the right to station occupation troops in Tonkin. On September 22, however, Japanese troops invaded from China, seizing the Vietnamese border towns of Dong Dang and Lang Son. As the French retreated southward, the Japanese encouraged Vietnamese troops to support the invasion. The communists in the Bac Son district border area moved to take advantage of the situation, organizing self-defense units and establishing a revolutionary administration. The French protested to the Japanese, however, and a cease-fire was arranged whereby the French forces returned to their posts and promptly put down all insurrection. Most of the communist forces in Tonkin were able to retreat to the mountains. In similar short-lived uprisings that took place in the Plain of Reeds area of Cochinchina, however, the communist rebel forces had nowhere to retreat and most were destroyed by the French.

Establishment of the Viet Minh

In early 1940, Ho Chi Minh returned to southern China, after having spent most of the previous seven years studying and teaching at the Lenin Institute in Moscow. In Kunming he reestablished contact with the ICP Central Committee and set up a temporary headquarters, which became the focal point for communist policymaking and planning. After thirty years absence, Ho returned to Vietnam in February 1941 and set up headquarters in a cave at Pac Bo, near the Sino-Vietnamese border, where in May the Eighth Plenum of the ICP was held. The major outcome of the meeting was the reiteration that the struggle for national independence took primacy over class war or other concerns of socialist ideology. To support this strategy, the League for the Independence of Vietnam (Viet Nam Doc Lap Dong Minh Hoi, *Viet Minh* for short--see Glossary) was established. In this new front group, which would be dominated by the party, all patriotic elements were welcomed as potential allies. The party would be forced in the short term to modify some of its goals and soften its rhetoric, supporting, for example, the reduction of land rents rather than demanding land seizures. Social revolution would have to await the defeat of the French and the Japanese. The Eighth Plenum also recognized guerrilla warfare as an integral part of the revolutionary strategy and established local self-defense militias in all villages under Viet Minh control. The cornerstone of the party's strategy, of which Ho appears to have been the chief architect, was the melding of the forces of urban nationalism and peasant rebellion into a single independence effort.

Ho Chi Minh, accompanied by Pham Van Dong, arriving in Paris, 1946
Courtesy New York Times, Paris Collection, National Archives

In order to implement the new strategy, two tasks were given priority: the establishment of a Viet Minh apparatus throughout the country and the creation of a secure revolutionary base in the Viet Bac border region from which southward expansion could begin. This area had the advantages of being remote from colonial control but accessible to China, which could serve both as a refuge and training ground. Moreover, the Viet Bac population was largely sympathetic to the Communists. Viet Minh influence began to permeate the area, and French forces attempted, but failed, to regain control of the region in 1941. The liberation zone soon spread to include the entire northern frontier area until it reached south of Cao Bang, where an ICP Interprovincial Committee established its headquarters. A temporary setback for the Communists occurred in August 1942, when Ho Chi Minh, while on a trip to southern China to meet with Chinese Communist Party officials, was arrested and imprisoned for two years by the Kuomintang. By August 1944, however, he had convinced the regional Chinese commander to support his return to Vietnam at the head of a guerrilla force. Accordingly, Ho returned to Vietnam in September with eighteen men trained and armed by the Chinese. Upon his arrival, he vetoed, as too precipitate, a plan laid by the ICP in his absence to launch a general uprising in the Viet Bac within two months. Ho did, however, approve the establishment of armed propaganda detachments with both military and political functions.

As World War II drew to a close, the ICP sought to have the Vietnamese independence movement recognized as one of the victorious Allied forces under the leadership of the United States. With this in mind, Ho returned again to southern China in January 1945 to meet with American and Free French units there. From the Americans he solicited financial support, while from the French he sought, unsuccessfully, guarantees of Vietnamese independence. On March 9, 1945, the Japanese gave the French an ultimatum demanding that all French and Indochinese forces be placed under Japanese control. Without waiting for the French reply, the Japanese proceeded to seize administrative buildings, radio stations, banks, and industries and to disarm the French forces. Bao Dai, the Nguyen ruler under the French, was retained as emperor, and a puppet government was established with Tran Trong Kim, a teacher and historian, as prime minister. Japan revoked the Franco-Vietnamese Treaty of Protectorate of 1883, which had established Indochina as a French protectorate, and declared the independence of Vietnam under Japanese tutelage.

The communists concluded that the approaching end of the war and the defeat of the Japanese meant that a propitious time for a general uprising of the Vietnamese people was close at hand. Accordingly, the ICP began planning to take advantage of the political vacuum produced by the French loss of control and the confinement of Japanese power largely to urban and strategic areas. Moreover, famine conditions prevailed in the countryside, and unemployment was rampant in the cities. In the Red River Delta alone, more than 500,000 people died of starvation between March and May 1945. Because Japan was considered the main enemy, the communists decided that a United Front should be formed that included patriotic French resistance groups and moderate urban Vietnamese bourgeoisie. The overall ICP strategy called for a two-stage revolt, beginning in rural areas and then moving to the cities. Accordingly Communist military forces responded to the plan. Armed Propaganda units under ICP military strategist Vo Nguyen Giap began moving south from Cao Bang into Thai Nguyen Province. To the east, the 3,000- man National Salvation Army commanded by Chu Van Tan began liberating the provinces of Tuyen Quang and Lang Son and establishing revolutionary district administrations. At the first major military conference of the ICP, held in April in Bac Giang Province, the leaders determined that a liberated zone would be established in the Viet Bac and that existing ICP military units would be united to form the new Vietnam Liberation Army (VLA), later called the People's Army of Vietnam (PAVN--see Glossary). Giap was named Commander in Chief of the VLA and chairman of the Revolution Military Committee, later called the Central Military Party Committed (CMPC). Meanwhile, the ICP was expanding its influence farther south by forming mass organizations known as national salvation associations (*cuu quoc hoi*) for various groups, including workers, peasants, women, youth, students, and soldiers. As a result of labor unrest in Hanoi, 2,000 workers were recruited into salvation associations in early 1945, and 100,000 peasants had been enlisted into salvation associations in Quang Ngai Province by mid-summer. In Saigon, a youth organization, Thanh Nien Tien Phong (Vanguard Youth), established by the communists in 1942, had recruited 200,000 by early summer. Thanh Nien Tien Phong became the focal point for the Communist effort in the south and soon expanded to more than one million members throughout Cochinchina. By June 1945, in the provinces of the Viet Bac, the Viet Minh had set up people's revolutionary committees at all levels, distributed communal and French-owned lands to the poor, abolished the corvee, established *quoc ngu* classes, set up local self-defense militias in the villages, and declared universal suffrage and democratic freedoms. The Viet Minh then established a provisional directorate, headed by Ho Chi Minh, as the governing body for the liberated zone, comprising an estimated one million people.

Despite its success in the north, the ICP faced a range of serious obstacles in Cochinchina, where the Japanese maintained 100,000 well-armed troops. In addition, the Japanese also supported the neo-Buddhist *Cao Dai* sect (see Glossary) of more than one million members, including a military force of several battalions. Another sect, the *Hoa Hao* (see Glossary), founded and led by the fanatical Huynh Phu So, eschewed temples and hierarchy and appealed to the poor and oppressed. Although lacking the military force of the Cao Dai, the Hoa Hao was also closely connected with the Japanese. Meanwhile, the Japanese had also gained control of the Viet Nam Phuc Quoc Dong Minh Hoi (League for the Restoration of Vietnam), established in 1939 as an outgrowth of Viet Nam Quang Pluc Hoi. Mobilized by the communists to face this array of forces in Cochinchina were the Vanguard Youth and the Vietnam Trade Union Federation, with 100,000 members in 300 unions.

The General Uprising and Independence

On August 13, 1945, the ICP Central Committee held its Ninth Plenum at Tan Trao to prepare an agenda for a National Congress of the Viet Minh a few days later. At the plenum, convened just after the dropping of the atomic bombs on Hiroshima and Nagasaki, an order for a general uprising was issued, and a national insurrection committee was established headed by ICP general secretary Truong Chinh. On August 16, the Viet Minh National Congress convened at Tan Trao and ratified the Central Committee decision to launch a general uprising. The Congress also elected a National Liberation Committee, headed by Ho Chi Minh (who was gravely ill at the time), to serve as a provisional government. The following day, the Congress, at a ceremony in front of the village *dinh*, officially adopted the national red flag with a gold star, and Ho read an appeal to the Vietnamese people to rise in revolution.

By the end of the first week following the Tan Trao conference, most of the provincial and district capitals north of Hanoi had fallen to the revolutionary forces. When the news of the Japanese surrender reached Hanoi on August 16, the local Japanese military command turned over its powers to the local Vietnamese authorities. By August 17, Viet Minh units in the Hanoi suburbs had deposed the local administrations and seized the government seals symbolizing political authority. Self-defense units were set up and armed with guns, knives, and sticks. Meanwhile, Viet Minh-led demonstrations broke out inside Hanoi. The following morning, a member of the Viet Minh Municipal Committee announced to a crowd of 200,000 gathered in Ba Dinh Square that the general uprising had begun. The crowd broke up immediately after that and headed for various key buildings around the city, including the palace, city hall, and police headquarters, where they accepted the surrender of the Japanese and local Vietnamese government forces, mostly without resistance. The Viet Minh sent telegrams throughout Tonkin announcing its victory, and local Viet Minh units were able to take over most of the provincial and district capitals without a struggle. In Annam and

Cochinchina, however, the Communist victory was less assured because the ICP in those regions had neither the advantage of long, careful preparation nor an established liberated base area and army. Hue fell in a manner similar to Hanoi, with the takeover first of the surrounding area. Saigon fell on August 25 to the Viet Minh, who organized a nine-member, multiparty Committee of the South, including six members of the Viet Minh, to govern the city. The provinces south and west of Saigon, however, remained in the hands of the Hoa Hao. Although the Hoa Hao and Cao Dai were anti-French, both were more interested in regional autonomy than in communist-led national independence. As a result, clashes between the Hoa Hao and the Viet Minh broke out in the Mekong Delta in September.

Ho Chi Minh moved his headquarters to Hanoi shortly after the Viet Minh takeover of the city. On August 28, the Viet Minh announced the formation of the provisional government of the Democratic Republic of Vietnam (DRV) with Ho as president and minister of foreign affairs. Vo Nguyen Giap was named minister of interior and Pham Van Dong minister of finance. In order to broaden support for the new government, several noncommunists were also included. Emperor Bao Dai, whom the communists had forced to abdicate on August 25, was given the position of high counselor to the new government. On September 2, half a million people gathered in Ba Dinh Square to hear Ho read the Vietnamese Declaration of Independence, based on the American Declaration of Independence and the French Declaration of the Rights of Man and the Citizen. After indicting the French colonial record in Vietnam, he closed with an appeal to the victorious Allies to recognize the independence of Vietnam.

Despite the heady days of August, major problems lay ahead for the ICP. Noncommunist political parties, which had been too weak and disorganized to take advantage of the political vacuum left by the fall of the Japanese, began to express opposition to communist control of the new provisional government. Among these parties, the nationalist VNQDD and Viet Nam Phuc Quoc Dong Minh Hoi parties had the benefit of friendship with the Chinese expeditionary forces of Chiang Kai-shek, which began arriving in northern Vietnam in early September. At the Potsdam Conference in July 1945, the Allies had agreed that the Chinese would accept the surrender of the Japanese in Indochina north of the 16°N parallel and the British, south of that line. The Vietnamese nationalists, with the help of Chinese troops, seized some areas north of Hanoi, and the VNQDD subsequently set up an opposition newspaper in Hanoi to denounce "red terror." The communists gave high priority to avoiding clashes with Chinese troops, which soon numbered 180,000. To prevent such encounters, Ho ordered VLA troops to avoid provoking any incidents with the Chinese and agreed to the Chinese demand that the communists negotiate with the Vietnamese nationalist parties. Accordingly, in November 1945, the provisional government began negotiations with the VNQDD and the Viet Nam Phuc Quoc Dong Minh Hoi, both of which initially took a hard line in their demands. The communists resisted, however, and the final agreement called for a provisional coalition government with Ho as president and nationalist leader Nguyen Hai Than as vice president. In the general elections scheduled for early January, 50 of the 350 National Assembly seats were to be reserved for the VNQDD and 20, for Viet Nam Phuc Quoc Dong Minh Hoi, regardless of the results of the balloting.

At the same time, the communists were in a far weaker political position in Cochinchina because they faced competition from the well-organized, economically influential, moderate parties based in Saigon and from the Hoa Hao and Cao Dai in the countryside. Moreover, the commander of the British expeditionary forces, which arrived in early September, was unsympathetic to Vietnamese desires for independence. French troops, released from Japanese prisons and rearmed by the British, provoked incidents and seized control of the city. A general strike called by the Vietnamese led to clashes with the French troops and mob violence in the French sections of the city. Negotiations between the French and the Committee of the South broke down in early October, as French troops began to occupy towns in the Mekong Delta. Plagued by clashes with the religious sects, lack of weapons, and a high desertion rate, the troops of the Viet Minh were driven deep into the delta, forests, and other inaccessible areas of the region.

Meanwhile, in Hanoi candidates supported by the Viet Minh won 300 seats in the National Assembly in the January 1946 elections. In early March, however, the threat of the imminent arrival of French troops in the north forced Ho to negotiate a compromise with France. Under the terms of the agreement, the French government recognized the DRV as a free state with its own army, legislative body, and financial powers, in return for Hanoi's acceptance of a small French military presence in northern Vietnam and membership in the French Union. Both sides agreed to a plebiscite in Cochinchina. The terms of the accord were generally unpopular with the Vietnamese and were widely viewed as a sell-out of the revolution. Ho, however, foresaw grave danger in refusing to compromise while the country was still in a weakened position. Soon after the agreement was signed, some 15,000 French troops arrived in Tonkin, and both the Vietnamese and the French began to question the terms of the accord. Negotiations to implement the agreement began in late spring at Fontainbleau, near Paris, and dragged on throughout the summer. Ho signed a modus vivendi (temporary agreement), which gave the Vietnamese little more than the promise of negotiation of a final treaty the following January, and returned to Vietnam.

United States Vice President Richard M. Nixon visiting Vietnam in 1953
Courtesy Indochina Archives

First Indochina War

Ho's efforts during this period were directed primarily at conciliating both the French themselves and the militantly antiFrench members of the ICP leadership. The growing frequency of clashes between French and Vietnamese forces in Haiphong led to a French naval bombardment of that port city in November 1946. Estimates of Vietnamese casualties from the action range from 6,000 to 20,000. This incident and the arrival of 1,000 troops of the French Foreign Legion in central and northern Vietnam in early December convinced the communists, including Ho, that they should prepare for war. On December 19, the French demanded that the Vietnamese forces in the Hanoi area disarm and transfer responsibility for law and order to French authority. That evening, the Viet Minh responded by attacking the city's electric plant and other French installations around the area. Forewarned, the French seized Gia Lam airfield and took control of the central part of Hanoi, as full-scale war broke out. By late January, the French had retaken most of the provincial capitals in northern and central Vietnam. Hue fell in early February, after a six-week siege. The Viet Minh, which avoided using its main force units against the French at that time, continued to control most of the countryside, where it concentrated on building up its military strength and setting up guerrilla training programs in liberated areas. Seizing the initiative, however, the French marched north to the Chinese border in the autumn of 1947, inflicting heavy casualties on the Viet Minh and retaking much of the Viet Bac region.

Meanwhile, in April 1947 the Viet Minh in Cochinchina had destroyed all chance for alliance with the religious sects by executing Huynh Phu So, leader of the Hoa Hao. Both the Hoa Hao and the Cao Dai formed alliances soon afterward with the French. The Committee for the South, which had seriously damaged the Communist image in Cochinchina by its hard-line approach, was replaced in 1951 by the Central Office for South Vietnam (COSVN, Trung Uong Cuc Mien Nam), headed by Le Duan. In the north, however, the political and military situation had begun to improve for the Communists by late 1948. The Viet Minh had increased the number of its troops to more than 250,000 and, through guerrilla activities, the Communists had managed to retake part of the Viet Bac as well as a number of small liberated base areas in the south. ICP political power was also growing, although lack of a land reform program and the continued moderate policy toward the patriotic landed gentry discouraged peasant support for the communists. In 1948, the French responded to the growing strength of the Viet Minh by granting nominal independence to all of Vietnam in the guise of "associated statehood" within the French Union. The terms of the agreement made it clear, however, that Vietnam's independence was, in reality, devoid of any practical significance. The new government, established with Bao Dai as chief of state, was viewed critically by nationalists as well as communists. Most prominent nationalists, including Ngo Dinh Diem (president, Republic of Vietnam, South Vietnam, 1955-63), refused positions in the government, and many left the country.

The United States recognized the Associated State of Vietnam in early 1950, but this action was counterbalanced a few days later with the recognition of the DRV by the new People's Republic of China. In March, Ho Chi Minh signed an agreement with Beijing that called for limited assistance to Hanoi. Shortly thereafter, Moscow also formally recognized the DRV, and the Viet Minh became more openly affiliated with the communist camp. Mao Zedong's model of revolution was openly praised in the Vietnamese press; and the ICP, which, on paper, had been temporarily dissolved in 1945 to obscure the Viet Minh's communist roots, surfaced under a new name in 1951 that removed all doubt of its communist nature. More than 200 delegates, representing some 500,000 party members, gathered at the Second National Party Congress of the ICP, held in February 1951 in Tuyen Quang Province. Renaming the ICP the Vietnam Workers' Party (VWP, Dang Lao Dong Viet Nam), the delegates elected Ho as party chairman and Truong Chinh as general secretary.

Treating wounded French solider at Dien Bien Phu, April 1954
Courtesy New York Times, Paris Collection, National Archives

Dien Bien Phu

With Beijing's promise of limited assistance to Hanoi, the communist military strategy concentrated on the liberation of Tonkin and consigned Cochinchina to a lower priority. The top military priority, as set by Giap, was to free the northern border areas in order to protect the movement of supplies and personnel from China. By autumn of 1950, the Viet Minh had again liberated the Viet Bac in decisive battles that forced the French to evacuate the entire border region, leaving behind a large quantity of ammunition. From their liberated zone in the northern border area, the Viet Minh were free to make raids into the Red River Delta. The French military in Vietnam found it increasingly difficult to convince Paris and the French electorate to give them the manpower and materiel needed to defeat the Viet Minh. For the next two years, the Viet Minh, well aware of the growing disillusionment of the French people with Indochina, concentrated its efforts on wearing down the French military by attacking its weakest outposts and by maximizing the physical distance between engagements to disperse French forces. Being able to choose the time and place for such engagements gave the guerrillas a decided advantage. Meanwhile, political activity was increased until, by late 1952, more than half the villages of the Red River Delta were under Viet Minh control.

The newly appointed commander of French forces in Vietnam, General Henri Navarre, decided soon after his arrival in Vietnam that it was essential to halt a Viet Minh offensive underway in neighboring Laos. To do so, Navarre believed it was necessary for the French to capture and hold the town of Dien Bien Phu, sixteen kilometers from the Laotian border. For the Viet Minh, control of Dien Bien Phu was an important link in the supply route from China. In November 1953, the French occupied the town with paratroop battalions and began reinforcing it with units from the French military post at nearby Lai Chau.

During that same month, Ho indicated that the DRV was willing to examine French proposals for a diplomatic settlement announced the month before. In February 1954, a peace conference to settle the Korean and Indochinese conflicts was set for April in Geneva, and negotiations in Indochina were scheduled to begin on May 8. Viet Minh strategists, led by Giap, concluded that a successful attack on a French fortified camp, timed to coincide with the peace talks, would give Hanoi the necessary leverage for a successful conclusion of the negotiations.

Accordingly, the siege of Dien Bien Phu began on March 13, by which time the Viet Minh had concentrated nearly 50,000 regular troops, 55,000 support troops, and almost 100,000 transport workers in the area. Chinese aid, consisting mainly of ammunition, petroleum, and some large artillery pieces carried a distance of 350 kilometers from the Chinese border, reached 1,500 tons per month by early 1954. The French garrison of 15,000, which depended on supply by air, was cut off by March 27, when the Viet Minh artillery succeeded in making the airfield unusable. An elaborate system of tunnels dug in the mountainsides enabled the Viet Minh to protect its artillery pieces by continually moving them to prevent discovery. Several hundred kilometers of trenches permitted the attackers to move progressively closer to the French encampment. In the final battle, human wave assaults were used to take the perimeter defenses, which yielded defensive guns that were then turned on the main encampment. The French garrison surrendered on May 7, ending the siege that had cost the lives of about 25,000 Vietnamese and more than 1,500 French troops.

The following day, peace talks on Indochina began in Geneva, attended by the DRV, the Associated State of Vietnam, Cambodia, Laos, France, Britain, China, the Soviet Union, and the United States. In July a compromise agreement was reached consisting of two documents: a cease-fire and a final declaration. The ceasefire agreement, which was signed only by France and the DRV, established a provisional military demarcation line at about the 17°N parallel and required the regroupment of all French military forces south of that line and of all Viet Minh military forces north of the line. A demilitarized zone (DMZ), no more than five kilometers wide, was established on either side of the demarcation line. The cease-fire agreement also provided for a 300-day period, during which all civilians were free to move from one zone to the other, and an International Control Commission, consisting of Canada, India, and Poland, to supervise the ceasefire . The final declaration was endorsed through recorded oral assent by the DRV, France, Britain, China, and the Soviet Union. It provided for the holding of national elections in July 1956, under the supervision of the International Control Commission, and stated that the military demarcation line was provisional and "should not in any way be interpreted as constituting a political territorial boundary." Both the United States and the Associated State of Vietnam, which France had recognized on June 4 as a "fully independent and sovereign state," refused to approve the final declaration and submitted separate declarations stating their reservations.

Charles DeGaulle and Ho Chi Minh are hanged in effigy during the National Shame Day celebration in Saigon, July 1964, observing the tenth anniversary of the July 1954 Geneva Agreements. Courtesy United States Army

The Aftermath of Geneva

The Geneva Agreements were viewed with doubt and dissatisfaction on all sides. Concern over possible United States intervention, should the Geneva talks fail, was probably a major factor in Hanoi's decision to accept the compromise agreement. The United States had dissociated itself from the final declaration, although it had stated that it would refrain from the threat or use of force to disturb the agreements. President Dwight D. Eisenhower wrote to the new Prime Minister of the Bao Dai government, Ngo Dinh Diem, in September

1954 promising United States support for a noncommunist Vietnam. Direct United States aid to South Vietnam began in January 1955, and American advisors began arriving the following month to train South Vietnamese army troops. By early 1955, Diem had consolidated his control by moving against lawless elements in the Saigon area and by suppressing the religious sects in the Mekong Delta. He also launched a "denounce the communists" campaign, in which, according to communist accounts, 25,000 communist sympathizers were arrested and more than 1,000 killed. In August 1955, Diem issued a statement formally refusing to participate in consultations with the DRV, which had been called for by the Geneva Agreement to prepare for national elections. In October, he easily defeated Bao Dai in a seriously tainted referendum and became president of the new Republic of Vietnam.

Northern Roman Catholic peasant refugee, 1954
Courtesy Indochina Archives

Despite the growing likelihood that national elections would not be held, the communist leadership in Hanoi decided for the time being to continue to concentrate its efforts on the political struggle. Several factors led to this decision, including the weakness of the party apparatus in the South, the need to concentrate on strengthening the war-weakened North, and pressure from the communist leadership of the Soviet Union, which, under General Secretary Nikita Khrushchev, had inaugurated its policy of peaceful coexistence with the West. By

1957, however, a shift to a more militant approach to the reunification of the country was apparent. Partly in response to Diem's anticommunist campaign, the Party stepped up terrorist activities in the South, assassinating several hundred officials of the Diem government. This led to the arrest of another 65,000 suspected Communists and the killing of more than 2,000 by the Saigon government in 1957. Repression by the Diem regime led to the rise of armed rebel self-defense units in various parts of the South, with the units often operating on their own without any party direction. Observing that a potential revolutionary situation had been created by popular resentment of the Diem government and fearing that the government's anticommunist policy would destroy or weaken party organization in the South, the VWP leadership determined that the time had come to resort to violent struggle.

Peasants suspected of being communists, 1966
Courtesy United States Army

Second Indochina War

By 1959 some of the 90,000 Viet Minh troops that had returned to the North following the Geneva Agreements had begun filtering back into the South to take up leadership positions in the insurgency apparat. Mass demonstrations, punctuated by an occasional raid on an isolated post, were the major activities in the initial stage of this insurgency. Communist-led uprisings launched in 1959 in the lower Mekong Delta and Central Highlands resulted in the establishment of liberated zones, including an area of nearly fifty villages in Quang Ngai Province. In areas under Communist control in 1959, the guerrillas established their own government, levied taxes, trained troops, built defense works, and provided education and medical care. In order to direct and coordinate the new policies in the South, it was necessary to revamp the party leadership apparatus and form a new united front group. Accordingly, COSVN, which had been abolished in 1954, was reestablished with General Nguyen Chi Thanh, a northerner, as chairman and Pham Hung, a southerner, as deputy chairman. On December 20, 1960, the National Front for the Liberation of South Vietnam, informally called the National Liberation Front (NLF, Mat Tran Dan Toc Giai Phong Mien Nam), was founded, with representatives on its Central Committee from all social classes, political parties, women's organizations, and religious groups, including Hoa Hao, Cao Dai, the Buddhists, and the Catholics. In order to keep the NLF from being obviously linked with the VWP and the DRV, its executive leadership consisted of individuals not publicly identified with the Communists, and the number of party members in leadership positions at all levels was strictly limited. Furthermore, in order not to alienate patriotic noncommunist elements, the new front was oriented more toward the defeat of the United Statesbacked Saigon government than toward social revolution.

The Fall of Ngo Dinh Diem

In 1961 the rapid increase of insurgency in the South Vietnamese countryside led President John F. Kennedy's administration to decide to increase United States support for the Diem regime. Some $US65 million in military equipment and $US136 million in economic aid were delivered that year, and by December 3,200 United States military personnel were in Vietnam. The United States Military Assistance Command, Vietnam (MACV) was formed under the command of General Paul D. Harkins in February 1962. The cornerstone of the counterinsurgency effort was the strategic hamlet program, which called for the consolidation of 14,000 villages of South Vietnam into 11,000 secure hamlets, each with its own houses, schools, wells, and watchtowers. The hamlets were intended to isolate guerrillas from the villages, their source of supplies and information, or, in Maoist terminology, to separate the fish from the sea in which they swim. The program had its problems, however, aside from the frequent attacks on the hamlets by guerrilla units. The self-defense units for the hamlets were often poorly trained, and support from the Army of the Republic of Vietnam (ARVN--see Glossary) was inadequate. Corruption, favoritism, and the resentment of a growing number of peasants who were forcibly being forced to resettled plagued the program. It was estimated that of the 8,000 hamlets established, only 1,500 were viable.

In response to increased United States involvement, all communist armed units in the South were unified into a single People's Liberation Armed Force (PLAF) in 1961. These troops expanded in number from fewer than 3,000 in 1959 to more than 15,000 by 1961, most of whom were assigned to guerrilla units. Southerners trained in the North who infiltrated back into the South composed an important element of this force. Although they accounted numerically for only about 20 percent of the PLAF, they provided a well-trained nucleus for the movement and often served as officers or political cadres. By late 1962, the PLAF had achieved the capability to attack fixed positions with battalionsized forces. The NLF was also expanded to include 300,000 members and perhaps 1 million sympathizers by 1962. Land reform programs were begun in liberated areas, and by 1964 approximately 1.52 million hectares had been distributed to needy peasants, according to Communist records. In the early stages, only communal lands, uncultivated lands, or lands of absentee landlords were distributed. Despite local pressure for more aggressive land reform, the peasantry generally approved of the program, and it was an important factor in gaining support for the liberation movement in the countryside. In the cities, the Workers' Liberation Association of Vietnam (Hoi Lao Dong Giai Phong Mien Nam), a labor organization affiliated with the NLF, was established in 1961.

Diem grew steadily more unpopular as his regime became more repressive. His brother and chief adviser, Ngo Dinh Nhu, was identified by regime opponents as the source of many of the government's repressive measures. Harassment of Buddhist groups by ARVN forces in early 1963 led to a crisis situation in Saigon. On May 8, 1963, ARVN troops fired into a crowd of demonstrators protesting the Diem government's discriminatory policies toward Buddhists, killing nine persons. Hundreds of Buddhist bonzes responded by staging peaceful protest demonstrations and by fasting. In June a bonze set himself on fire in Saigon as a protest, and, by the end of the year, six more bonzes had committed self-immolation. On August 21, special forces under the command of Ngo Dinh Nhu raided the pagodas of the major cities, killing many bonzes and arresting thousands of others. Following demonstrations at Saigon University on August 24, an estimated 4,000 students were rounded up and jailed, and the universities of Saigon and Hue were closed. Outraged by the Diem regime's repressive policies, the Kennedy administration indicated to South Vietnamese military leaders that Washington would be willing to support a new military government. Diem and Nhu were assassinated in a military coup in early November, and General Duong Van Minh took over the government.

Escalation of the War

Hanoi's response to the fall of the Diem regime was a subject of intense debate at the Ninth Plenum of the VWP Central Committee held in December 1963. It appeared that the new administration of President Lyndon B. Johnson (who assumed office following the assassination of President Kennedy on November 22) was not planning to withdraw from Vietnam but, rather, to increase its support for the new Saigon government. The VWP leadership concluded that only armed struggle would lead to success and called for an escalation of the war. The critical issues then became the reactions of the United States and the Soviet Union. Hanoi clearly hoped that the United States would opt for a compromise solution, as it had in Korea and Laos, and the party leaders believed that a quick and forceful escalation of the war would induce it to do so. Hanoi's decision to escalate the struggle was made in spite of the risk of damage to its relations with Moscow, which opposed the decision. The new policy also became an issue in the developing rift between Beijing and Moscow because China expressed its full support for the Vietnamese war of national liberation. As a result, Moscow's aid began to decrease as Beijing's grew.

Escalation of the war resulted in some immediate success for the struggle in the South. By 1964 a liberated zone had been established from the Central Highlands to the edge of the Mekong Delta, giving the communists control over more than half the total land area and about half the population of the South. PLAF forces totaled between 30 and 40 battalions, including 35,000 guerrillas and 80,000 irregulars. Moreover, with the completion of the so-called *Ho Chi Minh Trail* (see Glossary) through Laos, the number of PAVN troops infiltrated into the South began to increase. ARVN control was limited mainly to the cities and surrounding areas, and in 1964 and 1965 Saigon governments fell repeatedly in a series of military and civilian coups.

The Johnson administration remained hesitant to raise the American commitment to Vietnam. However, in August 1964, following the reputed shelling of United States warships in the Gulf of Tonkin off the North Vietnamese coast, Johnson approved air strikes against North Vietnamese naval bases. At President Johnson's urgent request, the United States Congress passed the Gulf of Tonkin Resolution, which gave the president the power "to take all necessary measures to repel any armed attack against the forces of the United States and to prevent further aggression." This tougher United States stance was matched in Moscow in October when Leonid Brezhnev and Aleksey Kosygin took over control of the government following the fall from power of Nikita Khrushchev. The new Soviet government pledged increased military support for Hanoi, and the NLF set up a permanent mission in Moscow.

United States support for South Vietnam, which had begun as an effort to defend Southeast Asia from the communist threat, developed into a matter of preserving United States prestige. The Johnson administration, nevertheless, was reluctant to commit combat troops to Vietnam, although the number of United States military advisers including their support and defense units had reached 16,000 by July 1964. Instead, in February 1965 the United States began a program of air strikes known as Operation Rolling Thunder against military targets in North Vietnam. Despite the bombing of the North, ARVN losses grew steadily, and the political situation in Saigon became precarious as one unstable government succeeded another. General William C. Westmoreland, commander of MACV from June 1964 to March 1968 urged the use of United States combat troops to stop the Communist advance, which he predicted, could take over the country within a year. The first two battalions of U.S. Marines (3,500 men) arrived in Vietnam in March 1965 to protect the U.S. airbase at Da Nang. The following month, Westmoreland convinced the administration to commit sufficient combat troops to secure base areas and mount a series of *search and destroy missions* (see Glossary). By late 1965, the United States expeditionary force in South Vietnam numbered 180,000, and the military situation had stabilized somewhat. Infiltration from the north, however, had also increased, although still chiefly by southerners who had gone north in 1954 and received military training. PLAF strength was estimated to be about 220,000, divided almost equally between guerrillas and main force troops, the latter including units of PAVN regulars totalling about 13,000 troops.

The United States decision to escalate the war was a surprise and a blow to party strategists in Hanoi. At the Twelfth Plenum of the Central Committee in December 1965, the decision was made to continue the struggle for liberation of the South despite the escalated American commitment. The party leadership concluded that a period of protracted struggle lay ahead in which it would be necessary to exert constant military pressure on the Saigon government and its ally in order to make the war sufficiently unpopular in Washington. Efforts were to be concentrated on the ARVN troops, which had suffered 113,000 desertions in 1965 and were thought to be on the verge of disintegration. In early 1965, Hanoi had been encouraged by Moscow's decision to increase its economic and military assistance substantially. The resulting several hundred million dollars in Soviet aid, including surface-to-air missiles, had probably been tied to a promise by Hanoi to attend an international conference on Indochina that had been proposed by Soviet premier Kosygin in February. As preconditions for these negotiations Hanoi and Washington, however, had each presented demands that were unacceptable to the other side. The DRV had called for an immediate and unconditional halt to the bombing of the north, and the United States had demanded the removal of PAVN troops from the South. Although both Hanoi and Washington had been interested in a negotiated settlement, each had preferred to postpone negotiations until it had achieved a position of strength on the battlefield.

By mid-1966 United States forces, now numbering 350,000, had gained the initiative in several key areas, pushing the communists out of the heavily populated zones of the south into the more remote mountainous regions and into areas along the Cambodian border. Revolutionary forces in the South, under the command of General Nguyen Chi Thanh, responded by launching an aggressive campaign of harassment operations and full-scale attacks by regiment-sized units. This approach proved costly, however, in terms of manpower and resources, and by late 1966 about 5,000 troops, including main force PAVN units, were being infiltrated from the North each month to help implement this strategy. At the same time, North Vietnam placed its economy on a war footing, temporarily shelving non-war-related construction efforts. As a consequence of the heavy United States bombing of the North, industries were dismantled and moved to remote areas. Young men were conscripted into the army and their places in fields and factories were filled by women, who also served in home defense and antiaircraft units. Such measures were very effective in countering the impact od the bombing on the North's war effort. The Johnson administration, however, showed no sign of willingness to change its bombing strategy or to lessen its war effort.

During this difficult period, the communists returned to protracted guerrilla warfare and political struggle. The party leadership called for increased efforts to infiltrate moderate political parties and religious organizations. The underground communist leadership in Saigon was instructed to prepare for a general uprising by recruiting youths into guerrilla units and training women to agitate against the city's poor living conditions and the injustices of the Saigon government. Total victory, according to the party leadership, would probably occur when military victories in rural areas were combined with general uprisings in the cities.

Citizens of Tay Ninh welcome the United States Army's 25th Infantry Division, August 1966.
Courtesy United States Army

In mid-1967, with United States troop levels close to the half million mark, Westmoreland requested 80,000 additional troops for immediate needs and indicated that further requests were being contemplated. United States forces in Tay Ninh, Binh Dinh, Quang Ngai, and Dinh Tuong provinces had initiated major offensives in late 1966 and in early 1967, and more troops were needed to support these and other planned operations. As a result of these deployments, United States forces were scattered from the DMZ to the Mekong Delta by mid-1967. Opposition to the war, meanwhile, was mounting in the United States; and among the Vietnamese facing one another in the South, the rising cost of men and resources was beginning to take its toll on both sides. The level of PLAF volunteers declined to less than 50 percent in 1967 and desertions rose, resulting in an even greater increase in northern troop participation. Morale declined among communist sympathizers and Saigon government supporters alike. In elections held in South Vietnam in September 1967, former generals Nguyen Van Thieu and Nguyen Cao Ky were elected president and vice president, respectively. A number of popular candidates, including Buddhists and peace candidates, were barred from running, and newspapers were largely suppressed during the campaign. Even so, the military candidates received less than 35 percent of the vote, although the election took place only in areas under the Saigon government's control. When proof of widespread election fraud was produced by the defeated candidates, students and Buddhists demonstrated and demanded that the elections be annulled.

The Tet Offensive

In mid-1967 the costs of the war mounted daily with no military victory in sight for either side. Against this background, the party leadership in Hanoi decided that the time was ripe for a general offensive in the rural areas combined with a popular uprising in the cities. The primary goals of this combined major offensive and uprising were to destabilize the Saigon regime and to force the United States to opt for a negotiated settlement. In October 1967, the first stage of the offensive began with a series of small attacks in remote and border areas designed to draw the ARVN and United States forces away from the cities. The rate of infiltration of troops from the North rose to 20,000 per month by late 1967, and the United States command in Saigon predicted a major Communist offensive early the following year. The DMZ area was expected to bear the brunt of the attack. Accordingly, United States troops were sent to strengthen northern border posts, and the security of the Saigon area was transferred to ARVN forces. Despite warnings of the impending offensive, in late January more than one-half of the ARVN forces were on leave because of the approaching Tet (Lunar New Year) holiday.

On January 31, 1968, the full-scale offensive began, with simultaneous attacks by the communists on five major cities, thirty-six provincial capitals, sixty-four district capitals, and numerous villages. In Saigon, suicide squads attacked the Independence Palace (the residence of the president), the radio station, the ARVN's joint General Staff Compound, Tan Son Nhut airfield, and the United States embassy, causing considerable damage and throwing the city into turmoil. Most of the attack forces throughout the country collapsed within a few days, often under the pressure of United States bombing and artillery attacks, which extensively damaged the urban areas. Hue, which had been seized by an estimated 12,000 Communist troops who had previously infiltrated the city, remained in communist hands until late February. A reported 2,000 to 3,000 officials, police, and others were executed in Hue during that time as counterrevolutionaries.

The Tet offensive is widely viewed as a turning point in the war despite the high cost to the communists (approximately 32,000 killed and about 5,800 captured) for what appeared at the time to be small gains. Although they managed to retain control of some of the rural areas, the communists were forced out of all of the towns and cities, except Hue, within a few weaks. Nevertheless, the offensive emphasized to the Johnson administration that victory in Vietnam would require a greater commitment of men and resources than the American people were willing to invest. On March 31, 1968, Johnson announced that he would not seek his party's nomination for another term of office, declared a halt to the bombing of North Vietnam (except for a narrow strip above the DMZ), and urged Hanoi to agree to peace talks. In the meantime, with U.S. troop strength at 525,000, a request by Westmoreland for an additional 200,000 troops was refused by a presidential commission headed by the new United States secretary of defense, Clark Clifford.

Interment for 300 unidentified victims of communist occupation of Hue in 1968
Courtesy United States Army

Following the Tet Offensive, the communists attempted to maintain their momentum through a series of attacks directed mainly at cities in the delta. Near the DMZ, some 15,000 PAVN and PLAF troops were also thrown into a three-month attack on the United States base at Khe Sanh. A second assault on Saigon, complete with rocket attacks, was launched in May. Through these and other attacks in the spring and summer of 1968, the Communists kept up pressure on the battlefield in order to strengthen their position in a projected a series of four-party peace talks scheduled to begin in January 1969 (that called for representatives of the United States, South Vietnam, North Vietnam, and the National Liberation Front to meet in Paris). In June 1969, the NLF and its allied organizations formed the Provisional Revolutionary Government of the Republic of South Vietnam (PRG), recognized by Hanoi as the legal government of South Vietnam. At that time, communist losses dating from the Tet Offensive numbered 75,000, and morale was faltering, even among the party leadership.

Newly arrived United States troops board buses at the Bien Hoa Air Terminal, February 1970.
Courtesy United States Army

Peace Negotiations

With negotiations making little progress, the United States military commander in Saigon, General Creighton W. Abrams, who had held that post since mid-1968, requested and was given permission by President Richard M. Nixon to launch secret bombing attacks, beginning March 18, 1970, on what were described as Vietnamese communist sanctuaries and supply routes inside Cambodia. In late March, Prince Norodom Sihanouk of Cambodia was ousted as chief of state in a military coup led by Premier and Defense Minister, General Lon Nol. Shortly thereafter, the Lon Nol government cancelled an agreement that had allowed North Vietnam to use the port at Sihanoukville. Hanoi reacted by increasing support to the Khmer (Kampuchean) Communist Party, by then under the leadership of the radical Pol Pot. In April, Nixon authorized the invasion of Cambodia by a joint United States-ARVN force of 30,000 troops for the purpose of destroying Communist bases across the border. Little more than short-term gains were accomplished by the invasion, which resulted in massive protests in the United States, leading to the passage of legislation by Congress requiring the removal of United States troops from Cambodia by the end of June.

In 1971 and 1972, the communists faced some serious problems unrelated to United States offensive operations. The Saigon government began to gain some support in the Mekong Delta because of the implementation of a "land-to-the-tiller" reform program pressed on the Thieu government by Washington in 1970. Almost 400,000 farmers received a total of 600,000 hectares, and by 1972 tenancy reportedly had declined from about 60 percent to 34 percent in some rural areas. In addition, a People's Self-Defense Force Program begun about this time had some success in freeing ARVN troops for combat duty, as United States forces were gradually withdrawn. Although it wasn't clear at the time whether the withdrawal of United States troops would cause the ARVN to crumble instantly, as predicted by the communists, the decisive defeat of an ARVN operation mounted against the Ho Chi Minh Trail in Laos in March 1971 was an early indication. At the time of the ARVN defeat, however, the communists were coping with deteriorating morale and with dwindling numbers of troops; a rising desertion rate and falling recruitment levels had reduced PLAF strength from 250,000 in 1968 to less than 200,000 in 1971.

Bicycles used to transport rice on the Ho Chi Minh Trail, captured during United States operations in Cambodia, spring 1970. Courtesy United States Army

Both on the battlefield and at the conference table, a stalemate of sorts was reached by mid-1971. In negotiations there was some flexibility, as Washington offered a unilateral withdrawal of United States forces provided Hanoi stopped its infiltration of the South; and Hanoi countered by agreeing to a coalition government in Saigon along with a United States troop withdrawal and to a cease-fire following the formation of a new government. The main point of debate was the retention of President Thieu as head of the South Vietnamese government, which Washington demanded and Hanoi rejected. To break the deadlock, the party leadership in Hanoi turned again to the strategy of a general offensive and uprising. Accordingly, the so-called Easter offensive was launched beginning on March 30, 1972, with a threepronged attack across the DMZ through the A Shau Valley. The following day the communists attacked the city of Kontum and the provinces of Binh Dinh and Phuoc Tuy, threatening to cut South Vietnam in two. A few days later, three PAVN divisions attacked Binh Long Province along the Cambodian border, placing the capital, An Loc, under siege. In

May the communists captured Quang Tri Province, including the capital, which was not recaptured by the ARVN until September. By that time, Quang Tri city had been virtually leveled by United States airstrikes. Although the Easter offensive did not result in the fall of the Saigon government, as the communists had hoped, it did further destabilize the government and reveal the ARVN's weaknesses. The costs were great on both sides, however, and by October both Hanoi and Washington were more inclined to negotiate. By then Hanoi had agreed to accept Thieu as president of a future Saigon government in exchange for the removal of United States forces without a corresponding removal of PAVN troops. Thieu's objections to the failure to require the removal of North Vietnamese forces was in the end ignored, and the Agreement on Ending the War and Restoring Peace in Vietnam was signed in Paris on January 27, 1973.

The Final Campaign

Although the terms of the peace agreement were less than the communists had hoped for, the accords did permit them to participate in the new government legally and recognized their right to control certain areas. Most important, the removal of United States forces gave the communists a welcome breathing space, allowing them to concentrate on political efforts. In the initial period after the signing of the agreement, the party leadership viewed armed struggle as a last resort only because it was feared that the United States might reintroduce its forces. PLAF troops were instructed to limit their use of force to selfdefense . Meanwhile, the Thieu government embarked on pacification efforts along the central coast and in the Mekong Delta, which resulted in a reduction of the area under official communist control to about 20 percent of the South. The Saigon government, however, faced serious difficulties, including the negative effect on the economy of the withdrawal of United States forces and a critical refugee problem. During the course of the war, several million Vietnamese had been evacuated or had fled from their villages to find safety and jobs in urban areas. Most of these remained unemployed and, together with militant Buddhist groups, the Cao Dai, and the Hoa Hao, represented a sizable wellspring of discontent with the Thieu government.

In early 1974, the communists launched a campaign to regain the territory they had lost since the cease-fire. Raids were conducted on roads, airfields, and economic installations; the flow of supplies and equipment from the North was stepped up; and a 19,000-kilometer network of roads leading from the DMZ in Quang Tri Province to Loc Ninh, northwest of Saigon, was completed. By summer the communists were moving cautiously forward, seizing vulnerable areas in the Central Highlands and in the provinces around Saigon. There was no direct response from the United States, and the resignation of Nixon in August convinced the party leadership that further United States intervention was unlikely. ARVN forces continued to deteriorate, suffering high casualties and facing a lack of ammunition and spare parts. The party leadership met in October to plan a 1975 military offensive concentrating on the Cambodian border area and the Central Highlands. The taking of the Phuoc Lang province capital, Phuoc Binh (now Ba Ra in Song Be Province), in early January was followed by a surprise attack in March on Ban Me Thuot, the largest city in the Central Highlands. President Thieu ordered ARVN units at Pleiku and Kontum to leave the highlands and withdraw to the coast to regroup for a counter attack on Ban Me Thuot. The ARVN strategic withdrawal became a rout, however, because PAVN units had already cut the main roads to the coast and fleeing civilians clogged the secondary roads as panic ensued. By the end of March, eight northern provinces had fallen to the communist forces, including the cities of Hue and Da Nang. Buoyed by this stunning victory, the party leadership directed the commander of revolutionary forces in the South, General Van Tien Dung to prepare for an offensive against Saigon. In early April, PAVN and PLAF troops moved south and began an encirclement of the capital. On April 20, after ten days of stiff resistance, the ARVN Eighteenth Division, stationed thirty kilometers north of Saigon, finally crumbled under the attack of three PAVN divisions. With Saigon in a state of panic, President Thieu resigned the following day and was replaced by Vice President Tran Van Huong. Duong Van Minh, thought to be more acceptable to the communists, took over the presidency on April 28. The communists refused to negotiate, however, and fifteen PAVN battalions began to move toward Saigon. On April 30, communist forces entered the capital, and Duong Van Minh ordered ARVN troops to lay down their arms.

Nearly thirty years had passed since Ho Chi Minh first declared Vietnam's independence as a unified nation in September 1945. In the interim, an entire generation of Vietnamese had endured a divided Vietnam, knowing only continuous warfare. The events of April 1975 not only abruptly concluded the war but also prepared the way for the official reunification of the country the following year, when the Vietnamese people were brought together under one independent government for the first time in more than a century.

* * *

The body of literature in English on the history of Vietnam has increased dramatically since the mid-1960s. Most of the writing, however, has focused on the three decades of war in that country following World War II. The increased interest in Vietnam, nevertheless, has prompted a number of historians to take the longer view--the Vietnamese view--of history and to examine earlier time periods.

Based on Vietnamese and Chinese sources, and particularly useful for Vietnamese history from the earliest traditions up to the end of the Chinese millennium, is Keith Weller Taylor's *Birth of Vietnam*. Also treating this period, as well as the period up through World War II, is Thomas Hodgkin's, *Vietnam: The Revolutionary Path*. Hodgkin gives detailed coverage of the 900-year period of Vietnamese independence, while D.G.E. Hall's classic *History of South-East Asia* provides a description and analysis of that period within the larger Southeast Asian context. Another useful single-volume history of Vietnam up to 1968 is Joseph Buttinger's *Vietnam: A Political History*. Finally, Alexander Woodside in *Vietnam and the Chinese Model* presents an interesting analysis, based on Vietnamese and Chinese sources, of Chinese influence on Vietnamese education, administration, education, literature, and law during the nineteenth century.

J. F. Cady treats in detail the French conquest and early colonial period in *The Roots of French Imperialism in Eastern Asia*. David Marr uses Vietnamese source materials to examine the roots of Vietnamese nationalism in *Vietnamese Anticolonialism, 1885-1925*, and William Duiker in *The Rise of Nationalism in Vietnam, 1900-1941* carries the examination of the nationalist movement up to the early period of Japanese occupation. Duiker also traces the communist movement from its origins to the reunification of the country in *The Communist Road to Power in Vietnam*.

Although their focus is somewhat peripheral to an overview history of Vietnam, there are a number of accounts of the United States involvement in Vietnam that bear mentioning, including: William Turley's *The Second Indochina War*; Ronald Spector's *Advice and Support: The Early Years, 1941-1960*; R.B. Smith's *An International History of the Vietnam War*; Stanley Karnow's *Vietnam: A History*; and George Mc T. Kahin's, *Intervention: How America Became Involved in Vietnam*.

Kham Thien Street Memorial in Hanoi depicting a mother and child standing on a United States Air Force bomb fragment. Courtesy Bill Herod

THE SOCIETY AND ITS ENVIRONMENT

Several months before his death in 1969, Ho Chi Minh declared that Vietnam would "certainly be reunified under the same roof" no matter what difficulties and hardships might lie ahead. In 1976 the country was territorially reunited--under Hanoi's roof-- after more than twenty years of separation. This historic event proved, however, to be only the first step toward the ultimate test of reunification--the development of sociocultural, economic, and political processes that could best serve the aspirations and needs of the Vietnamese people. In 1987 Vietnam was, in some respects, still a divided nation and still at war-- not for liberation from the bondage of neo-colonialism but for the triumph of socialism in what was officially called the struggle between the socialist and the capitalist paths.

The struggle between socialism and capitalism unfolded in an environment of social and religious patterns molded by centuries of cultural influences from Confucianism, Buddhism, Taoism, indigenous animism and, more recently, Roman Catholicism. The communist government disparaged some of these influences as feudal, backward, superstitious, reactionary, or bourgeois and targeted them for reform. Others, including Buddhism, Catholicism, and minor faiths, were tolerated.

The Vietnamese people were continually urged to discard vestiges of the old society and to adopt instead new values associated with love of labor, collective ownership, patriotism, socialism, and the proletarian dictatorship under the Vietnamese Communist Party (VCP, Viet Nam Cong San Dan). In 1987 these values were at best an abstraction to most Vietnamese, except perhaps for a fraction of the party's fewer than 2 million members. Despite the increasing dependence of families, simply for subsistence, on organizations sponsored by collectives and the state, the strongest bond in the society by far was that of family loyalty. Such loyalty was particularly evident after the mid-1970s, when living conditions deteriorated amid indications of growing government corruption.

Much of Vietnam's contemporary history has been a grim struggle, not on behalf of patriotism or socialism but for survival. With a per capita income estimated at less than US$200 per year, the Vietnamese people in the 1980s remained among the poorest in the world. In 1987 the society was predominantly rural; more than 80 percent of the population resided in villages and engaged primarily in farming. Among the urban population, party and government officials supplanted the former elite, whose privileged status had been derived mainly from wealth and higher education. In theory, Vietnam had eliminated all exploiting classes by developing a class structure composed of workers, peasants, and socialist intellectuals. In practice, a small-scale bourgeoisie continued to operate in the South's industrial sector with the permission of the state, and, according to an official source, some cadres in the south were exploiting peasants in the tradition of former landowners.

Theoretically the society is multiracial, but actually it is dominated by an ethnic Vietnamese elite. Vietnamese, who outnumber other ethnic groups, are overwhelmingly lowlanders; minority peoples, who are divided into nearly sixty groups of various sizes and backgrounds, are mostly highlanders. With the exception of the Chinese, or *Hoa* (see Glossary), who are mostly lowlanders, the minority peoples traditionally lived apart from one another and from the Vietnamese. In the 1980s, however, the distance between the highland and lowland communities gradually narrowed as a result of the government policy of population redistribution and political integration.

Under this policy, lowlanders were sent to remote, uninhabited areas of the highlands both to relieve overcrowdingin the cities and in the congested Red River Delta-and to increase food production. Both aims were part of the government's effort to raise the standard of living, which in turn was linked to another urgent national priority--family planning. In 1987 the rate of population growth continued to outstrip food production. Given the people's traditional belief in large families, the government faced a major challenge in its attempt to reduce the annual rate of population growth to 1.7 percent or less by 1990.

Geography

Vietnam is located in the southeastern extremity of the Indochinese peninsula and occupies about 331,688 square kilometers, of which about 25 percent was under cultivation in 1987. The S-shaped country has a north-to-south distance of 1,650 kilometers and is about 50 kilometers wide at the narrowest point. With a coastline of 3,260 kilometers, excluding islands, Vietnam claims 12 nautical miles as the limit of its territorial waters, an additional 12 nautical miles as a contiguous customs and security zone, and 200 nautical miles as an exclusive economic zone.

The boundary with Laos, settled, on an ethnic basis, between the rulers of Vietnam and Laos in the mid-seventeenth century, was formally defined by a delimitation treaty signed in 1977 and ratified in 1986. The frontier with Cambodia, defined at the time of French annexation of the western part of the Mekong River Delta in 1867, remained essentially unchanged, according to Hanoi, until some unresolved border issues were finally settled in the 1982-85 period. The land and sea boundary with China, delineated under the France-China treaties of 1887 and 1895, is "the frontier line" accepted by Hanoi that China agreed in 1957- 58 to respect. However, in February 1979, following China's limited invasion of Vietnam, Hanoi complained that from 1957 onward China had provoked numerous border incidents as part of its anti-Vietnam policy and expansionist designs in Southeast Asia. Among the territorial infringements cited was the Chinese occupation in January 1974 of the Paracel Islands, claimed by both countries in a dispute left unresolved in the 1980s (see Foreign Relations).

Vietnam is a country of tropical lowlands, hills, and densely forested highlands, with level land covering no more than 20 percent of the area. The country is divided into the highlands and the Red River Delta in the north; and the Giai Truong Son (Central mountains, or the Chaîne Annamitique, sometimes referred to simply as the Chaîne), the coastal lowlands, and the Mekong River Delta in the south.

The Red River Delta, a flat, triangular region of 3,000 square kilometers, is smaller but more intensely developed and more densely populated than the Mekong River Delta. Once an inlet of the Gulf of Tonkin, it has been filled in by the enormous alluvial deposits of the rivers, over a period of millennia, and it advances one hundred meters into the gulf annually. The ancestral home of the ethnic Vietnamese, the delta accounted for almost 70 percent of the agriculture and 80 percent of the industry of North Vietnam before 1975.

The Red River (Song Hong in Vietnamese), rising in China's Yunnan Province, is about 1,200 kilometers long. Its two main tributaries, the Song Lo (also called the Lo River, the Riviere Claire, or the Clear River) and the Song Da (also called the Black River or Riviere

Noire), contribute to its high water volume, which averages 500 million cubic meters per second, but may increase by more than 60 times at the peak of the rainy season. The entire delta region, backed by the steep rises of the forested highlands, is no more than three meters above sea level, and much of it is one meter or less. The area is subject to frequent flooding; at some places the high-water mark of floods is fourteen meters above the surrounding countryside. For centuries flood control has been an integral part of the delta's culture and economy. An extensive system of dikes and canals has been built to contain the Red River and to irrigate the rich rice-growing delta. Modeled on that of China, this ancient system has sustained a highly concentrated population and has made double-cropping wet-rice cultivation possible throughout about half the region (see figure 1).

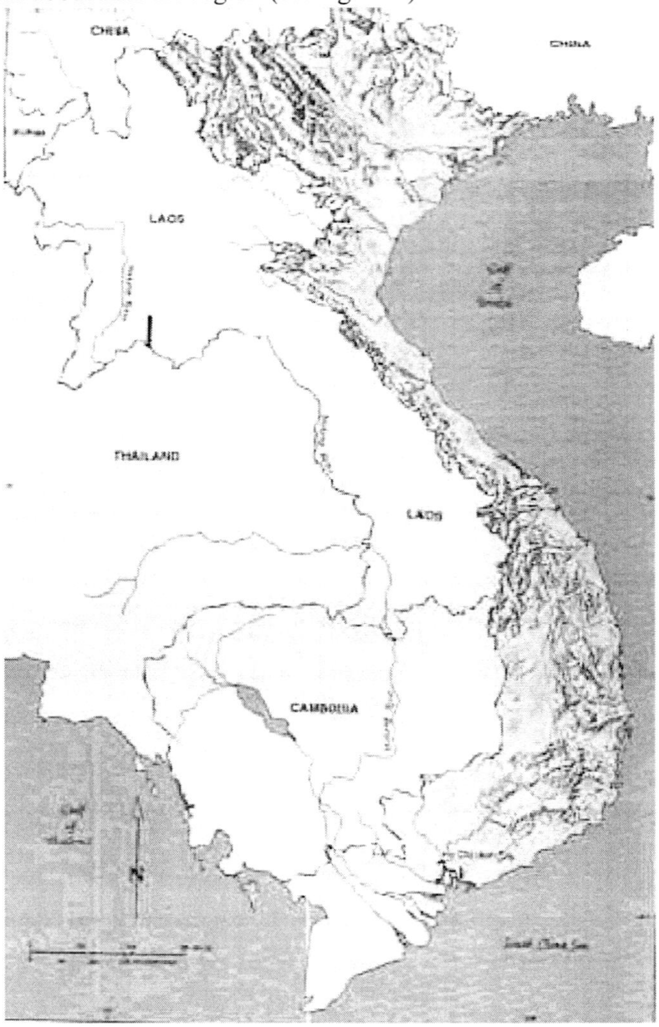

Figure 1. Topography and Drainage, 1987

The highlands and mountain plateaus in the north and northwest are inhabited mainly by tribal minority groups. The Giai Truong Son originates in the Xizang (Tibet) and Yunnan regions of southwest China and forms Vietnam's border with Laos and Cambodia. It terminates in the Mekong River Delta north of Ho Chi Minh City (formerly Saigon).

These central mountains, which have several high plateaus, are irregular in elevation and form. The northern section is narrow and very rugged; the country's highest peak, Fan Si Pan, rises to 3,142 meters in the extreme northwest. The southern portion has numerous spurs that divide the narrow coastal strip into a series of compartments. For centuries these topographical features not only rendered north-south communication difficult but also formed an effective natural barrier for the containment of the people living in the Mekong basin.

Within the southern portion of Vietnam is a plateau known as the Central Highlands (Tay Nguyen), approximately 51,800 square kilometers of rugged mountain peaks, extensive forests, and rich soil. Comprising 5 relatively flat plateaus of basalt soil spread over the provinces of Dac Lac and Gia Lai-Kon Tom, the highlands accounts for 16 percent of the country's arable land and 22 percent of its total forested land. Before 1975 North Vietnam had maintained that the Central Highlands and the Giai Truong Son were strategic areas of paramount importance, essential to the domination not only of South Vietnam but also of the southern part of Indochina. Since 1975 the highlands have provided an area in which to relocate people from the densely populated lowlands.

The narrow, flat coastal lowlands extend from south of the Red River Delta to the Mekong River basin. On the landward side, the Giai Truong Son rises precipitously above the coast, its spurs jutting into the sea at several places. Generally the coastal strip is fertile and rice is cultivated intensively.

The Mekong, which is 4,220 kilometers long, is one of the 12 great rivers of the world. From its source in the Xizang plateau, it flows through the Xizang and Yunnan regions of China, forms the boundary between Laos and Burma as well as between Laos and Thailand, divides into two branches--the Song Han Giang and Song Tien Giang--below Phnom Penh, and continues through Cambodia and the Mekong basin before draining into the South China Sea through nine mouths or *cuu long* (nine dragons). The river is heavily silted and is navigable by seagoing craft of shallow draft as far as Kompong Cham in Cambodia. A tributary entering the river at Phnom Penh drains the Tonle Sap, a shallow fresh- water lake that acts as a natural reservoir to stabilize the flow of water through the lower Mekong. When the river is in flood stage, its silted delta outlets are unable to carry off the high volume of water. Floodwaters back up into the Tonle Sap, causing the lake to inundate as much as 10,000 square kilometers. As the flood subsides, the flow of water reverses and proceeds from the lake to the sea. The effect is to reduce significantly the danger of devastating floods in the Mekong delta, where the river floods the surrounding fields each year to a level of one to two meters.

The Mekong delta, covering about 40,000 square kilometers, is a low-level plain not more than three meters above sea level at any point and criss-crossed by a maze of canals and rivers. So much sediment is carried by the Mekong's various branches and tributaries that the delta advances sixty to eighty meters into the sea every year. An official Vietnamese source estimates the amount of sediment deposited annually to be about 1 billion cubic meters, or nearly 13 times the amount deposited by the Red River. About 10,000 square kilometers of the delta are under rice cultivation, making the area one of the major rice-growing regions of the world. The southern tip, known as the Ca Mau Peninsula (Mui Bai Bung), is covered by dense jungle and mangrove swamps.

Vietnam has a tropical monsoon climate, with humidity averaging 84 percent throughout the year. However, because of differences in latitude and the marked variety of topographical relief, the climate tends to vary considerably from place to place. During the winter or dry season, extending roughly from November to April, the monsoon winds usually blow from the northeast along the China coast and across the Gulf of Tonkin, picking up considerable moisture; consequently the winter season in most parts of the country is dry only by comparison with the rainy or summer season. During the southwesterly summer monsoon, occurring from May to October, the heated air of the Gobi Desert rises, far to the north, inducing moist air to flow inland from the sea and deposit heavy rainfall.

Annual rainfall is substantial in all regions and torrential in some, ranging from 120 centimeters to 300 centimeters. Nearly 90 percent of the precipitation occurs during the summer. The average annual temperature is generally higher in the plains than in the mountains and plateaus. Temperatures range from a low of 5°C in December and January, the coolest months, to more than 37°C in April, the hottest month. Seasonal divisions are more clearly marked in the northern half than in the southern half of the country, where, except in some of the highlands, seasonal temperatures vary only a few degrees, usually in the 21°C-28°C range.

Population

According to Hanoi, the population of Vietnam was almost 60 million at the end of 1985 (Western sources estimated about a half million more than that in mid-1985). Vietnamese officials estimated that the population would be at least 66 million by 1990 and 80 million by the year 2000, unless the growth rate of 2 percent per year used for these estimates was lowered to 1.7 percent by 1990. With declining mortality rates achieved through improved health conditions, the population increased by 1.2 million or more per year between 1981 and 1986 (1.5 million in 1985 alone), worsening the country's chronic food shortage. In the 1980s, Vietnam needed to produce an additional 400,000 tons of food each year just to keep pace with its rapidly increasing population.

Census results of October 1979 showed the total population of reunified Vietnam to be 52.7 million of which 52 percent lived in the North and 48 percent in the South. About 19 percent of the population was classified as urban and 81 percent as rural. Females outnumbered males by 3 percent, and the average life expectancy at birth was 66 for females and 63 for males. With 52 percent of the total under 20 years of age, the population was young. Ethnically, 87 percent were Vietnamese-speaking lowlanders known as Viet or Kinh, and the remainder were Hoa or members of highland minority groups (see Ethnic Groups and Languages). In December 1986, Hanoi estimated that more than 1 million Vietnamese lived overseas, 50 percent of them in the United States. A Vietnamese source in Paris claimed that about half of Ho Chi Minh City's population lived completely or partially on family aid packages sent by Vietnamese emigres abroad.

Beginning in the early 1960s, the socioeconomic implications of rapid population growth became an increasing concern of the government in Hanoi. A family planning drive, instituted in 1963, was claimed by the government to have accounted for a decline in the annual growth rate in the North from 3.4 percent in 1960 to 2.7 percent in 1975. In the South, however, family planning was actively encouraged only after 1976, and the results were mixed, consistently falling short of announced goals. In 1981 Hanoi set a national goal of 1.7 percent growth rate to be achieved by the end of 1985: a growth rate of 1.3 to 1.5 percent was established for the North, 1.5 to 1.7 percent for the South, and 1.7 to 2.0 percent for the sparsely settled highland provinces. In 1987, the growth rate, according to Vietnamese sources, was about 2.0 percent (see Table 1).

Table 1. Population, 1979, 1984 and 1988(in thousands)

Place	1979 Census Population	Estimated 1984 Population	Estimated 1988 Population
Municipalities			
Hanoi	2,571	2,878	3,170
Haiphong	1,279	1,397	1,500
Ho Chi Minh City	3,420	3,564	3,685
Provinces			
An Giang	1,532	1,765	1,980
Bac Thai	815	903	980
Ben Tre	1,042	1,164	1,275
Binh Tri Thien	1,902	2,020	2,120
Cao Bang	480	540	595
Cuu Long	1,504	1,686	1,850
Dac Lac	490	611	735
Dong Nai	1,305	1,502	1,690
Dong Thap	1,183	1,314	1,430
Gia Lai-Kon Tum	596	692	785
Ha Bac	1,663	1,892	2,110
Ha Nam Ninh	2,781	3,061	3,315
Ha Son Binh	1,537	1,705	1,850
Ha Tuyen	782	881	975
Hai Hung	2,145	2,396	2,625
Hau Giang	2,233	2,495	2,735
Hoang Lien Son	778	866	950
Kien Giang	995	1,123	1,245
Lai Chau	322	378	432
Lam Dong	397	487	580
Lang Son	485	534	580
Long An	957	1,081	1,195
Minh Hai	1,220	1,550	1,900
Nghe Tinh	3,112	3,398	3,655
Nghia Binh	2,095	2,355	2,600
Phu Khanh	1,189	1,332	1,465
Quang Nam-Da Nang	1,530	1,678	1,810
Quang Ninh	750	812	870
Son La	488	562	635
Song Be	659	734	805
Tay Ninh	684	758	830
Thai Binh	1,506	1,653	1,790
Thanh Hoa	2,532	2,780	3,010
Thuan Hai	938	1,085	1,220
Tien Giang	1,265	1,388	1,505
Vinh Phu	1,488	1,656	1,805
Special Zone			
Vung Tau-Con Dao	92	94	98
TOTAL	52,742	58,770	64,385

Family planning was described as voluntary and dependent upon persuasion. The program's guidelines called for two children per couple, births spaced five years apart, and a minimum age of twenty-two for first-time mothers--a major challenge in a society where the customary age for women to marry, especially in the rural areas, was nineteen or twenty. Campaign workers were instructed to refrain tactfully from mentioning abortion and to focus instead on pregnancy prevention when dealing with people of strong religious conviction. Enlisting the support of Catholic priests for the campaign was strongly encouraged. In 1987 it was evident that the government was serious about family planning; a new law on marriage and the family adopted in December 1986 made family planning obligatory, and punitive measures, such as pay cuts and denial of bonuses and promotions, were introduced for non-compliance.

A substantial portion of the population had mixed feelings about birth control and sex education, and the number of women marrying before age twenty remained high. Typically, a woman of child-bearing age had four or more children. The 1986 family law that raised the legal marriage age for women to twenty-two met with strenuous opposition. Critics argued that raising the legal age offered no solution to the widespread practice among Vietnamese youth of "falling in love early, having sexual relations early, and getting married early." Some critics even advanced the view that the population should be increased to further economic development; others insisted that those who could grow enough food for themselves need not practice birth control. A significant proportion of the population retained traditional attitudes which favored large families with many sons as a means of insuring the survival of a family's lineage and providing for its security. Although problems associated with urban living, such as inadequate housing and unemployment, created a need for change in traditional family-size standards, old ways nevertheless persisted. They were perpetuated in proverbs like "If Heaven procreates elephants, it will provide enough grass to feed them" or "To have one son is to have; to have ten daughters is not to have."

Government authorities were concerned over the lack of coordination among agencies involved in family planning and the lack of necessary clinics and funding to provide convenient, safe, and efficient family planning services in rural areas. Even more disturbing was the knowledge that many local party committees and government agencies were only going through the motions of supporting the family planning drive. To remedy the situation, the government in 1984 created the National Committee on Family Planning (also known as the National Commission on Demography and Family Planning, or the National Population and Parenthood Commission). The commission was directed to increase the rate of contraceptive use among married couples from about 23 percent in 1983 to 70 percent by 1990 and to limit the population to between 75 and 80 million by the year 2000. The latter goal was to be based on an annual growth rate of 1.7 percent or less, a figure that in 1987 seemed unrealistically low. According to a National Committee on Family Planning report released in February 1987, the population grew by 2.2 percent in 1986 (Western analysts estimate the increase to have been between 2.5 and 2.8 percent). In light of the 1986 growth rate, the committee's target for 1987 was revised at the beginning of the year to 1.9 percent. Even if such a goal were met, Vietnam's population at the end of 1987 would stand in excess of 63 million inhabitants.

The average population density in 1985 was 179 persons per square kilometer. Population density varied widely, however, and was generally lower in the southern provinces than in the northern ones; in both North and South it was also lower in the highlands and mountainous regions than in the lowlands. The most densely settled region was the Red River Delta, accounting for roughly 75 percent of the population of the North. Also heavily settled was the Mekong River Delta, with nearly half of the southern population.

After 1976, population redistribution became a pressing issue because of food shortages and unemployment in the urban areas. A plan unveiled at the Fourth National Party Congress in December 1976 called for the relocation of 44 million people by 1980 and an additional 10 million by the mid-1990s. The plan also called for opening up 1 million hectares of virgin land to cultivation and introduced a measure designed to divert some armed forces personnel to the building of *new economic zones* (see Glossary). The relocation was to involve an interregional transfer of northerners to the South as well as an intraregional movement of lowlanders to upland areas in both the North and the South. Between 1976 and 1980, most of the 4 million people who were relocated to rural areas and the new economic zones were from Ho Chi Minh City and other southern cities. In the 1981-85 period, a total of about 0.6 million workers and 1.3 million dependents were relocated, causing the country's urban population to decline from 19.3 percent of the total in 1979 to 18 percent in 1985. The country's long-range goal, established in 1976, called for the population to be distributed more or less evenly throughout Vietnam's 443 districts with an average for each district of 200,000 persons living on 20,000 hectares.

Ethnic Groups and Languages

The ethnic Vietnamese are concentrated largely in the alluvial deltas and in the coastal plains, having little in common with the minority peoples of the highlands, whom they historically have regarded as hostile and barbaric. A homogenous social group, the Vietnamese exert influence on national life through their control of political and economic affairs and their role as purveyors of the dominant culture. By contrast, the ethnic minorities, except for the Hoa, are found mostly in the highlands that cover two-thirds of the national territory. The Hoa, the largest minority, are mainly lowlanders. Officially, the ethnic minorities are referred to as national minorities.

Vietnamese

The origins of the Vietnamese are generally traced to the inhabitants of the Red River Delta between 500 and 200 B.C., people who were a mixture of Australoid, Austronesian, and Mongoloid stock. Like their contemporary descendants, they were largely villagers, skilled in rice cultivation and fishing (see Early History).

Contemporary ethnic Vietnamese live in urban as well as rural areas, are engaged in a variety of occupations, and are represented at all levels on the socioeconomic scale. The power elite (senior officials in the party, government, and military establishments), in particular, is dominated by ethnic Vietnamese. Although predominantly Buddhist, the Vietnamese people's religious beliefs and practices nevertheless include remnants of an earlier animistic faith. A sizable minority is Roman Catholic. Despite some regional and local differences in customs and speech, the people retain a strong sense of ethnic identity that rests on a common language and a shared cultural heritage.

Tonkinese woman, late nineteenth century
Courtesy New York Times, Paris Collection, National Archives

Vietnamese, the official language, is the mother tongue of the vast majority of the people and is understood by many national minority members. According to a widely accepted theory, Vietnamese is believed to be related to the Austroasiatic family of languages, which includes various languages, dialects, and subdialects spoken in mainland Southeast Asia from Burma to Vietnam. Scholarship nonetheless is tentative on whether Vietnamese, which was spoken in the Red River Delta long before the Christian era, was influenced by Mon-Khmer or Tai, both Austroasiatic subsets.

Actually, the Vietnamese language was influenced more by classical Chinese than by any other language. During more than 1,000 years of Chinese rule and for centuries afterwards, Chinese was the language of officialdom, scholarship, and literature. The Chinese language had special status because of its identification with the ruling class of scholar-officials.

Nevertheless, Vietnamese continued to be the popular language, even though knowledge of Chinese was a prerequisite to government employment and social advancement.

Beginning in the eighth or ninth century, the Vietnamese devised a popular script based on Chinese characters to express written ideas and to standardize the phonetics of their own language. Well developed by the thirteenth century, this system, which combined ideographs and phonetics, became the medium for a growing popular literature. The system is known as *chu nom*, literally "southern character" or "southern writing," or simply *nom*. Although disdained by orthodox Confucian scholars, *chu nom* had a distinct place in the evolution of Vietnam's vernacular literature through the end of the nineteenth century.

In the seventeenth century, the Vietnamese language evolved further when Portuguese and French missionaries developed a new transcription that used roman letters instead of Chinese characters. The new system, called *quoc ngu*, was devised as a tool for their missionary activities, including the translation of prayer books and catechisms. By the end of the nineteenth century, it had become the common method of writing, gradually replacing classical Chinese and *chu nom*. *Quoc ngu* uses diacritical marks above or below letters to indicate variations in the pronunciation of vowels and of consonants, and differentiations in tones. Since most single syllables function as meaningful words identified only by tone, and each of these phonetic syllables can have numerous meanings, the diacritical marks are an essential part of the new written system (see Nine Centuries of Independence).

Under French rule, the French language was widely used in the cities, and it was read and spoken by all secondary-school graduates. Many less educated people, including merchants, lowranking civil servants, army veterans, and domestics working for French households, also had some familiarity with the language, although their knowledge might be limited to a form of pidgin French. In the rural areas the language generally was less wellknown , but a number of minority peoples learned its rudiments in school or during service with the French army. Use of the French language resulted in minor changes in the grammatical structure of Vietnamese and in the addition of some new technical, scientific, and popular terms.

Minorities

Living somewhat separately from the dominant ethnic Vietnamese are the numerous minorities. The 1979 census listed fifty-three minorities accounting for 12.7 percent (6.6 million persons) of the national population. This figure included the Hoa (Han Chinese), the single largest bloc--representing approximately 1.5 percent of the total population, or about 935,000 people--in the lowland urban centers of both the North and the South. Of the other minority groups, thirty, comprising 68 percent of the minority population (4.5 million persons), resided in the North, while the remaining twenty-two groups, comprising 32 percent of the minority population (2.1 million persons) lived in the South. The size of each community ranged from fewer than 1,000 to as many as 0.9 million persons, and 10 major groups comprised about 85 percent of the minority population (see table 2).

Minorities that live in the mountainous regions are known by their generic name, Montagnards. The Vietnamese also disparagingly call them "moi," meaning savage. The government attributes the backwardness of the Montagnards to the overwhelming influence of their history as exploited and oppressed peoples. They are darker skinned than their lowland neighbors.

Table 3. Ethnic Composition, 1979

Ethnic group	Alternate names	Principal areas of residence (provinces)	Population [1]
Viet	Kinh	Throughout the nation	46,065,400
Hoa (Han, Chinese)	Trieu Chau, Phuc Kien, Quang Dong, Hai Nam, Ha, Xa Phang	Ho Chi Minh City, Hanoi, Hau Ginag, Dong Nai, Minh Hai, Kien Giang, Haiphong Cuu Long	935,100
Tay	Tho, Ngan, Phen, Thu, Lao, Pa, Zi	Cao Bang, Lang Son, Ha, Tuyen, Bac Thai, Hoang Lien Son, Quang Ninh, Ha Bac, Lam Dong	901,800
Thai	Tai, Tai Khao (White Thai), Tay Dam (Black Thai), Tai Moui, Tai Thanh (Man Thanh, Hang Tong (Tai Muong), Pu Thay, Tho Da Bac	Son La, Nghe Tinh, Thanh Hoa, Lai Chau, Hoang Lien, Ha Son Binh, Lam Dong	766,700
Khmer	Cur, Cul, Cu, Tho, Khmer-Vietnamese, Khmer Krom	Hau Giang, Cuu Long, Kien Giang, Minh Hai, Ho Chi Minh City, Song Be Tay Ninh	717,300
Muong	Mol, Mual, Moi, Moi Bi, Ao Ta (Au Ta)	Ha Son Binh, Thanh Hoa, Vin Phu, Hoang Lien Son, Son La, Ha Nam Ninh	686,100
Nung	Xuong, Giang, Nung An, Phan Sinh, Nung Chao, Loi, Quy Rin, Khen Lai	Cao Bang, Lang Son, Bac Thai, Ha Tuyen, Ha Bac, Hoang Lien Son, Quang Ninh, Ho Chi Minh City, Lam Dong	559,700
Hmong (Meo)	Meo Hoa, Meo Xanh, Meo Do, Meo Den, Na Mieo, Man Trang	Ha Tuyen, Hoang Lien Son, Lai Chau, Son La, Cao Bang, Lang Son, Nghe Tinh	411,100
Zao	Man, Dong, Trai, Xa, Ziu, Mien, Kiem Mien, Quan Chet, Lo Gang, Zao Tien, Thanh Thah Y, Lan Ten, Dai Ban, Tieu Ban Coc Ngang, Coc Mun Son Dau	Ha Tuyen, Hoang Lien Son, Cao Bang, Lang Son, Bac Thai, Lai Chau, Son La, Ha Son Binh, Vinh Phu, Ha Bac, Thanh Hoa, Quang Ninh	346,800
Jarai	Giorai, Chorai, Tobuan, Hobau, Hdrung, Chor	Gia Lai-Kon Tum	184,500
Ede	Rhade, De, Kpa, Adham, Krung Ktul, Dlie Rue, Blo, Epan, Mdhur, Bih	Dac Lac, Phu Khanh	140,900
Bahnar	Golar, Tolo, Gho long, (Y-lang), Rengao, Ro Ngao, Kren, Roh, Kon Kde, A-la Kong, Kpang Kong, Bo Man	Gia Lai-Kon Tum, Nghia Binh, Phu Khanh	109,100
San Chay (Cao Lan-San Chi)	Cao Lan, Man Cao Lan, Hon Ban, San Chi (also called Son Tu but excludes the San Chi of Bao Lac and Cho Ra)	Bac Thai, Quang Ninh, Ha Bac, Cao Bang Lang Son, Ha Tuyen	77,100
Cham	Chiem Thanh, Hroi	Thuan Hai, An Giang, Ho Chi Minh City, Nghia Binh, Phu Khan	77,000
Sadang	Xo Teng, Hdang, To Trah, Mo Nam, Ha Lang, Ka Dong, Km Rang, Con Lan, Bri La, Tang	Gia Lai-Kon Tum, Quang Nam-Da-Nang	73,100
Kohor	Xre, Nop (Tu-lop), Codon Chil, Lat (Lach), Trinh	Lam Dong, Thuan Hai	70,500
Hre	Cham Re, Chom, Kre, Luy	Nghia Binh	66,900
San Ziu	San Zeo, Trai, Trai Dat, Man Quan Coc	Bac Thai, Vinh Phu, Ha Bac, Quang Ninh, Ha Tuyen	65,800
Raglai	Ra Clay, Rai, Noang, La Oang	Thuan Hai, Phu Khanh	58,000
Mnong	Phong, Nong, Pre, Bu Zang, Di Pri, Biat, Gar, Ro-lam, Chil	Dac Lac, Lam Dong, Song Be	46,000
Stieng	Xa dieng	Song Be, Tay Ninh	40,800
Bo Ru Van Kieu	Bru, Van Kieu, Mang Cong, Tri, Khua	Binh Tri Thien	33,100
Kho Mu	Khmu, Xe Cau, Mun Xen, Pu Thenh, Tenh, Tay Hay	Nghe Tinh, Son La, Lai Chau, Hoang Lien Son	32,100

Giay	Nhang, Dang, Pau Thin Pu, Na, Cui Chu, Xa	Hoang Lien Son, Ha Tuyen, Lai Chau	27,900
Ko Tu	Ka tu, Cao, Ha, Phuong, Ka Tang	Quang Nam-Da Nang, Binh Tri Thien	27,000
Tho	Keo, Mon, Cuoi, Ho, Dan Lai, Ly Ha, Tay Pong, Con Kha, Xa La Vang	Nghe Tinh, Thanh Hoa	24,900
Ta Oi	Toi Oi, Pa Co, Pa Hi (Ba Hi)	Binh Tri Thien	20,500
Ma	Chau Ma, Ma Ngan, Maxop Ma To, Ma Krung	Lam Dong, Dong Nai	20,300
Jehtrieng	Jeh, Gie, Dgieh, Tareh, Giang Ray, Pin, Trieng, Treng, Ta Rieng, Ve (Veh), La Ve, Ka Tang	Quang Nam-Da Nang, Gia Lai-Kon Tum	16,800
Co	Cor, Col, Cau, Trau	Nghia Binh, Quang Nam-Da Nang	16,800
Ha Nhi	U Ni, Xa U Ni	Lai Chau, Hoang Lien Son	9,400
Cho Ru	Chru, Che-ru, Chu	Lam Dong, Thuan Hai	7,700
Cho Ro	Zo Ro, Chau Ro	Dong Nai	7,100
Xing Mun	Puoc, Pua	Son La, Lai Chau	7000
Phu La	Bo Kho Pa, Mu Zi Pa, Xa Pho, Pho, Va Xo Lao, Pu Zang	Hoang Lien Son, Lai Chau	6,900
Lao	Lao Boc, Lao Noi	Lai Chau, Son La, Thanh Hoa, Hoang Lien Son	6,800
La Chi	Cui Te, La Qua	Ha Tuyen	5,900
La Hu	Khu Xung, Co Xung, Kha Qay	Lai Chau	4,300
La Ha	Xa Khao, Khla Phlao	Lai Chau, Son La	3,200
Lu	Nhuon (Zuon)	Lai Chau	3,000
Chut	Sach, May, Ruc, Ma Lieng, A Rem, Tu Yang, Pa Leng, Xo Lang, To Hung, Cha Cu, Tac Cui, U Mo, Xa La Vang	Binh Tri Thien	3,000
Lo Lo	Mun Zi	Cao Bang, Lang Son, Ha Tuyen	2,700
Mang	Mang U, Xa La Vang	Lai Chau	2,400
Khang	Xa Khao, Xa Sua, Xa Don Xa Dang, Xa Hoc, Xa Ai, Xa Bung, Quang Lam	Lai Chau, Son La	2,300
Pathen	Pa Hung, Tong	Ha Tuyen	2,200
Ngai	Xin, Le, Dan, Khanh Gia	Quang Ninh, Cao Bang, Lang Son	1,300
Boy	Chung Cha, Trong Gia, Tu Zi, Tu Zin	Hoang Lien Son, Ha Tuyen	1,300
Co Lao	none	Ha Tuyen	1,200
Cong	Xan Khong, Mong Nhe, Xa Xeng	Lai Chau	800
Si La	Cu De Xu, Kha Pe	Lai Chau	400
Pu Peo	Ka Beo, Pen Ti, Lo Lo	Ha Tuyen	300
Brau	Brao	Gia Lai-Kon Tum	100
O Du	Tay Hat	Nghe Tinh	100
Romam	n.a.	Gia Lai-Kon Tum	100
Other (including foreign residents)			43,400
Total			52,742,000

[1] 1979 census figures rounded to the nearest 100.

Source: Based on information from *Vietnam Courier*, [Hanoi], June 1987, 28-31; and Committee for Social Sciences, Socialist Republic of Vietnam, *Vietnam Social Sciences,* [Hanoi], March and April 1986, 172-76.

The origins of the non-Vietnamese minorities are far from clear, but scholars generally believe that some, like the Hmong (Meo), Zao, Nung, San Chay, Cao Lan, Giay, and Lolo, are descendants of the ancient migrants from southern China who settled in the northern border regions. Others, like the Tay, Muong, and Thai are believed to be related to the lowland natives of Malay stock who were forced into the highlands by successive invasions of Mongoloid peoples from China. Among these indigenous minorities are the Cham of central Vietnam, remnants of a kingdom that ruled the central coast of the country until overrun by the Vietnamese in the fifteenth century, and the Khmer, whose Cambodian forebears controlled the Mekong delta region until displaced in the late eighteenth century by the Vietnamese (see Nine Centuries of Independence). The Khmer and the Cham are lowlanders of the south and are considered, along with the Tay, Muong, and Thai of the north, to be culturally more developed than other minority ethnic groups but less so than the Vietnamese.

The non-Chinese minority peoples, however, are for the most part highlanders who live in relative independence and follow their own traditional customs and culture. They are classified as either sedentary or nomadic. The sedentary groups, the more numerous of the two kinds, are engaged mainly in the cultivation of wet rice and industrial crops; the nomadic groups, in slash- and-burn farming where forested land is cleared for a brief period of cultivation and then abandoned. Both groups inhabit the same four major areas: the northern Chinese border region and the uplands adjacent to the Red River Delta, the northwestern border region adjoining Laos and China, the Central Highlands and the area along the Giai Truong Son, and parts of the Mekong River Delta and the central coastal strip. These groups are notable for their diverse cultural characteristics. They are distinguished from one another not only by language but also by such other cultural features as architectural styles, colors and shapes of dress and personal ornaments, shapes of agricultural implements, religious practices, and systems of social organization.

The number and variety of languages used by Vietnam's minorities reflect the country's ethnic complexity. Minority groups are distinguished by more than a dozen distinct languages and numerous dialects; the origins and distribution of many of these languages have not yet been conclusively established. They can, however, be classified loosely into three major language families, which in turn can be divided into several subgroups. Eleven of the minority groups--Tay, Thai, Nung, Hmong, Muong, Cham, Khmer, Kohor, Ede, Bahnar, and Jarai--have their own writing systems.

Religious practices among highland minorities tend to be rooted in animistic beliefs. Most worship a pantheon of spirits, but a large number are Catholics or Protestants. In contrast to the Mahayana Buddhist beliefs of the majority of Vietnamese, the Khmer practice Theravada (or Hinayana) Buddhism, and the Cham subscribe to both Islam and Hindu beliefs (see Religion).

Before the arrival of the French in the nineteenth century, the highland minorities lived in isolation from the lowland population. Upon the consolidation of French rule, however, contacts between the two groups increased. The French, interested in the uplands for plantation agriculture, permitted the highlanders their linguistic and cultural autonomy, and administered their areas separately from the rest of Vietnam. Conferring this special status gave the French a free hand in cultivating the largely unexploited highlands, where their administrators and Christian missionaries also set up schools, hospitals, and leprosariums.

Often, however, conflicts arose between the upland communities and the French, who were distrusted as exploitative, unwelcome interlopers. The French, however, eventually overcame the unrest and successfully developed some of the highland areas, especially those of the Ede and Jarai, where they established large rubber, coffee, and tea plantations.

After the mid-1950s, North and South Vietnam dealt with the minorities differently. The Hanoi regime in the North, recognizing the traditional separatist attitudes of the tribal minorities, initiated a policy of accommodation by setting up two autonomous zones for the highlanders in return for their acceptance of Hanoi's political control. By offering limited self-government, Hanoi's leaders hoped that integration of the minorities into Vietnamese society could eventually be achieved. By contrast, the noncommunist Saigon administration in the South, under Ngo Dinh Diem, opted for direct, centralized control of the tribal minorities and incurred their enduring wrath by seizing ancestral tribal lands for the resettlement of displaced Catholic refugees from the North.

After Diem's death in 1963, successive Saigon administrations granted a modicum of autonomy, but the strategic hamlet program, introduced in the South in the 1960s, caused further disruption by forcing highlanders to relocate to fortified enclaves. The program was proposed to improve the physical security of montagnards as well as to deny food and services to *Viet Cong* (see Glossary) guerrillas, but it largely embittered its minority participants, who wanted to be left alone to continue living on their ancestral lands in the traditional manner. In an act of resistance, some tribal leaders gathered in 1964 to announce the formation of the Unified Front for the Struggle of Oppressed Races (Front Unifie pour la Lutte des Races Opprimees--FULRO), representing the Bahnar, Cham, Ede, Hre, Jarai, Mnong, Raglai, Sadang, Stieng, and other groups.

After 1975 a number of northern minority cadres were sent to the Central Highlands to lay the groundwork for socio-economic development. In 1977 a university was set up at Buon Me Thuot, capital of the Dac Lac Province, to train a corps of minority cadres. These tactics were designed to narrow the socioeconomic gap not only between the highlanders and the lowlanders but also among the minorities themselves.

In the mid-1980s, the party and media expressed satisfaction with the cadres' training and commended certain highland provinces for progress in agricultural cooperativization, noting that a growing number of slash-and-burn farmers had turned to sedentary farming and that further improvements in cultural and health facilities were planned. By 1986 about 43 percent of the estimated 2.2 million nomadic minority members were reported to have adopted a more sedentary life. There were also glowing claims that minorities were now full-fledged participants in national affairs, as was evidenced by their representation in the *National Assembly* (see Glossary) and in other government and party organizations.

A cursory examination reveals, however, that progress was spotty. The living conditions of highlanders continued to lag behind those of lowlanders. In remote areas, "backward customs and practices" remained unchanged, minority groups were insufficiently represented among cadres, and sorely needed resources for material improvements were lacking. Official claims that closer unity and greater harmony were being achieved in a multinational Vietnam were belied by the government's frequent admonishments against "narrow nationalism" (the parochialism of the minority groups) and against "big nationality prejudices" (the ingrained Vietnamese biases against minorities). To be sure, the number of minority cadres with either general or college- level education was growing, but in 1987 these cadres represented only a small portion of the functionaries serving in the highland provinces, districts, towns, and villages. In Dac Lac Province, 91 percent of the district-level cadres and 63 percent of the key village and lower level cadres had been transferred from other places, presumably from the North or the lowlands of the South.

Under the government program of population redistribution, lowlanders continued to emigrate to the Central Highlands. In 1980 about 52 percent of the Central Highlands population consisted of ethnic Vietnamese. In 1985, as pressure mounted on the Vietnamese government to produce grain and industrial crops, a greater influx of ethnic Vietnamese was anticipated. By 1987 it seemed clear that minority groups were likely to remain unequal partners in the management of their local affairs, despite official protestations to the contrary, as increasing numbers of Vietnamese settled in the Central Highlands.

The minority question remained an issue because of its implications not only for integration but also for internal security. In the mid-1980s, there were occasional official allusions to counterrevolutionary activities attributed to FULRO. Hanoi was quick to assert, however, that these rebel activities were blown out of proportion by the Western media. Nonetheless, the authorities were concerned about the northern border areas, where renegades of such groups as the Hmong, Zao, and Giay were said to have participated in China's anti-Vietnamese activities after 1979 as "special gangs of bandits." Official literature supported the construction of "a border cultural defense line to counter the multifaceted war of sabotage waged by the Chinese expansionists."

Hoa

The Hoa, or ethnic Chinese, are predominantly urban dwellers. A few Hoa live in small settlements in the northern highlands near the Chinese frontier, where they are also known as *ngai*. Traditionally, as elsewhere in Southeast Asia, the Chinese have retained a distinctive cultural identity, but in 1955 North Vietnam and China agreed that the Hoa should be integrated gradually into Vietnamese society and should have Vietnamese citizenship conferred on them (see Foreign Relations).

Before 1975 the northern Hoa were mainly rice farmers, fishermen, and coal miners, except for those residing in cities and provincial towns. In the South they were dominant in commerce and manufacturing. According to an official source, at the end of 1974 the Hoa controlled more than 80 percent of the food, textile, chemical, metallurgy, engineering, and electrical industries, 100 percent of wholesale trade, more than 50 percent of retail trade, and 90 percent of export-import trade. Dominance over the economy enabled the Hoa to "manipulate prices" of rice and other scarce goods. This particular source further observed that the Hoa community constituted "a state within a state," inasmuch as they had built "a closed world based on blood relations, strict internal discipline, and a network of sects, each with its own chief, to avoid the indigenous administration's direct interference." It was noted by Hanoi in 1983 that as many as 60 percent of "the former bourgeoisie" of the south were of Chinese origin.

In mid-1975 the combined Hoa communities of the North and South numbered approximately 1.3 million, and all but 200,000 resided in the South, most of them in the Saigon metropolitan area. Beginning in 1975, the Hoa bore the brunt of socialist transformation in the South, especially after the communist government decided in early 1978 to abolish private trade. This, combined with external tensions stemming from Vietnam's dispute with Cambodia and China in 1978 and 1979 caused an exodus of about 250,000 Hoa, of whom 170,000 fled overland into China from the North and the remainder fled by boat from the South (see Foreign Relations).

The Social System

Traditional Patterns

For centuries Vietnamese society was knit together by Confucian norms based on five relationships: the subordination of subject to ruler, son to father, wife to husband, and younger brother to elder brother, and the mutual respect between friends. These norms influenced the evolution of Vietnam as a hierarchic, authoritarian society in which Confucian scholarship, monarchical absolutism, filial piety, the subordinate role of women, and the family system were regarded as integral to the natural order of the universe.

The traditional society was stratified on the basis of education and occupation into four groups: scholar-officials or mandarins, farmers, artisans, and merchants. At the pinnacle was the emperor, who ruled with the "mandate of heaven." Next were the scholar-officials, recruited through rigorous civil service examinations in Chinese classical literature and philosophy. Once a person passed the triennial examinations he became an accredited scholar or degree holder and was eligible for appointment to the imperial civil service, the most prestigious route to power, status, and wealth. Together, the emperor, his family, and the scholar-officials constituted the ruling class.

In theory, the mandarinate was not a closed social group. Commoners were permitted to apply for the examinations, and the status of scholar-official could not be inherited. In practice, however, these officials became a self-perpetuating class of generalist-administrators, partly because their sons could afford years of academic preparation for the examinations whereas most commoners could not. Education, the key to upward mobility, was neither free nor compulsory and tended to be the preserve of the mandarins.

Although social eminence and political power were thus concentrated in the hands of the mandarins, economic power was based on landholdings and was more widely diffused as a result of progressive dismantling of the hereditary feudal nobility after the fifteenth century. This process was accomplished by breaking up the nobility's vast holdings and redistributing smaller parcels to others, such as families of royal blood, prominent scholar-officials, and influential local notables. The wealthier of these notables formed a kind of landed gentry that wielded influence in the rural towns and villages.

The society was further transformed in the nineteenth century by the imposition of French rule, the introduction of Western education, the beginnings of industrialization and urbanization, and the growth of commercial agriculture. The establishment of a new, French-dominated governing class led to a rapid decline in the power and prestige of the emperor and the mandarins, whose functions were substantially reduced. When the triennial examinations were held in 1876 and 1879, an average of 6,000 candidates took them; in 1913, only 1,330 did.

In place of the old imperial bureaucracy, in the late nineteenth and early twentieth centuries a new intellectual elite emerged that emphasized achievement in science, geography, and other modern subjects instead of the Confucian classics. The new Vietnamese intelligentsia was impressed by the power of the French and by the 1905 naval victory at Tsushima of a modernized Japan over tsarist Russia. Having viewed some of the achievements of Western culture in Europe during World War I, when nearly 150,000 Vietnamese were recruited for work in French factories, the new elite proclaimed their country's need for a modern, Western educational focus. By 1920, even in the conservative city of Hue, the last Confucian outpost, wealthy families refused to marry their daughters to the sons of distinguished scholarofficial families unless the young men had acquired a modern, Western-style education. The traditional civil service examinations were held for the last time in 1919.

Traditional Confucian village schools, accustomed to teaching in Chinese, introduced instruction in Vietnamese and French into the existing curriculum. Vietnamese who had successfully acquired a higher education at home or abroad entered government service as administrators or were absorbed as doctors, engineers, and teachers as the government expanded its role in the fields of health, public works, and education. Others took up professions outside government, such as law, medicine, chemistry, and journalism. The new elite was composed mainly of Vietnamese from Tonkin and Annam rather than from Cochinchina, a regional bias perhaps attributable to the location in Hanoi of the country's only institution of Western higher education.

The French period also produced a new group of Vietnamese absentee landowners who possessed riches far in excess of the wealth anyone in the older society had enjoyed. This new group came into existence as a result of the French development of vast new tracts of land in Cochinchina. A few of these large holdings were retained by French companies or citizens, but most were held by enterprising, Western-oriented, urban Vietnamese from Annam and Tonkin who lived mainly in Hanoi and Hue. By investing in light industry and medium-sized trading concerns, they became Vietnam's first modern industrialists and entrepreneurs.

In urban centers the demand of both the expanding French government bureaucracy and the private sector for secretaries, clerks, cashiers, interpreters, minor officials, and labor foremen created a new Vietnamese white-collar group. The development of mining and industry between 1890 and 1919 also introduced a new class of workers. Because most of the natural resources as well as a large labor pool were located in the North, industrial development was concentrated there, and Hanoi and Haiphong became the country's leading industrial centers. At the same time, conditions of overcrowding and intensive farming in the North provided little room for agriculture on a commercial scale. In order to expand agriculture, the French turned their attention to the underdeveloped, warmer South, where French cultivation of such crops as rubber, coffee, tea, and, in Cochinchina, rice gave rise to a group of agricultural and plantation wage earners.

The colonial period also led to a substantial increase in the Hoa population. The country's limited foreign and domestic trade were already in the hands of Chinese when the French arrived. The French chose to promote the Chinese role in commerce and to import Chinese labor to develop road and railroad systems, mining, and industry. French colonial policy that lifted the traditional ban on rice exports at the end of the nineteenth century also attracted new waves of Chinese merchants and shopkeepers seeking to take advantage of the new export market. Vietnam's growing economy attracted even more Chinese thereafter, especially to the South. Already deeply involved in the rice trade, the Chinese expanded their interests to include ricemilling and established a virtual monopoly.

They also were a significant presence in sugar refining, coconut and peanut oil production, lumber, and shipbuilding. Many who began their careers as laborers on the French rubber plantations of Cochinchina eventually started their own tea, pepper, or rice plantations to supply local market needs. Chinese gardeners in the suburbs of Saigon monopolized the supply of fresh vegetables consumed in that city, and Chinese restaurants and hotels proliferated in virtually every urban center.

Society in the 1954-75 Period

North Vietnam

At the time of the 1954 partition, Vietnam was overwhelmingly a rural society; peasants accounted for nearly 90 percent of the total population. During the ensuing 20 years of political separation, however, the North and the South developed into two very different societies. In the North the communists had embarked on a program intended to revolutionize the socioeconomic structure. The focus of change was ostensibly economic, but its underlying motivation was both political and social as well. Based on the Marxist principle of class struggle, it involved no less than the creation of a totally new social structure. Propertied classes were eliminated, and a proletarian dictatorship was established in which workers and peasants emerged as the nominal new masters of a socialist and ultimately classless state.

As a prelude to the socialist revolution, a land reform campaign and a harsh, systematic campaign to liquidate "feudal landlords" from rural society were launched concurrently in 1955. Reminiscent of the campaign undertaken by communists in China in earlier years, the liquidation of landlords cost the lives of an estimated 50,000 people and prompted the party to acknowledge and redress "a number of serious errors" committed by its zealous cadres.

In urban sectors the party's intervention was less direct, initially at least, because large numbers of the bourgeoisie had fled the North in anticipation of the communists' coming to power. Many had fled to the South before the party gained full control. Those who remained were verbally assailed as exploiters of the people, but, because the regime needed their administrative and technical skills and experience, they were otherwise treated tolerantly and allowed to retain private property.

In 1958 the regime stepped up the pace of "socialist transformation," mindful that even though the foundations of a socialist society were basically in place, the economy remained for the most part still in the hands of the private, capitalist sector. By 1960 all but a small number of peasants, artisans, handicraft workers, industrialists, traders, and merchants had been forced to join cooperatives of various kinds.

Intellectuals, many of whom had earlier been supporters of the *Viet Minh* (see Glossary), were first conciliated by the government, then stifled. Opposition to the government, expressed openly during and after the peasant uprisings of 1956, prompted the imposition of controls that graduated to complete suppression by 1958. Writers and artists who had established their reputations in the pre-communist era were excluded from taking any effective role in national affairs. Many were sent to the countryside to perform manual labor and to help educate a new corps of socialist intellectuals among the peasants.

The dominant group in the new social order were the highlevel party officials, who constituted a new ruling class. They owed their standing more to demonstrations of political acumen and devotion to nationalism or Marxism-Leninism than to educational or professional achievements. Years of resistance against the French in the rural areas had inured them to hardship and at the same time given them valuable experience in organization and guerrilla warfare. Resistance work had also brought them into close touch with many different segments of the population.

At the apex of the new ruling class were select members of the Political Bureau of the communist Vietnamese Workers Party (VWP, Dang Lao Dong Viet Nam), and a somewhat larger body of Central Committee members holding key posts in the party, the government, the military, and various party-supported organizations. Below the top echelon were the rank and file party members (500,000 by 1960), including a number of women and members of ethnic minorities. Party cadres who possessed special knowledge and experience in technical, financial, administrative, or managerial matters were posted in all social institutions to supervise the implementation of party decisions.

Occupying an intermediate position between the party and the citizenry were those persons who did not belong to the party but who, nevertheless, had professional skills or other talents needed by the regime. Noncommunists were found in various technical posts, in the school system, and in the mass organizations to which most citizens were required to belong. A few even occupied high, though politically marginal, posts in the government. The bulk of the population remained farmers, workers, soldiers, miners, porters, stevedores, clerks, tradespeople, teachers, and artisans.

Social reorganization did little to evoke mass enthusiasm for socialism, and socialist transformation of the private sector into cooperative- and state-run operations did not result in the kind of economic improvement the government needed to win over the peasants and merchants. The regime managed to provide better educational and health care services than had existed in the pre1954 years, but poverty was still endemic. The party attributed the "numerous difficulties" it faced to "natural calamities, enemy actions, and the utterly poor and backward state of the economy," but also acknowledged its own failings. These included cadre incompetence in ideological and organizational matters as well as in financial, technical, and managerial affairs.

South Vietnam

South of the demarcation line after partition in 1954, the social system remained unchanged except that power reverted to a Vietnamese elite. The South's urban-rural network of roles, heavily dependent on the peasant economy, remained intact despite the influx of nearly a million refugees from the North; and land reform, initiated unenthusiastically in 1956, had little socioeconomic impact in the face of obstruction by the landowning class. In contrast to the North, there was no doctrinaire, organized attempt to reorganize the society fundamentally or to implant new cultural values and social sanctions. The regime of Ngo Dinh Diem was more concerned with its own immediate survival than with revolutionary social change, and if it had a vision of sociopolitical reform at all, that vision was diffusive. Furthermore, it lacked a political organization comparable in zeal to the party apparatus of Hanoi in order to achieve its goals.

In the 1960s, prolonged political instability placed social structures in the South under increasing stress. The communist insurgency, which prevented the government from extending its authority to some areas of the countryside, was partially responsible, but even more disruptive were the policies of the government itself. Isolated in Saigon, the Diem regime alienated large parts of the population by acting to suppress Buddhists and other minorities, by forcing the relocation of peasants to areas nominally controlled by the government, and by systematically crushing political opposition. Such policies fueled a growing dissatisfaction with the regime that led to Diem's assassination in November 1963 and his replacement by a series of military strongmen.

As the war in the South intensified, it created unprecedented social disruption in both urban and rural life. Countless civilians were forced to abandon their ancestral lands and sever their network of family and communal ties to flee areas controlled by the Viet Cong or exposed to government operations against the communists. By the early 1970s, as many as 12 million persons, or 63 percent of the entire southern population, were estimated to have been displaced; some were relocated to government-protected rural hamlets while others crowded into already congested urban centers. Few villages, however remote, were left untouched by the war. The urban-rural boundary, once sharply defined, seemed to disappear as throngs of uprooted refugees moved to the cities. Traditional social structures broke down, leaving the society listless and bereft of a cohesive force other than the common instinct for survival.

The disruption imposed by the war, however, did not alter conventional socioeconomic class identifiers. In the urban areas, the small upper class elite continued to be limited to highranking military officers, government officials, people in the professions, absentee landlords, intellectuals, and Catholic and Buddhist religious leaders. The elite retained a strong personal interest in France and French culture; many had been educated in France and many had sons or daughters residing there. In addition to wealth, Western education--particularly French education--was valued highly, and French and English were widely spoken.

The urban middle class included civil servants, lower and middle-ranking officers in the armed forces, commercial employees, school teachers, shop owners and managers, small merchants, and farm and factory managers. A few were college graduates, although the majority had only a secondary-school education. Very few had been able to study abroad.

At the bottom of the urban society were unskilled, largely uneducated wageworkers and petty tradespeople. While semiliterate themselves, they nevertheless were able to send their children to primary school. Secondary education was less common, however, particularly for girls. These children tended not to proceed far enough in school to acquire an elementary knowledge of French or English, and most adults of the lower class knew only Vietnamese unless they had worked as domestics for foreigners.

Village society, which embraced 80 percent of the population, was composed mostly of farmers, who were ranked in three socioeconomic groups. The elite were the wealthiest landowners. If they farmed, the work was done by hired laborers who planted, irrigated, and harvested under the owner's supervision. In the off-season, landowners engaged in moneylending, rice trading, or rice milling. Usually the well-to-do owners were active in village affairs as members of the village councils. After the mid-1960s, however, interest in seeking such positions waned as village leaders increasingly were targeted by Viet Cong insurgents.

The less prosperous, middle-level villagers owned or rented enough land to live at a level well above subsistence, but they tended not to acquire a surplus large enough to invest in other ventures. They worked their own fields and hired farm hands only when needed during planting or harvesting. A few supplemented their income as artisans, but never as laborers. Because of their more modest economic circumstances, members of this group tended not to assume as many communal responsibilities as did the wealthier villagers.

At the bottom of village life were owners of small farming plots and tenant farmers. Forced to spend nearly all of their time eking out a living, they could not afford to engage in village affairs. Because they could not cultivate enough land to support their families, most of them worked also as part-time laborers, and their wives and children assisted with the field work. Their children frequently went to school only long enough to learn the rudiments of reading and writing. This group also included workers in a wide range of other service occupations, such as artisans, practitioners of oriental medicine, and small tradespeople.

Vietnam after 1975

The sudden collapse of Saigon in April 1975 set the stage for a new and uncertain chapter in the evolution of Vietnamese society. The Hanoi government had to confront directly what communists have long called the struggle between the two paths of socialism and capitalism. At issue was Hanoi's ability to translate its wartime success and socialist revolutionary experience into postwar rehabilitation and reconstruction, now that it controlled the South territorially.

Foremost among the regime's imperatives was that of restoring order and stability to the war-torn South. The critical question, however, was whether or not the northern conquerors could inspire the southern population to embrace communism. Initially, Hanoi appeared sanguine; the two zones had more similarities than dissimilarities, and the dissimilarities were expected to be eliminated as the South caught up with the North in socialist organization.

The December 1975 *Vietnam Courier*, an official government publication, portrayed Vietnam as two distinct, incongruent societies. The South was reported to continue to suffer from what communists consider the neo-colonialist influences and feudal ideology of the United States, while the North was considered to serve as a progressive environment for growing numbers of a new kind of socialist human being, imbued with patriotism, proletarian internationalism, and socialist virtues. The class of social exploiter had been eliminated in the North, leaving the classes of workers collectivized peasant, and socialist intellectual, the last consisting of various groups. In contrast, the South was divided into a working class, peasantry, petit bourgeois, capitalist--or *comprador* (see Glossary)--class, and the remnant of a feudal landlord class.

In September 1976, Premier Pham Van Dong declared that his compatriots, North and South, were "translating the revolutionary heroism they [had] displayed in fighting into creative labor in the acquisition of wealth and strength." In the South particularly, the old society was undergoing active changes as the result of "stirring revolutionary movements" by the workers, peasants, youth, women, intellectuals, and other groups. In agriculture alone, "millions of people" participated in bringing hundreds of thousands more hectares under cultivation and in building or dredging thousands of kilometers of canals and ditches.

From all indications, however, these changes occurred more through coercion than volition. In Dong's own words, the party had initiated "various policies aimed at eliminating the comprador capitalists as a class and doing away with all vestiges of feudal exploitation." These policies radically realigned the power elite so that the ruling machine was controlled collectively by the putative vanguard of the working class--the party--and by the senior cadres of the party who were mostly from the North.

In its quest for a new socialist order in the South, Hanoi relied on other techniques apart from socialist economic transformation and socialist education. These included thought reform, population resettlement, and internal exile, as well as surveillance and mass mobilization. Party-sponsored "study sessions" were obligatory for all adults. For the former elite of the Saigon regime, a more rigorous form of indoctrination was used; hundreds of thousands of former military officers, bureaucrats, politicians, religious and labor leaders, scholars, intellectuals, and lawyers, as well as critics of the new regime were ordered to "reeducation camps" for varying periods. In mid1985 , the Hanoi government conceded that it still held about 10,000 inmates in the reeducation camps, but the actual number was believed to be at least 40,000. In 1982 there were about 120,000 Vietnamese in these camps. According to a knowledgeable American observer, the inmates faced hard labor, but only rarely torture or execution.

Population resettlement or redistribution, although heralded on economic grounds, turned out to be another instrument of social control in disguise. It was a means of defusing tensions in congested cities, which were burdened with unemployed and socially dislocated people even after most of the rural refugees had been repatriated to their native villages. These refugees had swelled the urban population to 45 percent of the southern total in 1975 (up from 33 percent in 1970). The authorities sought to address the problem of urban congestion by relocating many of the metropolitan jobless in the new economic zones hastily set up in virgin lands, often malaria-infested jungles, as part of a broader effort to boost agricultural output. In 1975 and 1976 alone, more than 600,000 people were moved from Ho Chi Minh City to these zones, in most instances, reportedly, against their will. Because of the barely tolerable living conditions in the new settlements, a considerable number of people escaped or bribed their way back to the city. The new economic zones came to be widely perceived as places of internal exile. In fact, the authorities were said to have used the threat of exile to such places against those who refused to obey party instructions or to participate in the activities of the mass organizations.

Surveillance was a familiar tool of the regime, which was bent on purging all class enemies. Counterrevolutionaries, real and suspected, were summarily interned in reform camps or forced labor camps that were set up separately from the new economic zones in several border areas and other undeveloped regions.

The Hanoi government has claimed that not a single political execution took place in the South after 1975, even in cases of grave war crimes. Generally, the foreign press corroborated this claim by reporting in 1975 that there seemed to be no overt indication of the blood bath that many Western observers had predicted would occur in the wake of the communist takeover. Some Western observers, however, have estimated that as many as 65,000 South Vietnamese may have been executed.

In March 1982, the Vietnamese Communist Party (VCP) convened its Fifth National Party Congress to assess its achievements since 1976 and to outline its major tasks for the 1980s. The congress was revealing if only because of its somber admission that revolutionary optimism was no substitute for common sense. Despite rigid social controls and mass mobilization, the party fell far short of its original expectations for socialist transition. According to the party's assessment, from 1976 through 1980 shortcomings and errors occurred in establishing transition goals and in implementing the party line.

The congress, however, reaffirmed the correctness of the party line concerning socialist transition, and directed that it be implemented with due allowances for different regional circumstances. The task was admittedly formidable. In a realistic appraisal of the regime's difficulties, *Nhan Dan*, the party's daily organ, warned in June 1982 that the crux of the problem lay in the regime itself, the shortcomings of which included lack of party discipline and corruption of party and state functionaries.

In 1987 the goal of establishing a new society remained elusive, and Vietnam languished in the first stage of the party's planned period of transition to socialism. Mai Chi Tho, mayor of Ho Chi Minh City and deputy head of its party branch, had told visiting Western reporters as early as April 1985 that socialist transition, as officially envisioned, would probably continue until the year 2000.

In the estimation of the party, Vietnamese society had succumbed to a new form of sociopolitical elitism that was just as undesirable as the much-condemned elitism of the old society. Landlords and comprador capitalists may have disappeared but in their places were party cadres and state functionaries who were no less status-conscious and self-seeking. The Sixth National Party Congress in December 1986 found it necessary to issue a stern warning against opportunism, individualism, personal gain, corruption, and a desire for special prerogatives and privileges. A report to the congress urged the party to intensify class struggle in order to combat the corrupt practices engaged in by those who had "lost their class consciousness." Official efforts to purify the ranks of the working class, peasantry, and socialist intellectuals, however, failed to strike a responsive chord. In fact, the proceedings of the Sixth Congress left the inescapable impression that the regime was barely surviving the struggle between socialism and capitalism and that an early emergence of a communist class structure was unlikely.

As ideally envisioned, the socialist sector was expected to provide 70 percent of household income and the "household economy," or the privately controlled resources of the home, was to make up the balance. In September 1986 cadres and workers were earning their living mainly through moonlighting and, according to a Vietnamese source, remained on "the state rolls only to preserve their political prestige and to receive some ration stamps and coupons." The source further disclosed that the society's lack of class consciousness was reflected in the party's membership, among whom only about 10 percent were identified as from the working class.

Religion

The Constitution of the Socialist Republic of Vietnam, adopted in 1980, proclaims that "citizens enjoy freedom of worship, and may practice or not practice a religion" but that "no one may misuse religions to violate state laws or policies." Despite the Constitution's ostensible protection of the practice of the religion, the status of such was precarious in Vietnam in late 1987.

Buddhism

Historically, most Vietnamese have identified themselves with Buddhism, which originated in what is now southern Nepal around 530 B.C. as an offshoot of Hinduism. Its founder was Gautama, a prince who bridled at the formalism of Hinduism as it was being interpreted by the priestly caste of Brahmans. Gautama spent years meditating and wandering as an ascetic until he discovered the path of enlightenment to nirvana, the world of endless serenity in which one is freed from the cycle of birth, death, and rebirth. According to Buddhist thought, human salvation lies in discovering the "four noble truths"--that man is born to suffer in successive lives, that the cause of this suffering is man's craving for earthly pleasures and possessions, that the suffering ceases upon his deliverance from this craving, and that he achieves this deliverance by following "the noble eightfold path." The foundation of the Buddhist concept of morality and right behavior, the eightfold path, consists of right views, or sincerity in leading a religious life; right intention, or honesty in judgment; right speech, or sincerity in speech; right conduct, or sincerity in work; right livelihood, or sincerity in making a living; right effort, or sincerity in aspiration; right mindfulness, or sincerity in memory; and right concentration, or sincerity in meditation.

Buddhism spread first from China to Vietnam's Red River Delta region in approximately the second century A.D., and then from India to the southern Mekong Delta area at some time between the third and the sixth centuries. The Chinese version, Mahayana Buddhism, became the faith of most Vietnamese, whereas the Indian version, Theravada (or Hinayana) Buddhism, was confined mostly to the southern delta region. The doctrinal distinction between the two consists of their differing views of Gautama Buddha: the Mahayana school teaches that Gautama was only one of many "enlightened ones" manifesting the fundamental divine power of the universe; the Theravada school teaches that Gautama was the one-and-only enlightened one and the great teacher, but that he was not divine. The Mahayana sect holds further that laypersons can attain nirvana, whereas the Theravada school believes that only ordained monks and nuns can do so.

Few Vietnamese outside the clergy, however, are acquainted with Buddhism's elaborate cosmology. What appealed to them at the time it was introduced was Mahayana ritual and imagery. Mahayana ceremony easily conformed to indigenous Vietnamese beliefs, which combined folklore with Confucian and Taoist teachings, and Mahayana's "enlightened ones" were often venerated alongside various animist spirits.

Before the country was unified under communism, Buddhism enjoyed an autonomy from the state that was increasingly threatened once the communists gained power. For pragmatic reasons, however, the regime initially avoided overt hostility toward Buddhism or any other organized religion. Instead, it sought to separate real and potential collaborators from opponents by co-optation and control. For example, within months after winning the South, the communist regime set up a front called the Patriotic Buddhist Liaison Committee. The committee's purpose was to promote the idea that all patriotic Buddhists had a duty to participate in building a new society liberated for the first time from the shackles of feudal and neo-colonialist influences. The committee also tried to show that most Buddhists, leaders and followers alike, were indeed rallying behind the new regime and the liaison committee. This strategy attempted to thwart the power of the influential, independent groups of Buddhist clergy, particularly the Unified Buddhist Church of Vietnam, which had been a major pre-1975 critic of the Saigon government and of the roughly twenty Buddhist sects in Vietnam the most vocal in opposing the war.

Communists also pressured monks and nuns to lead a secular life, encouraging them to take part in productive agricultural labor or to become actively involved in the work of the Patriotic Buddhist Liaison Committee. For their refusal to collaborate, some prominent clerical leaders in the South were placed under house arrest or imprisoned, their pagodas were converted to public use, and their holdings were confiscated. Such activity closely paralleled communist actions against Buddhists in the North in the 1950s. In addition, the party prevented Buddhist organizations from training monks and nuns in schools that previously had been autonomous. In April 1980, a national committee of Buddhist groups throughout the country was formed by the government. The government-controlled Vietnam Buddhist Church was established in November 1981, and it emerged as the only officially sanctioned organization authorized to represent all Buddhist groups both at home and abroad.

As a result of communist policy, the observance of Buddhist ritual and practice was drastically reduced. A 1979 study of a Red River Delta commune, reported to be "overwhelmingly Catholic," disclosed that the commune's two pagodas were "maintained and frequented regularly by the faithful (the majority of whom were old women), especially on the Buddhist feast days." No monks or nuns had been observed, however, and the study went on to note that pagodas had been eliminated entirely in nearby Hanoi. In 1987 occasional reports suggested that the observance of Buddhist ritual continued in some remote areas.

The communist government's attitude toward Buddhism and other faiths being practiced remained one of tolerance as long as the clergy and faithful adhered strictly to official guidelines. These guidelines inhibited the growth of religious institutions, however, by restricting the number of institutions approved to train clergy and by preempting the time of potential candidates among the youth whose daily routine might require study, work, and participation in the activities of communist youth organizations. In an apparent effort to train a new generation of monks and nuns, the Vietnam Buddhist Church reportedly set up one Buddhist academy in Hanoi in November 1981 and another in Ho Chi Minh City in December 1984. These academies, however, served as an arm of the state.

Catholicism

Despite the Roman Catholic Church's rejection of ancestor worship, a cornerstone of the Confucian cultural tradition, Roman Catholicism established a solid position in Vietnamese society under French rule. The French encouraged its propagation to balance Buddhism and to serve as a vehicle for the further dissemination of Western culture. After the mid-1950s, Catholicism declined in the North, where the communists regarded it as a reactionary force opposed to national liberation and social progress. In the South, by contrast, Catholicism expanded under the presidency of Ngo Dinh Diem, who promoted it as an important bulwark against North Vietnam. Under Diem, himself a devout Catholic, Roman Catholics enjoyed an advantage over non-Catholics in commerce, the professions, education, and the government. This caused growing Buddhist discontent that contributed to the eventual collapse of the Diem regime and the ultimate rise to power of the military. Roman Catholics in reunified Vietnam numbered about 3.0 million in 1984, of whom nearly 1 million resided in the North and the remainder in the South.

In 1955 approximately 600,000 Catholics remained in the North after an estimated 650,000 had fled to the South. That year the Liaison Committee of Patriotic and Peace-Loving Catholics was set up in the North by the communist regime in an attempt to win over those Catholics who had chosen to remain (but were slower than non-Catholics to embrace the regime) and to "reintegrate" them into northern society. The church was allowed to retain its link with the Vatican, although all foreign priests had either fled south or been expelled, and normal church activities were permitted to continue, albeit in the shadow of a campaign of harassment. The appearance of normalcy was misleading, however. The church was stripped of its traditional autonomy in running schools, hospitals, and orphanages. Its traditional right to own property was abolished, and priests and nuns were required to devote part of their time to productive labor in agriculture. Nevertheless, officials claimed that Catholics had complete freedom of worship as long as they did not question the principle of collective socialism, spurn manual labor, or jeopardize the internal and external security of the state.

In November 1977, the *Vietnam Courier* reported that the church in the North had changed from "opposition to acceptance and participation," but that the transformation had been difficult for Catholics. In the same month, the government unveiled a decree on religion that reaffirmed the constitution's position on religious freedom, but made it unequivocally clear that such freedom was conditional and depended on the compatibility of church activities with such higher imperatives as patriotism and socialism. The new decree not only prescribed the duties and obligations required of the clergy by the state but also imposed state control over the conduct of religious services, education, training, investitures, appointments, travels, and transfers.

Applicable to all religious communities in the North and South, the new law clearly introduced a period of more active state intervention in church affairs. The regime apparently acted out of concern that the church in the North, despite having coexisted with socialism for twenty-three years, was not progressive enough to lead in the socialist transformation of the Catholic community in the South. The *Vietnam Courier* suggested this link between the northern and southern situations in November 1977, after noting that the northern Catholic church would have to shoulder the additional task of helping to reintegrate Vietnam's entire Catholic population into the national community.

Catholics in the South in 1975 officially numbered about 1.9 million, including 15 bishops, 3,000 regular and diocesan priests, 1,200 brothers, and 6,000 nuns. Four-hundred priests and lay brothers and 56,000 lay Catholics were estimated already to have fled the country in anticipation of the communist victory. At the time of the imposition of communist rule, the South had 870 parishes in 15 dioceses; Ho Chi Minh City alone had a half million Catholics, who were served by 600 priests and 4,000 lay brothers and nuns. The North's less than 1 million Catholics were served by about 3,500 churches attended by nearly 400 priests, 10 bishops, and 2 archbishops.

The government claimed that after April 1975 the religious activities of Roman Catholics were quickly stabilized, major services were held, and many cathedrals and churches that had been damaged or destroyed in the war were rebuilt. The regime claimed further that there was no religious persecution, or if there was persecution, that it was directed at the activities of "reactionary forces" bent on taking advantage of "the backwardness of a number of the faithful . . . ." Nevertheless, the authorities acted to isolate and to neutralize hard-core opposition to party policy and to persuade less strongly opposed factions to join a party-controlled "renovation and reconciliation" movement. A considerable number of Northern and Southern Roman Catholics, however, remained opposed to communist authority.

In 1980 the Unified Bishops' Council of Vietnam was established to enlist the aid of "patriotic" bishops in persuading recalcitrant elements of the Catholic community to cooperate with the regime. Three years later, in November 1983, a Committee for Solidarity of Patriotic Catholics was created to unite all Catholics and channel their energy into the building of socialism. This committee, which replaced the Liaison Committee of Patriotic and Peace-Loving Catholics, was formed at a time when the regime's surveillance of the Catholic community had been stepped up, reportedly due to the suspicion that some Catholics were involved in antistate activities. The regime's growing concern was further reflected in the establishment in March 1985 of a Religious Affairs Committee to coordinate and supervise religious organizations more effectively. Hanoi's increasing involvement in church affairs reportedly produced new strains in its relations with the Vatican. In 1987 it nevertheless appeared critical to Vietnam's leaders to convey to the public the impression that the Roman Catholic Church was active in the affairs of the nation and that church members were significant contributors to the socialist cause.

Other Faiths

Religions with less of a following than Buddhism or Catholicism were treated similarly by the regime, with the exception of those the regime considered merely superstitious, which incurred its outright hostility. Two religious movements that enjoyed considerable followings before 1975 were the *Cao Dai* (see Glossary) and the *Hoa Hao* (see Glossary). Both were founded in this century in the Mekong River Delta. The Cao Dai, the older of the two and a self-styled reformed Buddhist sect, flourished in the rural areas of the southern delta region. An amalgam of different beliefs derived from Confucianism, Taoism, and Christianity, among other sources, it claimed 1 million to 2 million adherents. The Hoa Hao, with more than 1 million followers, identified itself as a reformed Theravada Buddhist sect, but, unlike the Cao Dai, it preserved a distinctive Buddhist coloration. Based mostly in the southernmost areas of the delta, it stressed individual prayer, simplicity, and social justice over icon veneration or elaborate ceremonies. Before 1975 both faiths sought, with some success, to remain neutral in the war between Hanoi and Saigon. After 1975, however, like Buddhists and Roman Catholics, they were under heavy pressure from the communist regime to join its ranks.

Protestants, numbered between 100,000 and 200,000 in the early 1980s, and were found mostly among the Montagnard communities inhabiting the South's central highlands. Because of their alleged close association with American missionaries of the Christian and Missionary Alliance, Protestants were reported to have suffered more than Catholics after 1975.

A painting at the Cao Dai Temple, Tay Ninh Province, depicting three of the Cao Dai movement's spiritual "father": founder of the Chinese Republic Sun Yat-sen, French poet and novelist Victor Hugo, and Vietnamese prophet Trang Thinh Courtesy United States Army

In addition to organized religions, there existed a melange of beliefs without institutional structure that nevertheless had an enduring impact on Vietnamese life well into the 1980s. These, beliefs derived partly from Confucianism, stressed the virtues of filial piety, loyalty, family solidarity, and ancestor veneration--all central to the family system of the old society. Taoism, another important system of belief introduced from China, emphasized the importance of an individual's relationship to nature and to the universe. Beliefs rooted in Taoism were condemned by the regime as superstitious.

Despite official disapproval of superstitious practices, most Vietnamese, regardless of their professed religion, level of education, or ideology, were influenced at one time or another by such practices as astrology, geomancy and sorcery. Diviners and other specialists in the occult remained in popular demand because they were believed to be able to diagnose supernatural causes of illness, establish lucky dates for personal undertakings, or predict the future. Moreover, many Vietnamese believed that individual destiny was guided by astrological phenomena. By consulting one's horoscope, one could make the most of auspicious times and avoid disaster. It was not unusual, for example, for a couple to consult an astrologer before marrying. He would determine if the betrothed were suitably matched and even fix the date of the ceremony.

The belief in good and evil spirits, or animism, antedated all organized faiths in Vietnam and permeated the society, especially in the rural areas and in the highlands. These beliefs held that all phenomena and forces in the universe were controlled by spirits and that the souls of the dead were instrumental in determining an individual's fate. If propitiated, they provided the living with protection; if ignored, they induced misfortune. Although officially condemned as "superstitious practices," these beliefs continued to proliferate in the rural and in the highland areas as well as in the cities in the 1980s.

Lang Son following 1979 Chinese invasion
Courtesy Bill Herod

FOREIGN RELATIONS

Until the fall of the South Vietnamese government in 1975, the VCP considered foreign policy interests to be subordinate to the overriding issue of national liberation and reunification. Only with the end of the war did Hanoi turn its full attention to foreign policy concerns. Among the more pressing were its relations with Laos, Cambodia, China, the Soviet Union, the member nations of the Association of Southeast Asian Nations (ASEAN), and the West. Like domestic policy, foreign policy required the reconciliation of ideology and nationalism.

From an ideological standpoint, the Vietnamese saw themselves as fulfilling their international socialist duty by defeating a major "imperialist" enemy and by carrying out a revolution that could be a model for the Third World. Communist ideology in turn served Vietnamese nationalism by providing a justification for the pursuit of its nationalist goals. A Marxist-Leninist historical view, for example, justified creating an alliance of the three Indochinese countries because such an alliance was instrumental in the struggle against imperialism. By the same reasoning, Hanoi's decision in 1978 to overthrow the Pol Pot regime in Cambodia was defensible on the grounds that a new government more closely dedicated to Marxist-Leninist principles was required in Cambodia in order to reestablish an effective alliance against imperialism. Ideological and nationalist goals thus were often interchangeable, and Vietnamese foreign policy could be construed as serving national interests and international communism at the same time. In the final analysis, however, nationalism and national security remained the primary foreign policy concerns.

Laos and Cambodia

In 1987 Vietnam's relationships with Laos and Cambodia did not differ substantially from their historic patterns. Contemporary Vietnamese attitudes reflected the conviction of cultural and political superiority that had prevailed during the nineteenth century when weaker monarchs in Laos and Cambodia had paid tribute to the Vietnamese court in a system modeled on Vietnam's own relationship to China (see The Chinese Millennium; Nine Centuries of Independence). In the 1980s, Laos and Cambodia had once more become Vietnam's client states. Laos, with a communist party long nurtured by the Vietnamese, entered the relationship with docility; Cambodia, however, under a ruthless, but anti-Vietnamese dictatorship of its own, resisted being drawn into the Vietnamese orbit. Tension between the two states escalated into open warfare and, in 1978, Hanoi launched an invasion that toppled the Pol Pot regime in Phnom Penh. In 1987 Cambodia remained a state governed precariously by a regime installed by Hanoi, its activities constrained by the presence of a substantial Vietnamese occupation force and a tenacious insurgency in the countryside. Repeated Vietnamese assurances that Hanoi would withdraw its troops from the beleaguered country by 1990 were received with skepticism by some observers.

The communist victory in Vietnam in 1975 was accompanied by similar communist successes in Laos and Cambodia. The impression of the noncommunist world at the time was that the three Indochinese communist parties, having seized control in their respective countries, would logically work together, through the fraternal bond of a single ideology, to achieve common objectives. What appeared to be a surprising deterioration in relations, however, was actually the resurfacing of historical conflict that ideological commonality could not override (see Early History). The victories of the Vietnamese communists and the Cambodian communist *Khmer Rouge* (see Glossary) in 1975 did not bring peace. Relations between the two parties had been strained since the close of the First Indochina War. The Geneva Agreements had failed to secure for the Khmer communists, as part of the first Cambodian national liberation organization, the United Issarak Front, a legitimate place in Cambodian politics. Some Khmer Communist and Issarak leaders subsequently went to Hanoi, but among those who stayed behind, Pol Pot and his faction, who later gained control of the Khmer (Kampuchean) Communist party, blamed Vietnam for having betrayed this party at Geneva. Pol Pot never lost his antipathy for Vietnam. Under his leadership, the

Khmer Rouge adhered for years to a radical, chauvinistic, and bitterly anti-Vietnamese political line. Skirmishes broke out on the Cambodian-Vietnamese border almost immediately following the communist victories in Saigon and Phnom Penh, and in less than four years Vietnam was again at war, this time with Cambodia. Vietnam offensive forces crossing the Cambodia border in December 1978 the took less than a month, to occupy Phnom Penh amd most of the country.

When tensions between Cambodia and Vietnam broke into the open, the reason was ostensibly Cambodian demands that Hanoi return territory conquered by the Vietnamese centuries earlier. Vietnam's offers to negotiate the territorial issue were rejected, however, because of more urgent Khmer concerns that Hanoi intended to dominate Cambodia by forming an *Indochina Federation* (see Glossary) or "special relationship." In any event, Vietnamese interest in resolving the situation peacefully clearly came to an end once the decisison was made to invade Cambodia.

The invasion and the subsequent establishment of a puppet regime in Phnom Penh were costly to Hanoi, further isolating it from the international community. Vietnam's relations with a number of countries and with the United Nations (UN) deteriorated. The UN General Assembly refused to recognize the Vietnamese-supported government in Phnom Penh and demanded a total Vietnamese withdrawal followed by internationally supervised free elections. The ASEAN nations were unified in opposing Vietnam's action. Urged by Thailand's example, they provided support for the anti-Phnom Penh resistance. In February 1979, China was moved to retaliate against Vietnam across their mutual border (see China).

The ensuing conflict in Cambodia pitted Vietnamese troops, assisted by forces of the new Phnom Penh government--the People's Republic of Kampuchea (PRK)--against a coalition of communist and noncommunist resistance elements. Of these elements, the government displaced from Phnom Penh by the Vietnamese, Pol Pot's communist Khmer Rouge (which had established the government known as Democratic Kampuchea in Cambodia in 1975), was the strongest and most effective military force, mainly because of support from the Chinese. The extremism and brutality of the Khmer Rouge's brief reign in Phnom Penh, where it may have been responsible for as many as 2 million deaths, made it infamous. ASEAN's concern that the reputation of the Khmer Rouge would lessen the international appeal of the anti-Vietnamese cause led it to press the Khmer Rouge and noncommunist resistance elements into forming a coalition that would appear to diminish the Khmer Rouge's political role. The tripartite Coalition Government of Democratic Kampuchea (CGDK) was formed on June 22, 1982. In addition to the Khmer Rouge, it comprised a noncommunist resistance force called the Kampuchean People's National Liberation Front (KPNLF)--under the leadership of a former official of Prince Norodom Sihanouk's government, Son Sann--and Sihanouk's own noncommunist force (the Armee Nationale Sihanoukiste-- ANS). The Cambodian government in exile needed the added legitimacy that noncommunist factions and the prestige of Sihanouk's name could contribute. The Chinese were reluctant to withdraw their support from the Khmer Rouge, which they viewed as the only effective anti-Vietnamese fighting force among the three coalition members. They were persuaded, however, to support the coalition and eventually began supplying arms to Son Sann and Sihanouk as well as Pol Pot.

Despite an extensive record of internal squabbling, the coalition government in 1987 provided the international community with an acceptable alternative to the Vietnamese-supported Heng Samrin regime in Phnom Penh. From 1982 to 1987, the coalition survived annual Vietnamese dry-season campaigns against its base camps along the Thai-Cambodian border, and, by changing its tactics in 1986 to emphasize long-term operations deep in the Cambodian interior, increased its military effectiveness. The coalition's military operations prevented the Vietnamese from securing all of Cambodia and helped create a stalemate.

In 1987 the situation remained deadlocked. Despite the costs, Vietnam's negotiating position remained inflexible. Hanoi apparently perceived itself to have gained enormously in terms of national security. The "special relationship" it had futilely sought with Pol Pot was effected almost immediately with the new Phnom Penh government when, in February 1979, a Treaty of Friendship and Cooperation was signed. In 1982 and 1983 a substantial number of Vietnamese reportedly settled in Cambodia, although Vietnam did not seem to be making a concerted effort to colonize the country. Instead, Hanoi appeared to be striving to build an indigenous regime that would be responsive to general Vietnamese direction and become part of an Indochinese community under Vietnamese hegemony.

In contrast to its relationship with Cambodia, Vietnam's relations with communist Laos have been fairly stable. Historically, the ethnic tribes comprising present-day Laos had been less resistant to Vietnamese subjugation, and relations had never reached the level of animosity characteristic of the Vietnam-Cambodia relationship.

Although Hanoi was a signatory to the Geneva Agreement of 1962 that upheld the neutrality of Laos, it has failed to observe the agreement in practice. During the *Second Indochina War* (see Glossary), for example, the North Vietnamese obtained the cooperation of the Lao People's Revolutionary Party (Pathet Lao) in constructing and maintaining the *Ho Chi Minh Trail* (see Glossary), an unauthorized road communications network that passed through the length of Laos. Thousands of Vietnamese troops were stationed in Laos to maintain the road network and provide for its security. Vietnamese military personnel also fought beside the Pathet Lao in its struggle to overthrow Laos' neutralist government. Cooperation persisted after the war and the Lao communist victory. In 1976, agreements on cooperation in cultural, economic, scientific, and technical fields were signed between the two countries, followed in 1977 by a twenty-five-year Treaty of Friendship and Cooperation. The treaty was intended to strengthen ties as well as sanction Vietnam's military presence in, and military assistance to, Laos. Following Vietnam's invasion of Cambodia, Laos established links with the Vietnamese- supported PRK in Phnom Penh. Meanwhile, Hanoi maintained 40,000 to 60,000 troops in Laos. In 1985 the three governments discussed coordinating their 1986-90 five-year plans, and Vietnam assumed a larger role in developing Lao natural resources by agreeing to joint exploitation of Laotian forests and iron ore deposits. Nevertheless, such growth in cooperation prompted some debate on the Lao side over the country's growing dependence on Vietnam.

China

The deterioration of Sino-Vietnamese relations was gradual, commencing perhaps most dramatically with Richard M. Nixon's 1972 visit to China (which Hanoi later called the beginning of China's betrayal of Vietnam), but in the mid-1970s the signs of an impending breakdown were barely discernible. Until 1977 the Vietnam-Cambodia dispute appeared to the outside world to be purely bilateral and China's strategic considerations seemed only distantly connected to the skirmishes taking place on the Vietnamese-Cambodian border. The Chinese in the 1976-77 period were preoccupied with internal affairs, including the deaths of Mao Zedong and Zhou Enlai, the arrest of Mao's widow, and the return to power of Deng Xiaoping. As the situation between Vietnam and Cambodia deteriorated, the signs of a potential SinoVietnamese rift became clearer the more Cambodia's strategic importance for both China and Vietnam. appeared at risk. Aside from risking the return of the Khmer Rouge, Vietnam, viewed a disengagement from Cambodia as paramount to inviting China to create a two-front threat by establishing a foothold on a second Vietnamese frontier. In China's view, Vietnam's sustained presence in Cambodia not only precluded such an accomplishment, but conferred territory, once administered by an acknowledged Chinese ally, to the authority of an historic Asian adversary that was closely allied with a contemporary superpower rival, the Soviet Union.

Vietnam's and China's shared modern experiences, namely their common exploitation by colonial powers and adaptations to communist ideology, did little to alter Vietnam's historical view of China, which was colored by lengthy periods of Chinese conquest and domination. During the Second Indochina War, China acted as North Vietnam's closest ally, but, according to later Vietnamese statements, the Chinese tried to dominate the relationship from the beginning. Vietnam's desperate need for Chinese assistance forced it to maintain good relations with Beijing for the duration of the war, despite Vietnamese suspicions that China's ultimate purpose was to weaken Vietnam (see The Chinese Millennium; Nine Centuries of Independence).

After the end of the Second Indochina War, underlying tensions between the two countries surfaced, and in 1978 a number of issues converged to bring the relationship to the breaking point. In addition to the growing dispute in Cambodia, these issues included territorial disagreements and Vietnam's treatment of its own largest minority group, the *Hoa* (see Glossary) or ethnic Chinese, who numbered nearly 2 million.

The territorial dispute involved primarily delineation of territorial waters in the Gulf of Tonkin and sovereignty over two archipelagos in the South China Sea, the Paracel and the Spratly Islands (the Xisha and the Nansha in Chinese; the Hoang Sa and Truong Sa in Vietnamese). A border dispute on land (over fewer than sixty square kilometers) was responsible for the relatively steady occurrence of low-level border clashes involving crossborder violations and the exchange of small-arms fire. In 1958 the two governments decided to defer settling their border differences until after victory had been achieved in the South.

Disagreement over territorial waters in the Gulf of Tonkin stemmed from agreements reached between China and France in 1887, stipulating a territorial limit of no more three nautical miles. These agreements had been adequate until 1973, when Hanoi announced to Beijing its intention to negotiate contracts with foreign firms for the exploration of oil in the

Gulf of Tonkin. The disputed islands in the South China Sea assumed importance only after it was disclosed that they were near the potential sites of substantial offshore oil deposits. In January 1974, Chinese military units seized islands in the Paracels occupied by South Vietnamese armed forces, and Beijing claimed sovereignty over the Spratlys. Following their conquest of South Vietnam in the spring of 1975, units of the People's Army of Vietnam (PAVN) nevertheless moved to occupy the Spratly Islands previously held by the Saigon regime.

Vietnam's treatment of the Hoa became an issue in 1978, when Hanoi instituted a crackdown on the Chinese community because of its pervasive role in domestic commerce in the South and its alleged subversive activities in the North. The government action forced an unprecedented exodus of thousands of Hoa across the border into China, prompting Beijing to accuse Vietnam of persecuting its Chinese community and of breaking a 1955 agreement that called for the gradual and voluntary integration of the Hoa into Vietnamese society. The situation was aggravated when Vietnam denied landing privileges to three Chinese ships dispatched to evacuate Hoa seeking voluntary repatriation to China. Beijing threatened Hanoi with unspecified retaliation, and Chinese activities on the Sino-Vietnamese border escalated.

The deterioration in bilateral relations became evident when China reduced in May 1978 and then cancelled on July 3 its remaining aid projects in Vietnam. The officical announcement followed by only a few days Hanoi's admission on June 29 to the Soviet-dominated Council for Mutual Economic Assistance (Comecon--see Glossary). A few months later, in November 1978, a new era in Soviet-Vietnamese relations began with the signing of a Treaty of Friendship and Cooperation that called for mutual assistance and consultation in the event of a security threat to either country. The document facilitated Soviet use of Vietnamese airports and port facilities, particularly the former United States military complex at Cam Ranh Bay. In return, it assured Vietnam of economic and military aid for the anticipated invasion of Cambodia and established the Soviet Union as a deterrent to possible Chinese intervention in Cambodia.

Vietnam's decision to align with the Soviets together with its invasion of Cámbodia and mistreatment of the Hoa, provoked Beijing to "teach Hanoi a lesson." A "self-defense counterattack," mounted by China along the Sino-Vietnamese border on February 17, 1979, ended less than a month later, on March 5, when Chinese leaders announced that their objectives had been met and proceeded to withdraw their forces. Despite the Chinese boast of having shattered the myth of Vietnam's invincibility, the invasion effected little more than the diversion of some Vietnamese troops from Cambodia. The bulk of the resistance reportedly was offered by local Vietnamese border units and regional forces. Outnumbered, they performed well, exposing significant weaknesses in Chinese tactics, strategy, logistics, equipment, and communications. In the final analysis, the results were far from conclusive. Peace negotiations were initiated following the disengagement of forces, but broke down several times before being discontinued in December 1979.

The Cambodian crisis, too, remained stalemated, and Vietnamese dependence upon the Soviet Union continued. In 1987 tensions along the Sino-Vietnamese border erupted in sporadic fighting. China believed that the Cambodian conflict would serve Chinese interests by draining the Vietnamese economically and weakening Hanoi. China's sustained pressure on Vietnam's northern border would also tax Vietnam militarily, while satisfying ASEAN's requests for Chinese assistance in the conflict and providing Chinese armed forces with invaluable combat experience. Consequently, Vietnam's dry-season campaigns to eliminate

CGDK resistance base camps along the Thai-Cambodian border were generally matched by corresponding Chinese acts along the SinoVietnamese border. China issued vague threats to Vietnam of a "second lesson" in the mid-1980s but as of 1987 had not acted on these threats.

China imposed the removal of Vietnamese troops from Cambodia as a precondition to improved Sino-Soviet relations, and diplomatic activity in late 1986 indicated that Vietnam might mend its differences with China in the event the Soviets moved closer to the Chinese. Despite Hanoi's desire to ease tensions with Beijing, however, it was not willing to do so at the expense of its position in Cambodia.

The Soviet Union

Since the earliest days of the VCP, when the party's primary mentor was the Comintern, the Soviet Union has played a complex role in VCP affairs. Many of Vietnam's leaders had trained in the Soviet Union and had formed personal ties with their Soviet contemporaries. Historically, however, the relationship between the two nations has been characterized by strain, particularly on the Vietnamese side, and the record suggests several instances of Soviet neglect or betrayal of Vietnamese interests. These included Moscow's indifference to the founding of the VCP in 1930; failure to support materially or otherwise the Vietnamese resistance war against the French in the 1930s and early 1940s; failure to recognize North Vietnam until five years after its founding; failure to support Vietnam's application for membership in the UN in 1948 and 1951; support for the partitioning of Vietnam at the Geneva Conference in 1954; and sponsorship of a proposal to admit both North and South Vietnam to the UN in 1956. These examples of Soviet policy reminded the Vietnamese of the peril inherent in placing too much trust in a foreign ally.

The Sino-Soviet split in the late 1950s favorably altered the Soviet attitude toward Vietnam. Beginning in 1965, the Soviets initiated a program of military assistance to Hanoi that proved invaluable in carrying on the Second Indochina War. Hanoi, however, continued to suspect Soviet motives and perceived that Soviet aid, when offered, was insufficient and given only grudgingly after repeated appeals.

Following the conquest of South Vietnam in 1975, Hanoi sought to retain the equilibrium of its wartime relations with both China and the Soviet Union, but mounting tensions with Beijing, culminating in the loss of Chinese aid in 1978, compelled Hanoi to look increasingly to Moscow for economic and military assistance. Beginning in late 1975, a number of significant agreements were signed between the two countries. One coordinated the national economic development plans of the two countries, and another called for the Soviet Union to underwrite Vietnam's first post-reunification Five-Year Plan. The first formal alliance was achieved in June 1978 when Vietnam joined Comecon. That organization, which facilitated the economic integration of the Soviet Union, six East European countries, Cuba, and Mongolia, was able to offer economic assistance for some of the projects abandoned by China.

Vietnam's decision to invade Cambodia, which the leadership apparently made shortly after joining Comecon, required more than economic assistance from the Soviets (see Laos and Cambodia). The possibility of a formal alliance between Hanoi and Moscow had apparently been discussed since 1975, but the Vietnamese had rejected the idea in order to protect their relationship with China. In 1978 that relationship had deteriorated to the point where protecting it was no longer a consideration, and circumstances in Cambodia confirmed the need for Vietnamese-Soviet military cooperation. In spite of Vietnam's needs, it is likely that the November 1978 Treaty of Friendship and Cooperation was imposed by the Soviets as a condition for military assistance. As a result of the treaty, the Vietnamese granted the Soviets access to the facilities at Da Nang and Cam Ranh Bay. Use of the bases represented a substantial regional strategic gain for Moscow, whose naval bases in the Pacific Ocean, until then, had been limited to the Soviet Far East.

Soviet support sustained Vietnamese operations in Cambodia. Military aid in 1978 approached US$800 million annually, but after the Vietnamese invasion of Cambodia and the Chinese attack on Vietnam in February 1979, the figure rose to almost US$1.4 billion. The sharp increase, reflecting the Soviet effort to replace quickly Vietnamese equipment losses on the Sino-Vietnamese border, was subsequently reduced to between US$800 and 900 million in 1980 and between US$900 million and 1 billion in 1981. Military aid increased to 1.7 billion annually in the 1982- 85 period, and decreased to an estimated US$1.5 billion in 1985. Reported Soviet dissatisfaction with Hanoi's handling of Cambodia, stemming from the stalemated battlefield situation and its high costs, did not appear to affect Moscow's decision to continue to provide assistance for the war. At the end of 1987, there was no indication that the Soviets were pressing Vietnam to resolve the conflict.

In addition to its role as Vietnam's exclusive donor of military aid, the Soviet Union in 1987 was also Vietnam's largest contributor of economic aid and its biggest trade partner. During the Third Five-Year Plan (1981-85), the Soviets provided some US$5.4 billion in balance-of-payments aid, project assistance, and oil price subsidies. Total economic aid for 1986 was an estimated US$1.8 billion. The Soviets also have been a major supplier of food and commodity aid on a mostly grant-aid or softcurrency basis. By 1983 they were supplying 90 percent of Vietnam's petroleum, iron and steel, fertilizer, and cotton imports and 70 percent of its grain imports.

Soviet-Vietnamese ties in the mid-1980s were sound, although troubled by some underlying strain. The Vietnamese distrusted Soviet intentions and resented Hanoi's dependent role; the Soviets in turn distrusted the Vietnamese for not confiding in them. Reportedly, on a number of occasions Moscow learned of major Vietnamese policy plans and changes only after the fact. According to some foreign observers, the Soviets were not entirely prepared for the sudden deterioration in Sino-Vietnamese relations in 1978, and they may not have been aware of the full extent of Vietnamese plans in Cambodia. Others believe the Soviet Union was aware of the deterioration and was allowing Vietnam to play the role of proxy in Moscow's own dispute with Beijing.

Friction was particularly evident in economic relations. The Soviets resented the enormous burden of their aid program to Vietnam and felt that much of it was wasted because of Vietnamese inefficiency. In turn, the Vietnamese were offended by Moscow's 1980 decision to reduce aid in the face of severe economic hardships in Vietnam. In the mid-1980s, aid continued at a reduced rate although Vietnam's economic situation had worsened.

The prospect of an improvement in the state of Sino-Soviet relations in the mid-1980s did not appear to threaten the Soviet Union's ties with Vietnam. Although China demanded that Moscow ensure Vietnam's withdrawal from Cambodia as a condition to normalizing the Sino-Soviet relationship, Vietnamese leaders proceeded as if they were sure their existing policy in Cambodia would not be threatened. The Soviets even went so far as to promote improved relations between Hanoi and Beijing. At Vietnam's Sixth Party Congress in December 1986, the senior member of the Soviet delegation suggested that the normalization of relations between Vietnam and China would improve the situation in Asia and the world as a whole. The Vietnamese agreed with this premise but were unwilling to seek improved ties at the expense of weakening their position in Cambodia.

Eastern Europe

In addition to relations with the Soviet Union, Vietnam maintained close relations with other members of Comecon and the Warsaw Pact. Eastern Europe provided Vietnam with some US$844 million in aid between 1965 and 1975, amounting to 18 percent of all aid received during that period. Between November 1976 and June 1977, Vietnam signed commodity and payments agreements with eight communist countries, cultural agreements with four, scientific cooperation agreements with eight, and separate agreements for economic, scientific, or technical cooperation with five. Its relations with Czechoslovakia, the German Democratic Republic (East Germany), and Hungary were particularly close.

The United States

The Communist victory in South Vietnam in 1975 abruptly concluded three decades of United States intervention in Vietnam and brought to a close a painful and bitter era for both countries. The war generated considerable social and political discord in the United States, massive disruption in Vietnam, and was enormously costly to both sides. Vietnam endured physical destruction--ravaged battle sites, leveled factories and cities, and untold numbers of military and civilian casualties. The United States escaped physical devastation, but it suffered the loss of 58,000 lives (2,400 unaccounted for) and spent roughly $150 billion in direct expenses to sustain the war. The war also divided and confused American society.

To the Vietnamese communists, the war against the United States simply extended the war for independence initiated against the French. In Hanoi's view, when the United States displaced the French in Indochina, it assumed the French role as a major-power obstacle to Vietnam's eventual reunification.

For the United States, intervention was derived from considerations that largely transcended Vietnam. In the closing months of World War II, the United States had supported the idea of an international trusteeship for all of Indochina. Subsequently, in spite of misgivings in Washington about French intentions to reimpose colonial rule in Indochina, the United States eventually tilted in support of the French war effort in the embattled region. Anticolonial sentiment in the United States after World War II thus failed to outweigh policy priorities in Europe, such as the evolving North Atlantic Treaty Organization (NATO) relationship. The formal creation of NATO and the communist victory in China, both of which occurred in 1949, led the United States to support materially the French war effort in Indochina. The perception that communism was global and monolithic led the administration of President Dwight D. Eisenhower to support the idea of a noncommunist state in southern Vietnam, after the French withdrawal under the Geneva Agreements of 1954. Although this goal arguably ran counter to two key features of the Geneva Agreements (the stipulation that the line separating North and South Vietnam be neither a political nor territorial boundary and the call for reunification elections), it was based on the United States assessment that the Viet minh--which, contrary to the agreements, had left several thousand cadres south of the demarcation line--was already in violation. The first United States advisers arrived in the South within a year after Geneva to help President Ngo Dinh Diem establish a government that would be strong enough to stand up to the communist regime in the North.

Although Washington's advisory role was essentially political, United States policy makers determined that the effort to erect a non-communist state in Vietnam was vital to the security of the region and would be buttressed by military means, if necessary, to inhibit any would-be aggressor. Defending Vietnam's security against aggression from the North and from southern-based communist insurgency was a mission Washington initially perceived as requiring only combat support elements and advisers to South Vietnamese military units. The situation, however, rapidly deteriorated, and in 1965, at a time when increasing numbers of North Vietnamese-trained soldiers were moving in South Vietnam, the first increment of United States combat forces was introduced into the South and sustained bombing of military targets in North Vietnam was undertaken. Nearly eight more years of conflict occurred before the intense involvement of the United States ended in 1973.

An "Agreement Ending the War and Restoring Peace in Vietnam" was signed in Paris on January 27, 1973, by Washington, Hanoi, Saigon, and the Provisional Revolutionary Government, representing the Vietnamese communist organization in the South, the *Viet Cong* (see Glossary--contraction of Viet Nam Cong San). The settlement called for a cease-fire, withdrawal of all United States troops, continuance in place of North Vietnamese troops in the South, and the eventual reunification of the country "through peaceful means." In reality, once United States Forces were disengaged in early 1973 there was no effective way to prevent the North from overwhelming the South's defenses and the settlement proved unenforceably. Following the fragile cease-fire established by the agreement, PAVN units remained in the South Vietnamese countryside, while Army of the Republic of Vietnam (ARVN--see Glossary) units fought to dislodge them and expand the areas under Saigon's control. As a result, the two sides battled from 1973 to 1975, but the ARVN, having to fight without the close United States air, artillery, logistical, and medevac (medical evacuation) support to which it had become accustomed, acquitted itself badly, losing more and more ground to the community.

The surprisingly swift manner in which the South Vietnamese government finally collapsed in 1975 appeared to confirm that the Paris agreement had accomplished little more than to delay an inevitable defeat for the United States ally, South Vietnam, and that Washington had been impotent to avert this outcome.

Following the war, Hanoi pursued the establishment of diplomatic relations with the United States, initially in order to obtain US$3.3 billion in reconstruction aid, which President Richard M. Nixon had secretly promised after the Paris Agreement was signed in 1973. Under Article 21 of the agreement, the United States had pledged "to contribute to healing the wounds of war and to postwar reconstruction of the DRV . . ." but had specifically avoided using terminology that could be interpreted to mean that reparations were being offered for war damages. Nixon's promise was in the form of a letter, confirming the intent of Article 21 and offering a specific figure. Barely two months after Hanoi's victory in 1975, Premier Pham Van Dong, speaking to the National Assembly, invited the United States to normalize relations with Vietnam and to honor its commitment to provide reconstruction funds. Representatives of two American banks--the Bank of America and First National City Bank--were invited to discuss trade possibilities, and American oil companies were informed that they were welcome to apply for concessions to search for oil in offshore Vietnamese waters.

Washington neglected Dong's call for normal relations, however, because it was predicated on reparations, and the Washington political climate in the wake of the war precluded the pursuit of such an outcome. In response, the administration of President Gerald R. Ford imposed its own precondition for normal relations by announcing that a full accounting of Americans missing in action (MIAs--see Glossary), including the return of any remains, would be required before normalization could be effected. No concessions were made on either side until President Jimmy Carter softened the United States demand from a full accounting of MIAs to the fullest possible accounting and dispatched a mission to Hanoi in 1977 to initiate normalization discussions.

Although the Vietnamese at first were adamant about United States economic assistance (their first postwar economic plan counted on the amount promised by President Nixon), the condition was dropped in mid-1978 when Hanoi made additional gestures toward normal relations. At that time, Vietnamese Foreign Minister Nguyen Co Thach and the United States government reached an agreement in principle on normalization, but the date was left vague. When Thach urged November 1978, a date that in retrospect is significant because he was due in Moscow to sign the Treaty of Friendship and Cooperation with the Soviet Union, Washington was noncommittal. During this period, United States officials were preoccupied with the question of the Indochinese refugees, and they were in the process of normalizing relations with China. This was an action that could have been jeopardized had Washington concurrently sought a rapprochement with Vietnam, a nation whose relationship with Beijing was growing increasingly strained. Policy makers in Hanoi correctly reasoned that the United States had opted to strengthen its ties with China rather than with Vietnam, and they moved to formalize their ties with the Soviets in response. Their original hope, however, had been to gain both diplomatic recognition from the United States and a friendship treaty with Moscow, as a double guarantee against future Chinese interference.

In the United States, the issue of normalizing relations with Vietnam was complicated by Vietnam's invasion of Cambodia in December 1978, the continuing plight of Vietnamese refugees, and the unresolved MIA issue. In 1987, under President Ronald Reagan, the United States continued to enforce the trade embargo imposed on Hanoi in 1975 and barred normal ties as long as Vietnamese troops occupied Cambodia. Any efforts to improve relations remained closely tied to United States willingness to honor its 1973 aid commitment to Vietnam and to Hanoi's failure to account for the whereabouts of more than 2,400 MIAs in Indochina. From the signing of the Paris agreements in 1973 until mid-1978, the Vietnamese had routinely stressed the linkage between the aid and MIA issues. Beginning in mid-1978, however, Hanoi dropped its insistence that the MIA and aid questions be resolved as a precondition for normalization and stopped linking the MIA question to other unresolved matters between the two countries. Vietnamese leaders contrasted their restraint on the MIA issue with its alleged political exploitation by the United States as a condition for normal relations. As additional signs of goodwill, Hanoi permitted the joint United States-Vietnamese excavation of a B-52 crash site in 1985 and returned the remains of a number of United States servicemen between 1985 and 1987. Vietnamese spokesmen also claimed during this period to have a two-year plan to resolve the MIA question but failed to reveal details.

Although Vietnam's Sixth National Party Congress in December 1986 officially paid little attention to relations with the United States, the report of the congress noted that Vietnam was continuing to hold talks with Washington on humanitarian issues and expressed a readiness to improve relations. Although ambivalent in tone, the message was more positive than the 1982 Fifth National Party Congress report, which had attributed the stalemated relationship to Washington's "hostile policy." The improved wording was attributable to the influence of newly appointed Party General Secretary Nguyen Van Linh, who was expected to attach high priority to expanding Vietnam's links with the West.

Within a few months of the Sixth National Party Congress, however, Hanoi began to send conflicting signals to Washington. In mid-1987 the Vietnamese government, having determined that cooperation had gained few concessions from the United States, reverted to its pre-1978 position linking the aid and MIA issues. The resumption of its hardline stand, however, was brief. A meeting between Vietnamese leaders and President Reagan's special envoy on MIAs, General John W. Vessey, in August 1987 yielded significant gains for both sides. In exchange for greater Vietnamese cooperation on resolving the MIA issue, the United States agreed officially to encourage charitable assistance for Vietnam. Although the agreement fell short of Hanoi's requests for economic aid or war reparations, it marked the first time that the United States had offered anything in return for Vietnamese assistance in accounting for the MIAs and was an important step toward an eventual reconciliation between the two countries.

Ho Chi Minh City poster portrays American and Chinese "aggressors," 1979.
Courtesy Bill Herod

ASEAN

The Association of Southeast Asian Nations (ASEAN) was formed in 1967 as a regional, economic, cultural, and social cooperative organization. The original five member nations--Indonesia, Malaysia, the Philippines, Singapore, and Thailand (the sixth member, Brunei, was admitted in January 1984)--had little in common in their culture, history, or politics. Nevertheless, after a slow start the organization flourished; by 1987 it had the fastest growing GNP of all economic groups in the world and was a key force for regional stability.

ASEAN's charter declares that membership is open to all states in the region--a gesture toward Vietnam that Hanoi repeatedly rebuffed. Before Vietnam's invasion and occupation of Cambodia in December 1978, integration of the three Indochinese states and ASEAN into a larger regional organization was discussed within the ASEAN community as a possible solution to regional problems. The proposal surfaced at an ASEAN summit meeting held in Bali in January 1976, when, following reunification, Vietnam requested observer status at ASEAN meetings. It was understood at the time, however, that the inclusion of communist states within a grouping of free-market countries was unprecedented, and the idea was interpreted to be more a goodwill gesture than a serious proposition.

From 1976 to 1978, ASEAN's differences with Vietnam were both symbolic and real. ASEAN, for example, proposed establishing Southeast Asia as a zone of peace, freedom, and neutrality and invited Vietnam to support the proposal. Hanoi refused but countered with its own proposal, calling instead for a region of peace, independence, and neutrality. Apparently, the Vietnamese objected to the term freedom because of their vulnerability to criticism on human rights issues. The term *Independence*, on the other hand, was promoted by the Vietnamese as a concept opposing all foreign military bases in Southeast Asia, an idea that many of the ASEAN nations did not share.

During the Second Indochina War, each ASEAN state pursued its own Vietnam policy. Malaysia and Indonesia maintained strict neutrality, whereas Thailand and the Philippines contributed personnel and materiel to South Vietnam. Perceptions of Vietnam as a possible threat to the region also varied among member nations. Indonesia and Malaysia viewed Vietnam as a buffer against Chinese expansionism, whereas Thailand, wary of possible repetition of historic patterns of confrontation with Vietnam, turned to China for protection following the war's end and the subsequent withdrawal of United States forces from Thailand.

Following the 1978 invasion of Cambodia, however, the ASEAN nations were united in their condemnation of Hanoi. They took the lead in mobilizing international opinion against Vietnam, and, in the UN General Assembly, they annually sponsored resolutions calling for withdrawal of Vietnamese troops and for internationally supervised elections. The ASEAN nations also were instrumental in preventing the Vietnam-sponsored Heng Samrin regime in Phnom Penh from taking over Cambodia's UN seat. In June 1982, ASEAN was instrumental in persuading three disparate Cambodian resistance elements to merge into a coalition resistance government (see Laos and Cambodia).

ASEAN's position on Cambodia was important to Hanoi, because it was through ASEAN's efforts at the UN that the world's attention continued to focus on Cambodia in the late 1980s. The Vietnamese thus saw ASEAN as having the power to confer upon them or to deny them legitimacy in Cambodia. Vietnamese diplomats sought to convince the ASEAN countries that the invasion of Cambodia was intended to eliminate the threat posed by Pol

Pot's alignment with China. Rather than have its activity in Cambodia perceived as potentially damaging to ASEAN's security, Vietnam wanted to assure ASEAN members that it was in the group's interest to join with Vietnam in countering the Chinese threat to the region. Cultivating goodwill with key ASEAN members was an important part of this strategy. Thus, in 1978 Vietnam and the Philippines agreed to negotiate but failed to settle their conflicting claims to the Spratly Islands. Foreign Minister Thach, during a late-1982 visit to Indonesia, took a conciliatory position in discussing Vietnam's and Indonesia's competing claims to the Natuna Islands, and in 1984 Hanoi made a similar gesture to Malaysia in order to help resolve their conflicting claims over Amboyna Cay. In 1987, however, resolving the war in Cambodia remained the key to any further resolution of differences between Vietnam and ASEAN.

Thailand

As the ASEAN member most vulnerable to a Vietnamese attack, Thailand was foremost among the ASEAN partners opposing Vietnam's 1978 invasion of Cambodia. Thailand's suspicion of Vietnamese long-term objectives and fear of Vietnamese support for an internal Thai communist insurgency movement led the Thai government to support United States objectives in South Vietnam during the Second Indochina War. In 1979, after Vietnam's military occupation of Cambodia had raised these same concerns again, Bangkok was compelled once again to ally with, an adversary of Vietnam and looked to Beijing for security assistance. In both instances, Thailand's actions hardened Hanoi's attitude toward Bangkok.

In 1973 a new civilian government in Thailand created a chance for some degree of reconciliation with Vietnam, when it proposed to remove United States military forces from Thai soil and adopt a more neutralist stance. The Vietnamese responded by sending a delegation to Bangkok, but talks broke down before any progress in improving relations could be made. Discussions resumed in August 1976. They resulted in a call for an exchange of ambassadors and for an opening of negotiations on trade and economic cooperation, but a military coup in October 1976 ushered in a new Thai government that was less sympathetic to the Vietnamese. Contact was resumed briefly in May 1977, when Vietnam, Thailand, and Laos held a conference to discuss resuming work on the Mekong Development Project, a major cooperative effort that had been halted by the Second Indochina War. Beginning in December 1978, however, the conflict in Cambodia dominated diplomatic exchanges, and seasonal Vietnamese military offensives that included incursions across the Thai border and numerous Thai casualties particularly strained the relationship.

Other Noncommunist Nations

Relations with noncommunist nations were still in the early stages of development in the mid-1970s to mid-1980s. Noncommunist aid, nevertheless, was a significant part of Hanoi's budget prior to Vietnam's invasion of Cambodia in December 1978. In 1976 and 1977, for example, aid from noncommunist nations amounted to US$438.5 million, of which Sweden, France, Japan, and UN-related organizations accounted for 78 percent. With the exception of aid from Sweden, however, such aid was either significantly curtailed or terminated following the invasion.

Trade ties, after the invasion, suffered similarly. In 1976 four noncommunist trading partners--Japan, Hong Kong, France, and Sweden--accounted for 44 percent of Vietnam's imports, and more than half of Vietnam's exports went to noncommunist buyers such as Singapore, Hong Kong, Japan, and France. A decade later, in 1986, only 20 percent of Vietnam's imports were of noncommunist origin, and 40 percent of its exports were reaching noncommunist markets.

By the mid-1980s, however, Vietnam was actively seeking to improve its economic and political ties with the noncommunist world community in order to stimulate aid, trade, and investment. With few exceptions, noncommunist nations were prepared to reciprocate. The one obstacle preventing their doing so remained Hanoi's continued occupation of Cambodia and the absence of a resolution to the conflict.

International Organizations

Vietnam was admitted to the UN in September 1977 and gained membership in some of the organization's specialized agencies, such as the Food and Agriculture Organization, the World Bank (see Glossary), the International Civil Aviation Organization, the International Monetary Fund (see Glossary), the UN Development Program, the UN Educational, Scientific, and Cultural Organization, the World Health Organization, and the World Intellectual Property Organization. Hanoi also successfully claimed the seat formerly occupied by South Vietnam in the Asian Development Bank (see Glossary). In the 1980s, it was a member of the Colombo Plan (see Glossary), the Economic and Social Commission for Asia and the Pacific, INTELSAT (see Glossary), and the Mekong Development Project Committee and actively participated in the Nonaligned Movement (see Glossary) and the Group of 77 (see Glossary).

GLOSSARY

Army of the Republic of Vietnam (ARVN)

The military ground forces of the South Vietnamese government (Republic of Vietnam) until its collapse in April 1975. ARVN originated in the Vietnamese military units raised by French authorities to defend the Associated State of Vietnam in the early 1950s. During the Second Indochina War (*q.v.*), it grew to over 1 million men and women organized into eleven army divisions (plus specialized units, such as Rangers and Special Forces) deployed in four Corps Tactical Zones (redesignated as Military Regions in 1971).

Asian Development Bank (ADB)

Established in 1966, the ADB assists in economic development and promotes growth and cooperation in developing member countries. Membership includes both developed and developing countries in Asia and developed countries in the West.

Black Flag forces

A band of mostly Chinese adventurers who fled to northern Vietnam after the collapse of the Taiping Rebellion (1851-64) in China. They eventually placed themselves at the service of the imperial court in Hue and fought the French forces in the 1883-84 Tonkin campaign.

boat people

Refugees who fled Vietnam by sea after 1975. Many fell victim to pirate attacks in the Gulf of Thailand, drowned, or endured starvation and dehydration as a result of their escape in ill- equipped and undersized vessels. Those who reached safety in neighboring Southeast Asian countries were accorded temporary asylum in refugee camps while awaiting permanent resettlement in industrialized Western nations willing to accept them.

bonze

A general term for a Buddhist monk (as opposed to the more specific *bhikku*, meaning an ordained monk).

Cao Dai

Indigenous Vietnamese religion centered in Tay Ninh Province, southern Vietnam. It was founded and initially propagated by Ngo Van Chieu, a minor official who, in 1919, claimed to have had a series of revelations. The faith grew under the leadership of Le Van Trung, its first "pope" or Supreme Chief, chosen in 1925. Doctrinally, the religion is a syncretic blend of Christianity, Buddhism, Taoism, Confuciancism and Western nineteenth-century romanticism. Before the fall of Saigon, the Cao Dai had about 1 to 2 million adherents.

chi-bo

A party chapter composed of a collection of party cells (*to dang*), the lowest organizational echelon of the Indochinese and later the Vietnamese Communist Party.

chua

A lord or prince. The hereditary title used by the Trinh and Nguyen families, who ruled Vietnam in the name of the emperor during the later Le Dynasty in the sixteenth through the eighteenth centuries.

Colombo Plan

Founded in 1951 and known as the Colombo Plan for Cooperative Economic Development in South and Southeast Asia until it was expanded in 1977 and called the Colombo Plan for Cooperative Economic Development in Asia and the Pacific. It is an arrangement that permits a developing member country to approach a developed member country for assistance on a one-to- one basis. Assistance may be technical or in the form of capital or commodity aid.

Co Mat Vien

An advisory council set up by Emperor Minh Mang following the rebellion of Le Van Khoi in the 1830s.

Committee for Coordination of Investigations of the Lower Mekong Basin

Established in 1957 under the sponsorship of the United Nations Economic and Social Commission for Asia and the Pacific, the Committee aims to develop water resources in the lower Mekong basin through improvements in hydroelectric power, irrigation, flood control, watershed management, and navigation. Its membership is limited to Laos, Thailand, and Vietnam.

Communist International

Also called the Comintern or Third International, it was founded in Moscow in 1919 to coordinate the world communist movement. Officially disbanded in 1943, the Comintern was replaced from 1947 to 1954 by the Cominform (Communist Information Bureau), in which only the Soviet and the ruling East European communist parties (except for Yugoslavia, which was expelled in 1948) and the French and the Italian communist parties were represented. The Cominform was dissolved in 1956.

comprador

Vietnamese communist term (used originally in China to mean purchasing agent) applied disparagingly to the middleman who extracts a profit without engaging in economic production, that is, a "comprador capitalist." The term is also applied to an entrepreneur in Cholon, Ho Chi Minh City's predominantly Chinese sister city.

Council for Mutual Economic Assistance (Comecon)

Also abbreviated CEMA and CMEA, the organization was established in 1949 to promote economic cooperation among socialist bloc countries and is headquartered in Moscow. Its members in the 1980s included the Soviet Union, Bulgaria, Czechoslovakia, East Germany, Hungary, Poland, Romania, Cuba, Mongolia, and Vietnam.

democratic centralism
A basic Marxist-Leninist organizational principle accepted by all communist parties, including the Vietnamese (most recently at the Fourth National Party Congress in December 1976). It prescribes a hierarchical framework of party structures purportedly established through democratic elections.

dong (D)
Vietnam's monetary unit, which in mid-1989 had an exchange rate of US$1 to D4,500.

First Indochina War (1946-54)
The anticolonial conflict, also known as the Viet Minh War, between France and the Viet Minh, a Vietnamese communist-dominated coalition of Indochinese nationalist elements led by veteran revolutionary Ho Chi Minh. The French defeat at Dien Bien Phu in May 1954 marked the final episode of the war. The conflict was brought to an end officially by the Geneva Conference of July 1954 and its resulting agreements.

fiscal year (FY)
January 1 to December 31.

gross domestic product (GDP)
The value of domestic goods and services produced by an economy over a certain period, usually one year. Only output of goods for final consumption and investment are included because the values of primary and intermediate production are assumed to be included in final prices. Reductions for depreciation of physical assets are normally not included.

Group of 77
Founded in 1964 as a forum for developing countries to negotiate with developed countries for development aid, the original 77 developing nations had expanded by the 1980s to include the 127 members of the Nonaligned Movement (*q.v.*).

Hoa
Term applied by the Vietnamese to the ethnic Chinese residents of Vietnam.

Hoa Hao
Indigenous Vietnamese religion centered in An Giang Province, southern Vietnam. It was founded in the 1930s by Huynh Phu So, the son of a village elder in Chau Doc Province. Doctrinally, the faith is a variant of Mahayana Buddhism, but allows no intermediary between man and the Supreme Being. Before the fall of Saigon in 1975, the Hoa Hao had more than 1 million adherents.

Ho Chi Minh Trail
An intricate network of jungle trails, paths, and roads leading from the panhandle of northern Vietnam through Laos and Cambodia into the border provinces of southern Vietnam. At the height of the Second Indochina War (*q.v.*), it was a major resupply artery for Hanoi's armed forces operating in South Vietnam.

Indochina Federation

A political concept, never fully realized, joining the three Indochinese states into a confederation, first proposed at the Indochinese Communist Party Central Committee meeting in October 1930. The government of France resurrected the term in 1946 to describe a limited internal self-government granted to the states of Vietnam (including Cochinchina), Laos, and Cambodia. In the 1980s, the term was used disparagingly by some observers and analysts to categorize Vietnam's military presence in, and influence over, Laos and Cambodia.

International Monetary Fund (IMF)

Established along with the World Bank in 1945, the IMF is a specialized agency affiliated with the United Nations and is responsible for stabilizing international exchange loans to its members (including industrialized and developing countries) when they experience balance of payments difficulties. These loans frequently carry conditions that require substantial internal economic adjustments by the recipients, most of which are developing countries.

International Telecommunications Satellite Organization (INTELSAT)

Established by two international agreements concluded at Washington, D.C. in August 1971, and effective in February 1973, INTELSAT was formed to carry forward the development, construction, operation, and maintenance of the global commercial telecommunications satellite system. In the 1980s, there were 109 signatory member nations and 30 nonsignatory user nations.

Khmer Rouge

The name given to the Cambodian communists by Prince Norodom Sihanouk in the 1960s. Later, the term (although a misnomer) was applied to the insurgents of varying ideological backgrounds who opposed the Khmer Republic regime of Lon Nol. Between 1975 and 1978, it denoted the Democratic Kampuchea regime led by the radical Pol Pot faction of the Kampuchean (or Khmer) Communist Party. After being driven from Phnom Penh by the Vietnamese invasion of Cambodia in December 1978, the Khmer Rouge went back to guerrilla warfare and joined forces with two noncommunist insurgent movements to form the Coalition Government of Democratic Kampuchea.

missing-in-action (MIA)

United States military term for servicemen who remained unaccounted for at the end of the Second Indochina War (*q.v.*). In the 1980s, rumors persisted that some MIAs were still alive and had been detained involuntarily in Vietnam after the war.

National Assembly

The highest organ of government in Vietnam, according to the 1980 Constitution. The National Assembly is empowered with both constitutional and legislative authority. It can, theoretically at least, elect and remove members of upper-echelon government bodies, such as the Council of State and Council of Ministers; it may also pass laws, raise taxes, approve the state budget, and amend the constitution.

new economic zones
Population resettlement scheme undertaken in southern Vietnam after 1975 to increase food production and alleviate population pressure in congested urban areas, especially Ho Chi Minh City (Saigon). The sites selected for resettlement previously had been undeveloped or had been abandoned in the turbulence of war.

Nonaligned Movement (NAM)
Formed as the result of a series of increasingly structured nonaligned conferences, the first of which met at Belgrade, Yugoslavia in September 1961, the NAM's purpose is to insure the sovereignty and territorial integrity of nonaligned nations. In the 1980s, there were 127 member nations.

Parrot's Beak
The part of the Cambodian province of Svay Rieng that juts into the southern Vietnamese provinces of Tay Ninh and Long An. During the South Vietnamese and United States incursion into Cambodia in 1970, and again during the Vietnamese invasion that drove the Khmer Rouge from power in 1978, the area was the scene of heavy fighting.

People's Army of Vietnam (PAVN)
The military forces of the Democratic Republic of Vietnam (until 1976) and, after reunification, of the Socialist Republic of Vietnam. During the Second Indochina War (*q.v.*), PAVN bore the brunt of the fighting against the United States military forces in Vietnam, but was consistently able to recoup its losses and infiltrate units south by means of the Ho Chi Minh Trail (*q.v.*). Failing to topple the Saigon government during the Tet Offensive of 1968, PAVN undertook its first conventional invasion of South Vietnam in the Easter Offensive of 1972. This attempt ended in defeat, but PAVN's next effort, the Spring Offensive of 1975, quickly overran the ineffectual ARVN resistance and toppled the Saigon government, thereby bringing to a close the Second Indochina War.

Produced Nation Income (PNI)
A measure of an economy's material production that excludes income generated by the service sector and depreciation on capital equipment. It is used to measure controlled or communist economics where accounting procedures may ignore the service sector as "unproductive."

Ruble
Monetary unit of the Soviet Union, which in mid-1989 had an exchange rate of US$1 to Ruble 0.63.

search and destroy missions
Offensive military operations undertaken by United States combat units in Vietnam to find and neutralize the enemy, especially when the enemy's strength and disposition had not been fixed precisely. The capture and holding of territory during such operations was not a priority.

Second Indochina War (1954-75)

Armed conflict that pitted Viet Cong insurgents native to southern Vietnam and regular PAVN (*q.v.*) units with Chinese and Soviet logistical and materiel support on one side against ARVN (*q.v.*), United States, and smaller forces from the Republic of Korea (South Korea), Australia, Thailand and New Zealand on the other. Most of the ground fighting occurred in southern Vietnam. However, part of the conflict also involved an intensive air war over North Vietnam and Laos from 1965-73 and combat between competing indigenous forces in Laos and Cambodia.

to dang

A party cell, the lowest organizational echelon of the Indochinese and later the Vietnamese Communist Party.

Viet Cong

Contraction of the term Viet Nam Cong San (Vietnamese communists), the name applied by the governments of the United States and South Vietnam to the communist insurgents in rebellion against the latter government, beginning around 1957. The Vietnamese communists never used the term themselves, but referred to their movement as the National Front for the Liberation of South Vietnam (also known as the National Liberation Front), formally inaugurated in December 1960.

Viet Minh

Contraction of the term Viet Nam Doc Lap Dong Minh Hoi (Vietnam Independence League), a coalition of nationalist elements dominated by the communists and led by veteran revolutionary Ho Chi Minh. The movement first identified itself in May 1941, when it called for an uprising against the French colonial government. It proclaimed the independence of Vietnam on September 2, 1945, and led the anti-French guerrilla war that followed, until the victory at Dien Bien Phu brought the conflict to an end.

World Bank

The informal name used to designate a group of three affiliated international institutions: the International Bank for Reconstruction and Development (IBRD), the International Development Association (IDA), and the International Finance Corporation (IFC). The IBRD, established in 1945, has the primary purpose of providing loans to developing countries for productive projects. The IDA, a legally separate loan fund administered by the staff of the IBRD, was set up in 1960 to furnish credits to the poorest developing countries on much easier terms than those of conventional IBRD loans. The IFC, founded in 1956, supplements the activities of the IBRD through loans and assistance designed specifically to encourage the growth of productive private enterprises in less developed countries. The president and certain senior officers of the IBRD hold the same positions in the ICF. The three institutions are owned by the governments of the countries that subscribe their capital. To participate in the World Bank group, member states must first belong to the International Monetary Fund (*q.v.*).

INDEX

A

B

C

D

E

F

G

H

I

J

K

L

M

V

W